Sybil Oldfield, the daughter of a _____ nd an English father, was born in _____ and was educated in New _____ een a lecturer in Engli_____ as founded. She is al_____ munity, is married _____ wes, Sussex. Describing _____ ron anti-militarist and nuclear _____ ked in the peace movement for the pa_____ years. After Hitler's accession to power in _____ any, her mother and grandmother had to burn the membership lists of the German section of the Women's International League in their kitchen stove, and this book, written fifty years later, owes much to their influence and inspiration.

Spinsters of This Parish started life as a biographical and literary study of F.M. Mayor. It was only after discovering from the electoral roll for Hampstead, 1933, that a Mary Sheepshanks had moved into Flora Mayor's house after Flora's death that Sybil Oldfield began pursuing Mary's trail. Discovering her to be the remarkable but neglected woman that she was, Sybil Oldfield decided to write not about one forgotten woman, but two.

If you would like to know more about Virago books, write to us at 41 William IV Street, London WC2N 4DB for a full catalogue.

Please send a stamped addressed envelope

SPINSTERS
OF THIS PARISH

THE LIFE AND TIMES OF
F.M. MAYOR AND
MARY SHEEPSHANKS

BY
SYBIL OLDFIELD

Remember the forgotten ones:
a new world opens out for you.
Maria von Ebner-Eschenbach, *Aphorismen*, 1911

TO TERESA ROTHSCHILD

Published by VIRAGO PRESS Limited 1984
41 William IV Street, London WC2N 4DB

Copyright © Sybil Oldfield 1984

British Library Cataloguing in Publication Data

Oldfield, Sybil
    Spinsters of this parish: the life and times of F.M. Mayor and Mary
    Sheepshanks.
    1. Mayor, F.M.   2. Authors, English — 20th century — Biography
    3. Sheepshanks, Mary   4. Women — Suffrage — Great Britain —
    Biography
    I. Title
    823′.912   PR6025.A
    ISBN 0-86068-391-5

Typeset by Leaper & Gard Ltd, Bristol
Printed in Great Britain by litho at
The Anchor Press, Tiptree, Essex

CONTENTS

PREFACE

This book charts the escape of two forgotten women —
'extraordinary enough to be interesting, ordinary enough
to be significant' — from their restrictive background of
late-Victorian England. Both Flora Mayor and Mary
Sheepshanks loved many other women, but they did not
love one another; they liked each other and kept in touch all
their lives, but their paths often diverged. Therefore, this
book is not the biography of a friendship but rather the
account of two contrasting, contemporaneous lives, one of
action and one of contemplation. The two women were
well aware of the many differences between them — so
much so that they even became symbols for one another of
those differences. They were less aware of the underlying
values that they shared. I have tried to do justice both to
what separated and to what united them. I have also tried to
hold the balance evenly between them; but it is inevitable,
given the liveliness of Flora Mayor's early letters and
journals, that it should be she who emerges first from the
shadows. Perhaps this book, beginning in the nineteenth
century, should itself be read somewhat like a nineteenth-
century novel in which one character emerges only to
retreat again as the light falls upon another.

Spinsters of this Parish could not have been written
without the trust and active help of three people: Flora
Mayor's niece, Lady Rothschild (née Teresa Mayor),
generously allowed me to have access to her family's
papers, including letters, journals, commonplace-books
and old photographs covering a period of more than 150
years. Few biographers can have been happier than I was
when I first looked inside the trunk in that Surrey attic.

vii

Then Mary Sheepshanks' niece, Mrs Pita Sheepshanks, located her Aunt Mary's unpublished memoirs and letters in Buenos Aires and sent them on to me.* And another Sheepshanks niece, Mrs Christina Bewley, first enabled me to understand something of what an extraordinary woman Mary Sheepshanks had been.

I am also very happy to acknowledge my debt to Ann Phillips, Tutor/Librarian of Newnham College, Cambridge; to David Doughan at the Fawcett Collection, City of London Polytechnic; to Kenneth Blackwell of the Bertrand Russell Archives, McMasters University, Hamilton, Ontario; to the Custodians of the Jane Addams Collections at Swarthmore, Pennsylvania and at Boulder, Colorado; and to Bet Inglis of the Leonard and Virginia Woolf Archive at my own University of Sussex.

Finally, I am most grateful to the following for their invaluable reminiscences: the late Dame Margery Corbett Ashby, Lord Fenner Brockway, the late Sir Christopher Cox, Miss Daisy Dobson, Dr Muriel Drew, Miss Elizabeth Jenkins, Dr Priscilla Johnston, Miss Peggy Lamert, Mrs Alexie Mayor, Mr Denis Richards, Miss Daphne Sanger, Lt. Col. John Sheepshanks, Mrs Susan Spencer, Lt. General and Mrs William Stawell, the late Dame Rebecca West and Mrs Diana Zvegintsov.

This book was completed with financial assistance from the University of Sussex Arts Research Fund, the Norman Angell Peace Research Fund and the British Academy.

Ben, Tess, Danny and Maggie Oldfield should be thanked for their seven years' patience with a preoccupied author. My gratitude also goes out to Mollie Potter for helping us bring up the children during this time; Derek, I took for granted.

---

* In quotes from the family papers, I have sometimes run together several excerpts to create a more rounded picture: where I have done so, I have indicated the different sources by a four-point ellipsis. In all other instances, a three-point ellipsis has been used.

PROLOGUE

At the end of October 1872, two baby girls were born into two very different Anglican clerical households. One, who was christened Mary Ryott Sheepshanks, grew up in a grim parish in the north of England, on the outskirts of the industrial port of Liverpool — a city that was already a byword for miserable poverty, chronic unemployment and violence. Superb carriages of the very rich could be seen driving through snow-covered streets where half-starved women and children walked barefoot.[1] Young Mary Sheepshanks herself occasionally saw the deprivation erupt into violence — for instance, between the Orange factions and the Roman Catholics who lived in slum streets near her home. Men and women 'fought with fenders and fire-irons in defence of their tenets or merely in drunken brawls.'[2] The other little girl, who was christened Flora Macdonald Mayor as a tribute to her famous royalist ancestress, was born in prosperous southern England, and grew up in the Royal Borough of Kingston-upon-Thames, in a large house overlooking the ancient oaks of Richmond Park where spotted deer cropped the grass.

Mary Sheepshanks' home until she was eighteen was St Mary's Vicarage in the Liverpool suburb of Anfield. It was a dark, austere house with no garden and no sun. The children had to sleep several to a room, and the general cheerlessness was aggravated by their parents' belief in

1

'plain living' — including cold baths, a monotonous if
wholesome diet, linoleum on the stairs and as few fires as
possible. The Reverend and Mrs Sheepshanks actively disapproved of their children 'having a good time'; they
insisted not only that Sunday should be a day of strenuous
and unrelieved religious observance, but also that every
Friday be kept as a fast day with little food and no pleasures:

All invitations to children's parties on a Friday were refused;
and as Friday was the usual and favourite day for parties in
the park villas, the arrival of an invitation bound to be refused
was an occasion of great bitterness.[3]

The Sheepshanks children were often ill, not least because
of the stinking dust heap at the bottom of their yard 'into
which garbage and cinders were thrown daily and only
collected twice a year.'[4]

Flora Mayor's family home, Queensgate House,
Kingston Hill, was all that was cultivated and comfortable.
A painting of the interior of the Mayors' drawing-room has
survived showing a rose carpet and chintz furnishings, with
many small watercolours and a large eighteenth-century
portrait by Romney on the wall. There are flowers on the
occasional table, a piano stands open, and books are
stacked or lying everywhere. An elderly Highland terrier is
stretched out at his ease in front of the fire. It is a light-filled,
consciously civilised and welcoming interior. And whereas
Mary Sheepshanks' nursery was bleak to a degree, without
decoration of any kind and almost without toys, Flora
Mayor's nursery was furnished with pictures, books, toys,
paintboxes, puzzles and games. Queensgate House even
had a croquet lawn as well as shrubberies to romp and hide
in and specially carpentered hutches for the Mayor children's many pets.

These two contrasting landscapes of childhood were to
influence both women's expectations of the world all their
lives.

1

TWO CHILDHOODS, 1872–1882

Mary Sheepshanks rarely spoke about her childhood. Grim surroundings and plain living do not necessarily produce infant unhappiness, but in Mary's case almost continuous unhappiness was the key-note of her early years. The cause of this unhappiness was not the place but the people. The Sheepshanks children's greatest misery was that there were so many of them — seventeen in all, including four who died in infancy. Almost every year for twenty-two years yet another Sheepshanks baby would appear — to the growing embarrassment of the older ones. Many people have enjoyed belonging to a large family but the Sheepshanks children did not. As Mary's youngest sister Dorothy recalls:

Those who [minded] most acutely were the elder members of the family — some of my sisters were really ashamed ...
[William and I] had a vague sense that the rest of the family wished we did not exist. We added to the numbers, and we felt we were a sort of reproach; even two fewer would have been less awful.[1]

Mary was the eldest girl, soon to be followed by seven younger brothers and five sisters.

'You must not mind if your mother is always out of temper', Mary's father is reported to have told her in an oblique reference to his young wife's current pregnancy.

Whenever Mrs Sheepshanks realized that she was preg-
nant again, she would have a terrible fit of crying, and the
Rev. Sheepshanks would go out and buy her a new tea-set
or dinner-set — he was particularly fond of collecting fine
porcelain. In her later years, once all her children were
quite grown up and had left home, Mrs Sheepshanks
would maintain, as Mary reported,

that hers had been a happy life; but in earlier years her nerves
were overstrained beyond endurance and the real sweetness
and generosity of her nature were sometimes over-clouded ...
The entire lack of the element of pleasure in our home-life
was no doubt largely due to the ceaseless worry and nervous
strain of her incessant child bearing ... my Mother was
swamped by babies ... She had had little education and, as
she somewhat pathetically said to me many years later, she
had never met any highly educated or intellectual women and
was at a loss in dealing with a daughter who seemed to have
that sort of bent.[2]

It was hardly to be expected that Mrs Sheepshanks could
give much individual attention or affectionate support to
her eldest daughter during her fourteen subsequent
pregnancies, nor did she. She was a woman who preferred
all her sons to any of her daughters, and of her six daughters, Mary was the one for whom she cared least, being the
plainest, the least feminine, and the most bookish as well as
the most implacable of all her girls. But all Mrs Sheepshanks' children were very devoted to *her* — as children so
often are to a mother of whose love they are deeply unsure.
Mary's youngest sister wrote:

Every one of her unruly and often quarrelsome and disagreeable children loved her with their whole hearts — that was the
one and only feeling we all shared ... though we did not
spend many hours in her company, she was the centre of our
lives ...[3]

A daughter's differences from her mother are, in a sense,
implicit criticisms of that mother. An 'undermothered' girl
like Mary, as Adrienne Rich suggests, may react

by denying her own vulnerability, denying she has felt any loss or absence of mothering. She may spend her life proving her strength in the 'mothering' of others ... in the role of teacher, doctor, political activist, psychotherapist. In a sense she is giving to others what she herself lacked; but this will always mean that she needs the neediness of others in order to go on feeling her own strength.[4]

Mary Sheepshanks grew up needing to find both alternative mothers and needy people to mother for much of her life.

Mary Sheepshanks' childhood was also much affected by her father. Eighty years later, Mary was still able to remember the bustle of the Rev. Sheepshanks' working week:

At Sunday night supper the curates discussed the week's tasks with him, mapping out and allotting the streets to be visited. It was settled who was to take certain classes in the day schools or for confirmation, the Band of Hope, the Sunday School, the weekly services, the baptisms, weddings and funerals ... The great church was packed to the doors for the Sunday morning and evening services, and there were many active workers, district visitors and helpers in every department. My Father was a thoroughly happy man ...[5]

Tall, 'wonderfully handsome', as his daughter Dorothy recalls, with a calmly powerful, authoritative presence, the Reverend John Sheepshanks had led an extraordinarily adventurous life after having graduated with 1st Class Honours from Cambridge. During the 1850s Mary's father had taken part in a mission to the North American Indians of British Columbia with whom he got on very well and with whose cause he sympathised against the victorious white land-grabbers; he vaccinated a whole tribe of Canadian Indians against the smallpox; he built his own log hut in the wilds of British Columbia and braved a mob's drunken violence on a mission to the Californian Gold Rush. Then he left America for Asia, crossing the Pacific by cargo boat and travelling through China by horse-cart and camel. In Canton he saw the execution ground where criminals — or rebels — were decapitated when hanging upon crosses, and their skulls left upon the ground. In 1860, without maps or medical aids, the Rev. Sheepshanks then crossed the great Gobi desert alone and unarmed, meeting only the nomad Mongol herdsmen whose Buddhism, closely akin to that of Tibet, greatly interested him. Finally, when crossing Siberia,

he had seen those terrible processions of men and women dragging along into exile and prison which were common in Tsarist Russia and had heard the clank of chains as the files of prisoners walked along manacled to each other.[6]

Listening to her father's accounts of such experiences was one of the most formative and positive elements in Mary's childhood, firing her with reformist indignation at the wrongs he so vividly described.

But the pity was that although her father was the most significant member of the family for Mary, Mary did not matter very much to him. She was neither a promising son nor a beautiful daughter. Time and again as a child and young girl she tried to impress him, but rarely, if ever, managed to do so. To counter her disappointment, Mary grew more critical of her father, weaning herself from her need of his praise and going her own way — even rejecting his religious faith. Yet she was the one among all his thirteen children who was most like him — sharing his mental and physical energy, his moral courage, his linguistic flair and his zest for travelling through dangerous and lonely parts of the globe. That part of her father to which she had whole-heartedly responded as a child — his sense of the justice due to others and the immovable courage of his convictions — Mary took into herself. Even in very old age her respect for this aspect of her father rings out:

Of public events before 1890 those that stand out most strongly in my memory are the Irish troubles, the Fenian

outrages and the Phoenix Park murders. My Father was a
Liberal Home Ruler and, while condemning the outrages, he
put them in perspective, saying that a small unarmed nation
had no other way of waging a war of liberation. In taking the
line he did about the Irish my Father showed, as always, his
independence of judgement and indifference to popularity.
Later on, he again took the unpopular line by defending the
Boer cause in the South African war.[7]

Mary's later causes such as socialism, feminism and
pacifism, too extreme for her father's Gladstonian Liberalism, were nevertheless her version of his altruistic conscience. Although she later rebelled against her father,
Mary never denied him by negating the values for which he
stood.

There remain Mary's many brothers and sisters. Her
own sense of her situation in her huge family was that she
was without a friend. Her elder brother Richard, who was
closest to her in age and also very clever, should have been a
beloved companion. But, in fact, he was given to implacable animosities and to outbreaks of sadistic violence. It
was said that his emotional nature had been permanently
damaged by traumatic bullying at his preparatory school —
for all the Sheepshanks boys were sent away to preparatory
and public schools, and one of the divisions within the
family was caused precisely by the educational advantages
(whatever they may have been psychologically) accorded to
all the boys, and to 'the greater interest taken in them.'[8]
Anger at this preference for sons over daughters, however
general at that time, did influence Mary's later feminism.
But Mary did not become the acknowledged leader of the
girls against the boys in the Sheepshanks family. Her next
sister was six years younger than she; then came two more
girls in quick succession, and these three together formed a
clique that successfully resisted all Mary's efforts to
dominate them. They were prettier, livelier, more generally popular than Mary, with her spectacles and her frown.
In addition to all this hostility between the older boys and

girls and between the middle girls and Mary, there was a constant state of war between the middle group of Sheepshanks children and the much younger Dorothy and William, made up of constant harassment by one side and constant surrenders or retreat by the other.

We began now to suffer from the incessant teasing of the older ones. It was customary in those days to tease children and we hated it. I had to put up with remarks about my lack of colour and washed-out cheeks and was called 'SLUGGEY' as a nickname by the older boys. Sometimes our legs were smartly hit with sticks, sometimes we were told to 'run for our lives' and chased upstairs. Sometimes we were held on the ground and cushions pressed over our faces. So, though I do not want to exaggerate, we had in general a hunted feeling and wanted to avoid the others. Luckily, as we considered it, they always used the great staircase, and we were forbidden to do so ... So we used exclusively the stone back-stairs, and we used to creep up them, anxiously watching as we climbed each flight lest the doors which led through to the main passages and rooms should open and we should be caught. ... I know quite well that none of those older ones had any idea of our feelings; they never meant to be unkind and never realized how nervous we were or how defenceless we felt against their greater strength, nor how we disliked the sharp things they would say ...[9]

Did they not, one wonders? Mary had left home sometime before this reign of terror became the order of the day at the Bishop's Palace, Norwich. (The Rev. Sheepshanks had been elevated to a bishopric c. 1890 by Gladstone.) Nevertheless, there is no evidence that she felt the slightest tenderness for any of her brothers or sisters, or that they had felt any for her. The struggle for psychic space, in Mary's own words, fighting 'for their own hand'[10] had simply been too bitter. The first surviving photograph of her shows her at twenty refusing either to smile or even to look at the camera; she had agreed to be included in the huge family group only on sufferance.

Although no photograph of Mary as a child has yet come to light it is possible, from descriptions of other members of the family, to visualize her as a large, plain baby, growing into a larger, plain little girl, who felt she had to stump in cross isolation around the house. Her attempts to find a place in her family were a preparation for life of a sort — a toughening-up process that strengthened her to withstand all her later experiences of hostility. She grew a thick protective shell which concealed a deep capacity for hurt and an immense, unsatisfied need to care and be cared for. Mary never found it easy to believe that people *did* care for her, and she herself was too quick to jump to hostile judgements on others. Her tongue, the expression of her exceptionally able mind, became her trusty sword — a weapon resorted to quickly and too often in later life when sharp defensive jabs at jeering brothers and sisters were no longer necessary but had become habitual.

The implacable rivalry and animosity between the gifted Sheepshanks children lasted in some cases all their lives. At no one time were they all on visiting or even on speaking terms with one another. Feuds lasted for decades, and even attempted deathbed reconciliations were rebuffed. But each of the others did at least have one or two friends among their brothers and sisters; Mary had none. Already as a young schoolgirl Mary diagnosed what she saw as the root cause of family unhappiness: 'My first speech at the High School debating society was against large families, and time has only strengthened that view.' To make her criticism of her own home so public, even at this age, was a devastating comment on the intensity and depth of her alienation from her family. Even more devastating, for all its surface calm, is Mary's account of her youthful reaction to the serious, sometimes nearly fatal, illnesses of her younger brothers and sisters:

Two happy memories of my youth are of the kindness and sympathy of a dear old Yorkshire woman, Mrs Robert

Reynard, most generous and understanding of women; and of the charming and cultivated Miss Gertrude Langton, at whose house I was sometimes a happy guest during the frequent epidemics and quarantine in our family. When any of the children had measles, chicken pox, scarlet fever or diphtheria they were nursed at home; and I was sent either into lodgings or, if invited, to stay with our excellent family doctor and his wife or with Miss Langton. These visits were to me a pleasant relief. I revelled in the quiet orderliness and elegance of Miss Langton's house and in the tête-à-tête talks or game of bézique in the evening after my day at school. (Mary Sheepshanks, *Autobiography*, ch. 1.)

Mary grew up to be a tireless rescuer of refugees, but first she had to learn what it meant to be in need of refuge herself. Of her own unpublished memoir of her childhood, Mary remarked:

I am afraid Katherine and Dorothy will be angry at my account of my youth in Liverpool, though I have softened it a good deal. They had a pleasant childhood in Norwich and won't believe how grim the Vicarage was. (Letter to her niece Pita, 1953.)

Flora Mayor was born just five days earlier than Mary Sheepshanks, on 20 October, 1872. 'Born on Sunday, twin daughters, the elder at 3.20, the younger at 4.0 p.m., very small and weakly,' their father noted in his commonplace-book, between recording his reading of Samuel Butler and of Froude. To be born one of twins is still regarded as a 'risk factor' by doctors, psychologists and social workers. But although Flora had poor physical health, psychologically her relationship with Alice proved immensely positive for much of her life. Some twins, especially 'identical twins' like Flora and Alice, suffer from confusion about their identities or engage in acute sibling rivalry, but both Flora and Alice Mayor seem to have had strong, individual, characters from birth. Their separate identities were actually reinforced by each girl's innermost consciousness of difference from the other and by their *bande à part* in relation to the rest of the world. Their lifelong mutual companionship, beginning in the Victorian perambulator, was very like a good marriage.

Whereas the Reverend John Sheepshanks was an evangelical Anglican in the industrial north, the Reverend Joseph Mayor was a scholarly divine. An authority on the Epistle of James and on Latin prosody, he held the Chair of Classics at King's College, University of London and later the Chair of Moral Philosophy there. The Mayor family was 'very comfortably off', and their home at Queensgate House, Kingston Hill, had the upper-middle-class support of a devoted staff of servants, including cook, maids, nanny and gardener. The nanny, Hannah, and the gardener, Thorogood, remained friends of the family all their lives. The childhood of Alice and Flora Mayor, like that of their elder brothers Robin and Henry, was the opposite of grim. Although, as children of a clerical family, they had to be regular attenders at church and Sunday school, the girls rather liked doing justice to their favourite hymns. 'How that child Flora does roar', wrote Flora herself to Alice after one Sunday's efforts to entertain poor children at the Sailors' Orphanage. And when they were not at church or paying visits or doing lessons with their mother or father, there was no end to the occupations that the four children thought up for themselves. Rainy afternoons or long winter evenings were spent reading or playing card games, or making up long serial stories together, or holding debates or writing their family newspaper, the *Queensgate Chronicle*, or singing around the piano or, best of all, dressing up and acting charades. Birthdays were traditionally celebrated with magic lantern shows or visits to the circus or to Gilbert and Sullivan. In summer there was kite-flying and battledore and fossicking by the sea; at Christmas their father would put up holly and ivy in the large entrance hall and light candles in the Chinese lanterns. And soon the Mayor children themselves were putting on their own versions of *Aladdin* or *Cinderella*. All these activities and many more figure over and over again in the hundreds of family letters and journal entries that cover the years of Flora's childhood.

Flora's father was forty-six and her mother forty-two when she, their last child and one of just two cherished daughters was born. Both Professor Mayor and his wife had had unhappy childhoods. Flora's mother, Jessie Grote, had been left motherless at five and fatherless at six. She had been reared first by her severe, Calvinist grandmother, and then passed from the care of one aunt or uncle to another. Flora's father had been the eighth of his parents' twelve children. He lost his father when he was fourteen and thereafter had to make his own way in the world, always under intense pressure from his mother to succeed at school:

I was grievously disappointed at not having a more cheering account of your present progress ... O my Joe if you knew how very much of your Mother's comfort and happiness was bound up in your well doing, I am sure you would be impelled by filial love to do your very utmost ... I hope and believe that you never suffer yourself to be influenced by the representations of idle boys who would of course wish others to get forward no better than themselves ... Are you doing your best my boy? Remember nothing less should satisfy your conscience and certainly nothing less will please me. (Mrs Charlotte Mayor to Joseph Mayor when he was at Rugby School.)

Professor and Mrs Joseph Mayor wanted their children to be happier and freer from constraint than they themselves had been. Thus, when Flora's elder brother Robin was born, his paternal grandmother, Mrs Charlotte Mayor, prayed for the child's soul, but his father, Professor Joseph Mayor, looked on his baby simply as a baby:

the baby has got over his troubles of yesterday and is doing something to win back his character; in appearance he is perhaps rather deteriorating, being redder than he was and keeping his eyes mostly shut. The only point on which we now pride ourselves is the beauty of the hands and nails which I dare say he shares with the rest of the baby world ... The nurse professes to admire his strength as proved in his powers of turning himself over without assistance, and his lusty smacking of his lips, which certainly is an amusing performance — I could hear him down in the room below ...[11]

This homely letter was written by Professor Joseph Mayor to his sister Fanny, the youngest of Flora Mayor's seven unmarried aunts. No evocation of the Mayor family life can leave out 'the Aunts' whose house in Hampstead provided a second indulgent home for Robin, Henry, Alice and Flora. Whenever there was illness at Queensgate House, Kingston, or whenever the parents took a holiday, one or more of the Mayor children would be collected and taken care of by 'the Aunts'; whenever a multiple disaster struck the family, one or more of 'the Aunts' would arrive to take a hand with the nursing, day and night.

Henry back from Hampstead, rather spoilt and passionate. ... Alice and Henry at Hampstead for three days, then changed for Flora and Robin. ... [Aunt] Georgie had been sleeping here to take the place of Hannah ... [Aunt] Fanny has arrived to help.

These are constantly recurring entries in the Rev. Mayor's commonplace-book. Aided by the redoubtable nanny, Hannah, the Aunts, especially Kate, Georgie and Fanny, were doting surrogate parents:

I think they are the sweetest pair I ever saw ... Flora looks such a little fat round child and has quite irrepressible spirits ... as they drove down to the station they were both singing 'Hold the Fort!' at the tops of their voices as we went along. (Kate Mayor to Joseph and Jessie Mayor, 1875.)

All the aunts were great characters. The eldest of them, clever and artistic Anna, refused the headship of a house of

Deaconesses, offered her by the Bishop of Salisbury, in order to stay in Rome and work for the conversion of the Italians to Protestantism, under the very nose of the Vatican. She did not succeed, but neither did she give up.[12] Next came Aunt Lizzie, also artistic, who was an active unpaid social worker in a poor district of London; then the two teachers, Charlotte and Kate:

November 19th, 1874, Kate here with scheme for taking part in a School at Sierra Leone — happily diverted to the idea of the Paris home for unprotected Englishwomen.[13]

Next came Emily, a keen hill-walker in the Lake District when she was not active in the Ladies' Church Defence League. And finally there were the two youngest — Georgie and Fanny, both pioneer nurses — Georgie being one of the most revered Nursing Sisters at the Great Ormond St Hospital for Sick Children. All 'the Aunts' could read French, German and Italian and were well-read in English literature, history and theology.

'The Aunts' were not all liked by Flora, but they were all respected and many of them were loved. Remembering their zest and seriousness, Flora Mayor was never guilty of amused condescension towards the Victorians. 'The Aunts' also contributed to her understanding of both the strains and supports within family life. In sharp contrast to the rivalries, bullying and 'bad blood' that existed within the Sheepshanks family, the ten surviving Mayor brothers and sisters of the older generation were bound to one another all their lives by ties of the deepest affection. They visited one another constantly, shouldered one another's burdens, rejoiced in one another's happiness or success, and finally nursed one another when dying. They also gave the four young Mayor children a great deal of love. Whereas Mary Sheepshanks left her family at the earliest possible moment, hardly ever to return, and ventured out to try and find alternative families in the world outside, Flora Mayor's extended family, together with a very few

close friends, became her entire world. Many hundreds of
family letters, as well as journals dating right back to the
1770s, were kept by the Mayors to be read and re-read by
one generation after another until Flora herself became the
family archivist. They survive to this day. Family *pietas*,
therefore, was an experienced reality to Flora Mayor and
her wish to 'conserve' all that was best in her own family's
traditions constituted a significant element in her later
conservatism.

Pre-eminent in the Mayor tradition was scholarship.
Almost all Flora's immediate forebears were people of
intellectual distinction. Her paternal grandmother,
Charlotte Mayor was the sister of Henry Bickersteth, Lord
Langdale, Master of the Rolls, and had herself been taught
Latin and Greek, French and Hebrew. Her twelve children
included the seven aunts as well as Flora's father, the Pro-
fessor of Classics and Moral Philosophy, Flora's uncle,
Robert Mayor, a distinguished mathematician and classi-
cist, and Fellow of St John's College, Cambridge, and
Flora's other uncle, John Mayor, also a Fellow of St John's
College, later Regius Professor of Latin at Cambridge and
reputedly one of the most learned men of his time. Flora's
mother was the niece of Professor George Grote, (friend of
Mill and Bentham, co-founder of the University of London
and pre-eminent historian of Greece), and of Professor
John Grote who held the Chair of Moral Philosophy at
Cambridge. Jessie Grote was a woman of wide culture. She
was exceptionally musical and had an extraordinary
capacity for mastering foreign languages, learning Italian
and German as a girl in Trieste and then teaching herself
Spanish, Portuguese, Danish, Dutch, Gaelic, 'and some
others'. Flora's mother translated the Icelandic Sagas into
English as well as a Zulu grammar from the Danish. There
was not the slightest danger that Mrs Mayor would feel
inferior to Flora in intellectual matters, as Mrs Sheepshanks felt with her daughter Mary.

When Flora's brothers Robin and Henry were nearly

ten, the time had come for them in their turn to show their intellectual prowess, and they were sent away to board at a Classical crammer's. After each term, their father would note in his commonplace-book the boys' academic reading and intellectual potential:

Mr Edgar thought Robin had the 'makings of a great scholar' ... As he only began Greek in April 1879 [i.e. when he was nine], this is satisfactory. ... Robin has been doing Analects off-hand, and is reading Herodotus by himself ... Henry reading Phaedrus with me. ... Robin top of his new class. Henry began Euclid and working steadily at his Latin.

But signs of strain, especially in Robin, were unmistakable:

Yesterday we had him back for the afternoon — it is curious what a change even these few days have wrought — he is a little subdued in manner and has a sweeter and more thoughtful expression. ... Robin here yesterday: still too subdued, but with a beautiful look about him like Christian starting on his pilgrimage. ... December 1880, Robin gets class prize. He is rather wanting in life and freedom as compared with Henry. ... Jan. 1882 — Children all writing tales. Henry in verse. Robin returned to school. His tale very bald, much less vivid than Henry's.[14]

Robin topped the entrance scholarship lists both to Clifton and to Eton before he was thirteen and Henry won a scholarship to Clifton.

The twins probably felt undervalued by their father — Professor Mayor never mentions Flora or Alice in his commonplace-book except in connection with their illnesses, until they are ten, when he merely notes that he has begun to give them lessons in arithmetic and grammar. But the girls did receive education from their mother as she attempted to make them more like her. In a letter Flora wrote to Alice when she was forty-four and their mother eighty-six, she throws some light on this:

In the evening Mother proposed that she should 'Give me a little reading in Dante.' I foresaw this would be very trying but thought it unkind to refuse. However I arranged to take prayers in ten minutes, but it *did* recall old days. I snubbed corrections in pronunciation but I think that kind of thing definitely put us off many intellectual things. Her knowledge of Dante and Italian is quite wonderful of course.

In a later letter Flora remarked of her mother: 'I don't think she ever can have been able to discuss, because she always thinks she's right. She cut herself off from discussion by that.' Mrs Mayor wanted to be proud of her two accomplished daughters but she never became really close to either of them. On occasion she could be frightening: 'I could see how terrifically formidable Mother would be if one was in her power' (Flora to Alice when they were fifty). That Flora never was in her mother's power, although she lived with her for much of her life, was due to her having Alice. To intimidate one little girl is not difficult; to intimidate two simultaneously is impossible. A sardonically raised eyebrow, secretly signalled from one to the other and back soon became part of Alice and Flora's response. The warmth within the Mayor family came less from the mother than from the children's nanny, Hannah, and from the Aunts.

The childhood photographs of Flora show an arrestingly mobile face, with very dark hair and blue eyes. Mary Sheepshanks, tall and strongly-built for her age, always the responsible eldest, was indulged hardly at all, whereas Flora, the delicate, appealingly eager and vivacious youngest, could usually rely on a little spoiling. Not surprisingly, Mary Sheepshanks grew up thinking that she was neither attractive nor precious to anyone, while Flora Mayor assumed, sometimes too readily, that she would always be a great social success. Flora's devotion to her twin Alice modified her narcissism, and though to the outside world it seemed that Flora was the dominant one, secretly, as Alice knew, Flora had the greatest respect for

Alice's caustic judgement — including Alice's judgement of Flora.

But Flora did not have only Alice, and Alice Flora. For the first ten years of their lives the two girls had Robin and Henry with them also. The four children, all of them bookish and close in age, really composed a unit. A letter from eleven-year-old Henry to Alice and Flora then nine-and-a-half (probably visiting the Aunts) evokes the ease and closeness of the children's shared lives. Nothing could be more natural, unconstrained, and reminiscent of Rousseau's *Émile*:

My dear F and A,

I am glad to say Zilla [one of the guinea-pigs] is much better, and will certainly get over it, though Thorogood thought one day that she would die. She is very tender, and you will not be able to nurse her, most likely, for over a month. Pappa and Mamma and Robin came back late yesterday evening. Thorogood and I waited for them at the park gate. I saw a lot of stag-beetles flying about, and with the help of Thorogood I managed to catch one ... Yesterday I went up to the 'Woodlands' and had a game at Cricket. Dora [the dog] is very well and was much pleased when they came home. Bonny and Bunny [the girls' rabbits] are very well and so is everything else. I am not quite sure whether you saw the new rabbit hutch before you went: it was made by one of the workmen who were here tarring the fence, and is capitally roomy. Tomorrow I am going at 5.0 to Mr Gooch, to play cricket with the choir-boys, like I did last year. We are having quantities of strawberries here. One day I got two baskets piled up and one of Thorogood's largest pots full of them.

Have you finished 'The last of the Mohicans' yet?

Please Answer

Yours affectionately,

H.B. Mayor

But all that changed once Robin and Henry were well and truly into their preparatory and public school regimen. Mary Sheepshanks felt that she had never had a real relationship with any of her brothers; Flora, in later life, knew what it was to have had one and to have lost it:

I am quite sure Robin and Henry have a steady brotherly feeling for us, but I don't think they in the least want to see us or have any intercourse with us. . . . I think Robin and Henry have made so little effort against coldness. They had sisters who were proud and delighted to have their affection. I think our love is nothing to either of them. They can't help being cold, but they could foster what they've got. . . . I did feel it a good deal last night. I simply feel one has to cross one's intercourse with one's brothers out of one's life, as one of the departed joys of youth and just face it as a disability, a very hard disability, of age. (Letters from Flora to Alice, c. 1906, 1912, 1922.)

That the Mayor children's early home life was basically happy is as indubitable as that the Sheepshanks children's was not. But there is no such thing as an invariably happy child. Significantly Flora wrote to Alice when they were in their fifties:

Doll has lent me a book about Quaker children more like my *Reminiscences* than anything I have yet read. Very interesting . . . The author in her childhood only remembered one *absolutely* happy day. From four onwards she was dogged by what was the object in life and why the torrents of generations. Very interesting. You'd better read it.[15]

Mary Sheepshanks identified all the external factors making for her unhappiness as a child — the excessive size of the family, the inadequate educational provision for girls, the Puritanical world-view which rejected pleasure for children on principle — and hence she campaigned actively for much of her life to eliminate pernicious ideas and to put right remediable wrongs. But for Flora Mayor the very absence of external reasons for her occasional acute misery as a child revealed to her that personal relationships can alone make a Heaven of Hell, a Hell of Heaven. The whole, absurd business of our dealings with one another — our fallings-out and struggles to fall back in — are contained in the first surviving letter Flora ever wrote:

Dearest Maudie,

Alice and I wanted to write to you to ask you to make it up; we have been so unhappy since we quarreled, and now Ethel is gone there is hardly anyone we know here, and the boys are *so* very un-pleasant, we don't know what to do.

If you will make it up come to tea on Friday and we can have a *nice* talk.

> With many kisses
>   Dear Maudie
> from your loving
> school-fellow
> Flora Mayor

TWO EDUCATIONS, 1883–1895

Long before Mary Sheepshanks and Flora Mayor first met, they were, without knowing it, one in spirit. Between the ages of ten and sixteen both girls became addicted to the reading of novels. What they were responding to as they sat for hours on end, engrossed in *Jane Eyre* or *The Mill on the Floss*, was nothing less than the articulation of their own secret dreams of rebellion and of heroism, expressed for the first time in literature by small, middle-class girls like themselves:[1]

'Wicked and cruel boy!' I said. 'You are like a murderer — you are like a slave-driver — you are like the Roman emperors!' ... He ran headlong at me: I felt him grasp my hair and my shoulders: he had closed with a desperate thing. I really saw in him a tyrant; a murderer ... I don't very well know what I did with my hands, but he called me 'Rat! rat!' and bellowed out aloud ... Four hands were immediately laid upon me, and I was borne upstairs.' (*Jane Eyre*, ch.1.)

'Oh, mother,' said Maggie in a vehemently cross tone, 'I don't want to do my patchwork.'

'What! not your pretty patchwork, to make a counterpane for your aunt Glegg?'

'It's foolish work,' said Maggie, with a toss of her mane, 'tearing things to pieces to sew 'em together again. And I don't want to do anything for my aunt Glegg — I don't like her.'

Exit Maggie, dragging her bonnet by the string ... (*The Mill on the Floss*, ch.1.)

Novels like *Jane Eyre* and *The Mill on the Floss* speak not only to the actual condition of clever, intense girls, chafing within the walls of a sometimes uncongenial home; they speak to the fantasies of deprivation, and of final, triumphant vindication that are familiar to every child. And it was precisely because they did not kick and scream like rebellious Jane Eyre, or shout ' "Oh, Mother," in a vehemently cross tone', that girls like Mary and Flora needed fictitious characters who would kick and shout for them. Jane Austen, the Brontës, Mrs Gaskell and George Eliot, however, did not only identify the false values of snobbish, mercenary worldliness or of mere passive conformity which must be kicked against; they also dramatised the positive values of integrity and self-assertion for women.[2] Marianne and Elinor Dashwood, Elizabeth Bennet, Fanny Price, Emma Woodhouse, Anne Elliot, Jane Eyre, Lucy Snowe, Maggie Tulliver, Jo March, Ethel May, Dorothea Brooke and Margaret Hale are by far the most interesting, the strongest and the most sensitive people in their respective worlds, and their girl-readers felt enormously strengthened on discovering them — both then and ever since:

I recognized myself in [Maggie Tulliver]. She too was dark, loved nature, and books and life, was too headstrong to be able to observe the conventions of her respectable surroundings, and yet was very sensitive to the criticism of a brother she adored. (Simone de Beauvoir, *Memoirs of a Dutiful Daughter*, 1958, Bk.II.)

Seeing myself as the ill-treated misunderstood Jane, I read on and on ... At the end I announced that I had changed my name to 'Janet', for that was what Rochester called his Jane in his fondest moments. By steadfastly refusing to answer to anything else, Janet I became, and am still. (Janet Hitchman, *King of the Barbareens*, 1960.)

Like Simone de Beauvoir, Flora was fired by all this reading of novels to dream of becoming a writer of novels herself; like Janet Hitchman, Mary needed the therapeutic fantasy within each novel, as it promised her that an Ugly Duckling heroine could grow up to be loved and valued at last.

Second only in significance to this compulsive novel-reading was the influence upon Mary and Flora of their experience of school. The two girls belonged to the first generation to attend Girls' High Schools in Britain. In 1880, Mary Sheepshanks' school, the Liverpool High School, was founded by the Girls' Public Day School Trust (GPDST), and in 1884, Flora and Alice Mayor's Surbiton High School was founded by the Church of England to counterbalance the undenominational religious education favoured by the GPDST.[3] Mary Sheepshanks was allowed to go to Liverpool High School when she was fourteen largely because she had made herself so un-enjoyable a member of the family at home. Not only did she outgrow the governess, as she herself says, but she let it be known that she had done so. Liverpool High School for Girls was situated in an imposing villa backing on to Princes Park at 17 Belvidere Road. 'Belvidere' was an anglicism for 'the vision beautiful', but to get to it Mary Sheepshanks had to walk to and from Anfield in all weathers, starting off on winter mornings alone in the dark. She was a brave, tough and determined girl, having no truck at all with Victorian restrictions on the behaviour considered proper or safe for a 'young lady'.

At that time there was no bus or tram for the cross-country route ... So at fourteen ... I had to walk to the other side of the town, three miles each way through dingy streets and across brickfields with stagnant pools and dead cats. (Mary Sheepshanks, *Autobiography*, ch.1.)

Despite the long cold walk there and back, the three hours' homework every evening and the absence of any games or recreation, Liverpool High School was an eye-opening and inspiring experience for Mary Sheepshanks. She found it greatly preferable to her life at home. Here her passionate earnestness and her bookishness could be affirmed rather than laughed at and it was at the Liverpool High School's debating society that Mary Sheepshanks began her life's career of bold public speaking — her first speech being the one in which she had dared to deplore large families. Stimulated by her opportunity of meeting other clever girls, several of whom were to win scholarships to university, Mary worked eagerly:

1889 Form V. English Literature, *Macbeth*.
      'On the whole, the work of the Form was satisfactory. M. Sheepshanks deserves mention.'
1889 Council's Certificate of Merit awarded for Distinction in 4 subjects in the Oxford and Cambridge Board Examinations in July, 1889. Form V. Distinguished in 4 subjects, Mary Sheepshanks.
1891 Cambridge Higher Local Examinations.
      Mary Sheepshanks, Hons. in French, German, and Literature.

Even more important than her intellectual debt, as Mary testified seventy years later, was her first real experience of loving friendship:

It was almost impossible to make friends, as all my schoolfellows lived in the better-class neighbourhood near the school and were thus out of reach. But my first day at school brought me a dear and life-long friend — Emily Japp, with her deepset grey eyes, dark hair falling over her shoulders and lovely disposition ...
    The Headmistress, Miss Huckwell, was inspiring and awe-inspiring. She was very small of stature, but of terrific personality, and she could make the boldest quake. Her lessons on English Literature were memorable. Another star and life-long friend was Lucy Silcox [later Headmistress of St Felix School, Southwold], who had taken both the classical and mathematical Triposes at Cambridge. Her flashing eyes and gypsy look gave a hint of a warm and tempestuous nature,

and her recherché and at times exotic dress expressed a love
of beauty which in her was a dominating passion ... Miss
Huckwell inspired respect; Lucy Silcox gave and inspired
love. (Mary Sheepshanks, *Autobiography*, ch. 1.)

Flora Mayor attended Surbiton High School with her
twin sister Alice. The school's motto was Kingsley's in-
junction: 'Be good, sweet maid and let who will be clever'
and this emphasis on goodness rather than on cleverness
permeated from the headmistress, Miss Nixon Smith,
down. But the goodness was real goodness. Three of the
headmistress's letters to the Mayor twins have survived:
'Will you understand all I should like to say dear. Your
loving K.H. Nixon Smith' is how she ended one letter to
Flora in 1888; and to Alice, when Flora achieved entry to
Newnham whilst Alice did not — 'Much love — I think it is
very good of you to have given up Flora'. Once again, as in
the relationship between Lucy Silcox and Mary Sheepshanks, there is that note of unconcealed, direct personal
feeling from teacher to girl which often nowadays would be
self-censored and erased.

The standard of teaching at Surbiton High School was
less distinguished than at Liverpool, and since Flora
Mayor's own family was so intellectual she was less
impressed by her teachers and contemporaries than Mary
Sheepshanks was by hers. What did matter to Flora was
that she should impress them. It was at school that Flora
first developed her appetite for 'popularity', by which she
meant being adored, cheered to the echo, a star. Flora
Mayor was never at any time a 'Rector's Daughter',
reconciled like her own later heroine, Mary Jocelyn, to
obscurity or insignificance in others' eyes. Instead, with
naïve, unblushing egotism, Flora retailed to Alice all their
talents and virtues, as listed by an admiring schoolfriend:

She said she had never heard anything against either of us.
She says our chief quality is supposed to be good nature, also
that we have not a grain of conceit, also that we're appallingly

clever, also that we have very good voices, also that we're awfully jolly girls ... She says she likes us best next to Elsie. Eddie thinks we're awfully jolly girls not silly with boys as lots of girls are. I feel quite proud.

Not content with ten out of ten for humility, Flora wanted to shine above the rest still more. Applause did come, literally, when her acting talent was first displayed at a school production of Molière's *L'Avare* when she was fourteen, and two years later Flora had another star part in the school's drama production of *Little Lord Fauntleroy*. In 1889, when they were seventeen, both the Mayor sisters were awarded Third Class Honours in the Oxford University Junior Local Examinations and Flora also won the Sixth Form Latin prize. All in all, Surbiton High School was a much gentler introduction to the world than was Mary's high school in Liverpool; it was perhaps too protective and affirming. Only much later did Flora remark ruefully to Alice: 'Of course I know we impressed dear Mary Walton as modest, but we were *terribly* vain, and too childish. We remained really seventeen for years.'

When Mary Sheepshanks was seventeen, in 1889, she was sent to Germany to 'finish' her schooling. It was the first time that she had been abroad and suddenly she found herself far away from Liverpool living alone in the cultured milieu of Kassel, with its

well laid out streets, fine buildings, concert halls, theatres and picture gallery ... I had never before seen a play, nor heard a concert nor had I seen any good pictures ... [But] theatre-going here was as much a matter of course as church-going was at home. Prices were low and early hours were kept. Six o'clock was the usual time for the play to begin, and at nine o'clock the maid, wearing a neat knitted hood, was at the theatre to escort me home. (Mary Sheepshanks, *Autobiography*, ch.2.)

Mary soon became a fluent speaker of German; her gift for German and for many other languages stayed with her all her life and was essential in her political work. But Mary learned something even more important than a thorough knowledge of another language — she learned to enjoy herself. There was her first German Christmas with German carols round the Christmas tree, then seeing the New Year in with hot punch, and, best of all, skating on the lake at Wilhelmshöhe. 'Skating on well-swept ice ... in bright sunshine to the music of a military band was intoxicating.' Mary Sheepshanks marvelled at the very possibility of pleasure: 'It seemed to be generally accepted that one should enjoy life.'

Having reported home that the Kassel school was not much good, Mary transferred after Easter to Potsdam. There she lived with the family of the court chaplain. Her father assumed that the chaplain would be a serious Christian, but Mary soon discovered the old pastor to be a bad-tempered, card-playing drunkard. Everything else about Mary's stay in Potsdam, however, was so idyllic, that she could recall its every detail more than half a century on:

We breakfasted and in mid-morning had a snack. At about 3 o'clock we had coffee in the large garden, with many shady trees under which hammocks were slung. Later we would go walking in the parks or swimming or spend long summer days sailing on the lakes of the river Havel in small boats with centre-boards. Last of all there'd be supper on the veranda balcony in the summer night ... Early in July the two old people went off to Switzerland where they spent a month on the Riga — so we were left happily to our own devices ... Twice a week the guards' band played in the gardens and we met our friends. Sometimes we were invited out in the evening, and very informally we would dance on the carpet in our day clothes, and finish up with a supper of herring salad and Rhine wine.

How right the old Romans were to realise that what the people wanted was bread and games — or otherwise food and fun. We were young and enjoyed anything that meant meeting other young people — no fuss, no frills. (Mary Sheepshanks, *Autobiography*, ch.2.)

Mary concluded 'it was certainly very unlike any English vicarage I have known.'

Mary was fitted out with pretty but inexpensive clothes by her new German friends and she 'blossomed from a schoolgirl into a young lady.' No photograph of her has survived from this period, but it must have been a real blossoming, for one German girl turned to Mary and said: 'You English girls have a good time at home and, not content with that, you come here and snap away the men from us'. Mary never felt so carefree or so attractive again. She wrote: 'That pleasant summer passed all too quickly.' It had been a revelation of nothing less than another way of life jolting and querying her in-bred Puritan censoriousness. Mary began, during her time in Germany, to distance herself from her family's and her country's Victorian assumptions about what was right and wrong in conduct. Her cultural and her moral horizons had widened immeasurably. Moreover Mary had gained in social confidence and self-reliance. She had survived a different way of life in a foreign country on her own and this helped her to grow up sooner than did Flora Mayor. That it was Germany which had given Mary Sheepshanks this year of happiness and shown her such a human, life-loving face, was to affect her profoundly in 1914 — and again in 1933 and 1945.

The year after Mary came back home to Liverpool from Potsdam, the Mayor twins were sent off together to the Moravian School of Montmirail in Switzerland to perfect their French. The boarding school to which they were sent had been most carefully selected by their mother as being devoutly Protestant, cultured, and very strictly regulated:

You can't do a single thing here without asking permission. You can't wear a different dress, you can't leave the room even without asking first — at least if you do somebody comes up with an awestruck face and says '*on ne doit pas*'. I'm not allowed to wear my boa here now because it's summer. I wanted something warm one day because I had a sore throat but it is considered *impoli* to wear fur in the summer, also to eat the skin of baked potatoes ... (Flora to her brothers, July 1890.)

In a later letter Flora added:

I don't hate being *seminaire* so much as most people except that when you're quietly walking in the garden one of the mistresses comes flying after you — one of the chairs is not exactly parallel with the table or there is a crumb on the floor and you have to hurry to put it straight.

Illustrated magazines sent from England were confiscated by the deputy headmistress, Mademoiselle Bibier, because they showed '*les jeunes gens dans les attitudes impossibles.*' Compositions were set on '*Pourquoi j'aime ma mère*', to which Flora responded with the two lines: '*J'aime ma mère, parce-qu'elle est ma mère, je pense qu'on ne peut trouver une meilleure raison que cela.*' 'The subject,' said Mlle Bibier, 'is not so arid as you seem to have thought, you will do it again.' Flora tried to treat the whole place as a joke, but that did not do at all. She was labelled 'supercilious' and said to have a disposition less *aimable* and *agréable* than that of Alice. Both the twins, now eighteen years old, were frequently corrected for their pride, their untidiness, talking too much English, banging the door, bad sewing, and for sitting with their legs crossed. Many of the English girls began to have attacks of hysteria and fainting fits. Flora reported home:

the fainting has been going on most merrily this week. On Saturday M. Reichel [the Proprietor] gave us a long discourse about it. He said he had come back from Germany to find not only physical illness but worse than that — a moral malady. There was a bad spirit about in the school. A few of the girls had spoken very unjustly about certain persons at Montmirail, had given out that they detested the school and had tried to persuade other girls to be discontented also in every way. He knew those same girls were physically unwell but the doctor had assured him that the fainting had been avoidable and a girl morally healthy would not have found it necessary

to faint about twice a day. All this had distressed M. Reichel
more than he would say; he had had serious intentions of
closing Montmirail at Xmas. (Flora to her brother Henry,
December 1890.)

The consequence was that one English mother came and
withdrew both her daughter and her daughter's friend
from the school and the Mayor girls themselves left soon
after the New Year. They moved in with a sensible woman
in Neuchâtel and Flora commented, 'it's nice to get to
civilization again.'

Flora's frustration and irritation at Montmirail can be
detected in her mediocre report:

Application: Might be better.
Français: Rather superficial.
Compositions: Few ideas and rather imperfect style.
Piano: Not much talents.
Ordre: Very indifferent.
Orthographie: Deficient.

Only her *Récitations* were 'pretty good'.

Flora left Montmirail with her *amour-propre* and her
insularity both still intact. But before leaving Switzerland
she did try to warn her mother that she now wanted to be
finished with 'finishing' — 'As to what we shall take up
when we come home we must have a consultation about it
... I don't think tho' we shall have time for another language as practising takes up such an awful time.' It is significant that Flora writes here of what '*we* shall take up', rather
than of what 'I shall'. She and Alice were still inseparable
and thought of themselves as a unit. But in October 1892
the Mayor twins, then aged twenty, were parted for the first
extended period in their lives. For what Flora did 'take up'
and Alice did not, was university education, at Newnham
College, Cambridge, where Mary Sheepshanks had
already settled in the year before.

What Mary and Flora both found, on going up to Cambridge in the early 1890s, was an academic world in which women students could participate only on sufferance. Women had been admitted to sit the Honours Tripos Exams on the same terms as men since 1881, but they were still refused degrees. *The Times*, the *Pall Mall Gazette* and the *Morning Post* all declared their opposition to women being granted degrees — it would be the thin end of the wedge, the professions would be overrun, all academic standards would be lowered — perhaps it would be better if there were no women students at Cambridge at all. 'Passive hostility and sniggers'[4] were commonplace, as were the more aggressive assertions that women were not intellectually capable of benefiting from a university education, or, if they were capable and eager to study at Cambridge, then they were not 'true women':

Those whose natures are the fullest, and who would turn to best account for the world whatever opportunities were afforded to them, are just those who are most likely to be deterred from coming to Cambridge for fear of the strain between their desire for knowledge with honour and their affection for those at home. The better girl of the family would not *want* to study away from home.[5]

Even within the circle of the Mayor family's own friends and relatives there were serious doubts about the 'niceness' and 'ladylikeness' of women university students: 'Aunt Minnie, [not one of the seven Mayor Aunts] hates Colleges and higher education and will never ask you to the house while you're at Newnham', Alice reported to Flora in 1894. And their old schoolfriend, Katherine Monro, herself a Girtonian, warned Flora that the male undergraduates at Cambridge considered all women students to be 'prigs' caring for nothing but study, and that they even selected the sneering epithet 'Unwashen' for the women at Newnham.

This uneasy, even embattled relationship between the new women's college and the ancient all-male University meant that Newnham during the 1890's had still to be very much a world unto itself. But it was a satisfying, even a fascinating world:

We read papers to one-another; we danced and acted; the musical ones played and sang.[6]

College life was ... in many ways a very free life in comparison with our home life.[7]

To come up from a home that was either dreary and lacking in affection as in Mary Sheepshanks' case or from a home that was almost too protective, as in Flora Mayor's and then to find oneself given a room of one's own, with a fire, book-shelves, a table for working at and armchairs for friends, was to discover a perfect combination of privacy and warmth, of intellectual stimulus and emotional support:

I loved it from the first night. Our first night was very stormy, do you remember? I drew the curtains and lit my lamp and sat and looked at my fire. I didn't do anything else the whole evening, it was so blissful to look at one's *own* fire.[8]

Writing in her eighties, Mary Sheepshanks remembered how:

College life meant for me a new freedom and independence ... The mere living in Cambridge was a joy in itself; the beauty of it all, the noble architecture, the atmosphere of learning were balm to one's soul ...

To spend some of the most formative years in an atmos-phere of things of the mind and in the acquisition of know-ledge is happiness in itself and the results and memories are undying. Community life at its best, as in a college, brings contacts with people of varied interests and backgrounds and studying a wide range of subjects. Friendships are formed and new vistas opened. For a few years at least escape is possible from the worries and trivialities of domestic life. (Mary Sheepshanks, *Autobiography*, ch. 3.)

Meta Tuke, who was a tutor at Newnham during Mary and

Flora's time, and later became Principal of Bedford College, University of London, gave as her tribute:

At Newnham I saw women more reasonable, more contented, less petty than I had known them elsewhere. I saw them seriously determined to understand some of the problems of the world, imbued with the expectation of what education could do for women, with aspirations for a good above that of everyday life.

If that last passage sounds almost too 'high-minded', it may be counter-balanced by the emotional side of the students' lives. For here were collected many of the most gifted and remarkable women in England at the most spirited period of their lives. Not surprisingly many of them came to love one another.

My education in Cambridge came entirely from my fellow-Newnhamites ... For the first time we made friends. The slow exploration of another human being, the discovery of shared perplexities and interests, the delight in our new companions' gifts and, maybe, beauty (for beauty was not wanting in those years) — these were excitements. Many of us made friends who remained faithful to us all our lives.[9]

Mary Sheepshanks' special flame was Melian Stawell, the Classical Scholar who translated Homer, Goethe and, later, the Cretan Script, and who was, according to Mary,

the most striking personality at Newnham at that time. She was an Australian student of outstanding ability, striking physical beauty and grace. On one occasion when she entered a room full of people a man exclaimed, 'At last the gods have come down to earth in the likeness of a woman!' ... She was in fact one of those rare individuals endowed with every gift ...

Melian Stawell was in her third year when I went up, and I saw a good deal of her and learnt much from her. Through her I first came to appreciate the writings of Walt Whitman, who was at that time her favourite poet. Meredith, Ibsen and Browning were also stars in our firmament then. (Mary Sheepshanks, *Autobiography*, ch. 3.)

As for Flora's admired ones:

> Miss Stahlknecht [a fellow-student] is most fascinating, like a
> heroine in a book, only a shade uncertain in temper. ... Miss
> Stephen [the Vice-Principal of Newnham] came to see me last
> night. She gives the sweetest hugs of anyone I know. ... Miss
> Sharpley [Classics tutor] is the one I'm principally mashed on
> now, because she's so enigmatic and coquettish. ... Margaret
> thinks the delightful girls' society at College makes men's
> boring afterwards. I agree to some extent. (Flora to Alice,
> October—December 1892.)

Some of these eager emotional responses were little more
than passing 'crushes', called *Grandes Passions* (or 'GPs' in
Newnhamese), but many of the bonds which were first
formed at Newnham did go deep and grew into reciprocal,
sustaining relationships that were to last until death.[10]

Alice Mayor had been very much afraid on Flora's first
going up to Newnham, that her twin — so like her in
appearance that they could only be told apart by the colour
of their sashes — would now desert her for some more
fascinating, brilliant new college friend. She even feared
that Flora might grow ashamed of her less intellectual
sister. But in fact Flora's intimacy with Alice prevented her
from ever seeking any other kindred spirit while at Cambridge, and during her four years there she wrote each day
to Alice, recounting every detail of her startlingly novel life.
Flora reassured Alice, with fierce indignation, that she
valued Alice's judgement far more than she did that of any
of her fellow-students, however 'brilliant' they might be.

One cannot be certain when or where Flora Mayor and
Mary Sheepshanks met during their Newnham days. Both
girls belonged to many college societies, both found
themselves invited out a good deal and both made their
mark as lively talkers and strong personalities within their
own 'sets'. But at one such college meeting or dinner-party
Flora and Mary did meet and they took to one another. It
was characteristic of them both at this time that Mary

should have been rather more impressed by Flora than Flora was by Mary. The photographs of both girls when at Newnham show Mary soft-faced and shy with eyes cast down and looking away from the camera — although she had conceded to take off her pince-nez for once — whereas Flora looks exceptionally vital and attractive, her eyes dancing with confidence and humour. Mary understood from the outset that Flora needed to be flattered: 'Mary Sheepshanks said: "I told Mrs Creighton what a splendid person you were so I hope you'll say something nice about me." However I never got the opportunity.' (Flora to Alice, c.1893.) Flora did then add to Alice apropos of Mary: 'I hope you will like her. I do very much indeed.' What had immediately struck Flora about Mary was her bold conversation — 'M. Sheepshanks is an awfully nice girl to talk to', she promised Alice, and soon Alice herself heartily agreed:

... we had lots of interesting talk. I think [Miss Sheepshanks] about the most interesting girl I know to talk to ... she talks a good deal about men and matrimony, religion, books, art (very intelligently which is more than most people do). ... She is certainly very keen on men and would get on with them admirably I'm sure ... it is inspiring to the intellect to have her to discuss things with, we differ exceedingly.' (Alice to Flora, 1895-6.)

Well-informed, trenchant and genuinely interested in other people's experiences and points of view, Mary was much sought-after as a dinner-table guest guaranteed to make the evening 'go'. She never set any great store by herself as a social asset, simply ascribing her invitations to dinner at the Trinity Master's Lodge or with the Provost of King's to the fact that she was a single girl; but the interesting talk she had there was talk that she helped to make interesting. Men like Bertrand Russell, C.P. Sanger, the Llewelyn Davies brothers, Vaughan Williams, G.M. Trevelyan, Geoffrey and Hilton Young and Charles

Buxton would hardly have made friends and stayed friends with Mary Sheepshanks as they did, had she not had something compelling about her.

Mary had been persuaded, after her successful studies in Germany, that she should read for the Mediaeval and Modern Languages Tripos, but she rapidly became very bored with Anglo-Saxon and Old High German — 'the lectures were uniformly dull ... I only obtained a Second Class.' (Mary Sheepshanks, *Autobiography*, ch. 3.) It would have made Mary happier all her life long if only she could have gained a First (like her elder brother Richard) and so have impressed her father at last. But what Mary did come to realise in the intervals of grinding away at Old High German was where her real intellectual interests lay. Economic and social history, political philosophy and psychology — all those modern concerns which had only recently surfaced at Cambridge were what really spoke to her:

Fortunately I was able to stay up for a fourth year, and I enjoyed a course in Moral Science, Psychology and History of Philosophy and Economics. How I wished I had entered for that course or for History from the beginning! (Mary Sheepshanks, *Autobiography*, ch. 3.)

When she was not talking animatedly, or studying Anglo-Saxon or rowing to Clay Hithe early on a summer morning, Mary was occupied by her first experiences of social work in a Cambridge that was far from prosperous. Out of 819 children born in Cambridge in 1904, 107 died before they were a year old.[11] The two pieces of social work which Mary did regularly were to teach the adult literacy classes in the poor working-class district of Barnwell which were organized by Newnham on Sunday mornings, and once a week to take round a few old age pensions granted by the Charity Organization Society. In addition, in May 1896, the North Hall Diary reports that 'Miss Sheepshanks gave an interesting address in the College hall' on the

Women's University Settlement in Southwark. Such social work did take time away from Old High German, but it also taught Mary Sheepshanks where her natural working bent would lie.

There was another aspect of Mary's years at Cambridge which had a life-long significance for her. As her youngest sister Dorothy recounted many years later: 'Mary came to hold very advanced views in many respects, views of which father disapproved.'[12] Dorothy did not say what Mary's 'very advanced views' were, but, given Mary's contact with the Bertrand Russell set and her own bent toward social work, one can only assume that they were 'free-thinking' in religion and 'radical' in politics. Presumably Mary would have refused to attend Divine Service during an early visit home after going up to Cambridge, (home being by now the Bishop's Palace, Norwich) and strong words then passed on both sides. Whether Mary had ever had very much religious faith to lose is doubtful, since nothing in her Liverpool years would have inclined her to believe in a loving personal God either in her own or in anyone else's case. Mary's father was so repelled by Mary's opinions that he would not allow his numerous younger children to risk contamination. Arrangements were made for Mary not to spend any of her future university vacations at home. This break with her family, most unusual for a Victorian middle-class girl, was almost complete before Mary had finished being an undergraduate. The fact that it was Mary who had outspokenly rejected what was sacred to her parents did not prevent her from feeling rejected by them. Both during and after her time at Cambridge Mary became a proselytizing agnostic, and there is a Sheepshanks family anecdote that during a royal garden party, given by the Bishop of Norwich and graced by King Edward VII, Mary sat herself at a table outside the Palace gate in Norwich and handed out atheist tracts.

Whereas Mary Sheepshanks looked outwards at Newnham and at Cambridge with the grateful, though not uncritical, attitude of a girl who does not feel that she is anything very special in looks or giftedness, Flora Mayor, with all the confidence of the attractive and the amusing, was largely preoccupied with how Newnham and Cambridge reacted to her. From the first, her letters home to Alice bubbled over with her extra-curricula goings-on:

We do have fun here. It's such a different life from usual. I shall look back to it as most doux. We have awfully interesting discussions usually after supper. We talk about religious things pretty often, also books a good bit ... The bicycle is fascinating ... it's much easier than skating — not so tiring. Mounting is a trial and one must have knickerbockers for it ... Has Judith said anything to you about the mock-Parliament debate? Yesterday I got up at 7 and played my tennis tie and beat her easily ... After dinner we had dancing. It was *lovely*. I do enjoy the dancing so. If you'll believe it I've had one or two compliments on my steering. Am reading *Wages of Sin*. Fiction Library has kept me horribly busy also I had to hold a beastly Newspaper meeting ... Miss Stawell was very nice and just think in the evening she asked me to dance with her and afterwards to come and see her. Unenlightened as you are you don't know what an honour that is but she is absolutely the Queen of the College ... I did feel proud. She dances most splendidly ... The Acting is simply lovely, infinitely nicer than our School for Scandal. Of course it's more fun to stage-manage and have the best part. I did funk doing that beastly washing scene but all, dons included, have been most complimentary. We gave a performance for Newnham yesterday, people yelled out 'Speech' but I wouldn't do that. They put me up for Vice-President of Debate which was rather jolly ... Altogether Newnham is as rapturous as ever.

Study took tenth place. Flora mentions just one essay on Political Economy: 'Mrs Marshall said mine showed thought and was a very fair paper indeed considering I'd never read anything.' The barb seems to have gone unperceived. In between the acting and the dancing, the talking, the bicycling, the debating and the Fiction Library,

Flora did become more aware of her own and other people's perspectives:

Had dinner with Miss Clough to meet two South Africans. They talked so *horribly* about natives my blood boiled. I had a long talk with Miss C. about it afterwards. She defended them and is keen on Rhodes. We both got so hot.

Within days of going up to Cambridge Flora reported having been lent her 'first definitely Unchristian book — I don't think it is even theist.' That book was *The Story of a South African Farm*. Flora's father, the Rev. Dr Joseph Mayor was swift to respond:

My dearest Flora
The book you speak of (*An African Farm*) shows the reaction from Calvinism resulting in the most dreary scepticism and opening the way to positive immorality. It is of course clever, and when the writer gets into more healthy surroundings, she may perhaps become a useful teacher, but it is not in the least the book for young and thoughtless girls. You will probably meet people of advanced views at Newnham, and some of our friends thought we were rash in letting you go there, but it is no longer possible for women to go through the world with their eyes shut, and if the highest education is reserved for those who have already a tendency to scepticism, or who belong to agnostic homes, it will be a very bad look-out for English society in the future. You, I think, ought to be able 'to prove all things and hold fast to truth'. Your position is probably better than that of most of your companions, both socially and intellectually, and in time you ought to be able to exercise some influence. That God's blessing may be with you through this eventful year is the earnest wish and prayer of your affectionate father.

The Rev. Mayor was Flora's 'ever affectionate father', unlike the Rev. Sheepshanks in relation to his 'advanced' daughter Mary, and this bond of love between the Mayors certainly helped to strengthen Flora's respect for religious belief. But there is considerable irony in the fact that in the very moment in which Flora's father is appealing to Flora to hold fast to spiritual truth, he is also appealing to her personal pride: 'Your position is probably better than that of most of your companions, both socially and intellectually', and pride was Flora's devil. For Flora's real God during these years, as her letters make abundantly clear, was her own delicious self:

This letter shall be devoted to compliments I've received as I know you like to hear them.

Miss Dant remarked that I have by far the prettiest figure in the whole College. Miss Tate-Reid said whilst admiring my black jacket 'But of course anything looks nice on you. Lots of people have admired your lovely figure.' Miss Fawcett asked me if I'd played hockey before and on hearing not said I showed *very great* promise. Miss Tate-Reid thinks I've got a lovely singing voice and also the prettiest speaking voice in the College. She really pays dozens of compliments. She has admired my legs and my French and my acting and my hockey. I've had other compliments on my dancing too. Miss Dant said I'd got a great deal of fun about me. I spoke at the Sharp Prac and Miss Todd said 'I congratulate you on your speech Miss Mayor, you set the tone to the whole evening.' (Flora to Alice, 1892.)

There follows a page of suggestions as to what Flora would like from Alice for her birthday, then:

Will you send me my tennis racket. Tennis shoes, penholder, my band. Oh, Mrs Marshall put 'Good' on two of my answers last time and read one out as being very good.

Finally, scrawled in the margin, 'My dear child it looks so awful writing all this twaddle down, I feel quite ashamed of it.' But the letter was sent all the same. Sharing her undisguised delight in all these 'comps.' with her identical twin, Flora felt, was as harmless as talking aloud to herself.[13] Flora continued to find herself charming for several terms more:

We proceeded to construct an ideal beauty out of us five — My eyes, lashes, chin, forehead, skin, hands, feet, neck and figure were chosen. I was rather proud ... People seem to think I have a striking face, but that does not seem complimentary to me ...

Why didn't you say anything about my speaking at the Political — I think it was frightfully exciting. I learnt my speech off by heart. I got heaps of congratulations from everybody so I expect it was all right. A Cambridge lady remarked what an exquisite complexion I'd got. (Flora to Alice, c. 1893-4.)

Anything less like her own later heroines, Henrietta Symons or Mary Jocelyn, than their author was at twenty could hardly be imagined. Many an evening was spent analysing Flora's interesting personality — not altogether favourably, but Flora would still faithfully report everything to Alice, even the hints that she was arrogant and perhaps not quite sincere in her displays of warmth.

Among the men at Cambridge Flora seems to have made less of an impression. Edward Marsh, for instance, wrote to Bertrand Russell:

I met a lovely person on Sunday. Miss Stawell, whom Dickinson was nice enough to ask me to meet. I think she's very superior indeed — she seems to have quite a rare feeling for beauty in art, I hope we shall see more of her. Mayor's sister was there too, she seemed rather common and flippant in comparison.

Flora's activities while at Newnham seem to have included a little of everything, always with gusto. She was frequently mentioned in the North Hall Diary:

The annual entertainment at Barnwell [the Adult Education Centre] took the form this year of theatricals. A very successful performance of *Good For Nothing* with Miss Mayor in the title role was given and repeated on the following night in the College Hall.

In May 1894, Flora opposed the motion at the Newnham College History Society that 'We are nearer true democracy than any ancient or mediaeval state.' At another meeting of the same society she was in the Chair and had to accept a censure motion against herself. 'It was a *mauvais quart d'heure* but people said I appeared absolutely composed so that's a blessing.' In 1895 Flora was one of the eighteen signatories to a petition to the Principal, Mrs Sidgwick, protesting against the woefully low standard of housekeeping at Newnham and pleading with much sweet reasonableness for a domestic bursar: 'the crockery is not clean; the vegetables are not strained; ... one small cauliflower is served for 10 people ...' During one Long Vacation Flora acted Mrs Malaprop in an open-air production of *The Rivals* in Cambridge, and at Commem in 1896, she was again one of those chosen to propose the toasts. 'When Flora was at Newnham she burnt the candle at both ends and her health never recovered,' said Alice forty years later, trying to warn her niece, then also a student at Newnham, against going the same way. There were several allusions to staying up talking until two or three in the morning, and many of the daily notes to Alice tail off in a scrawled 'Too dead for more, Flora.' The doctor was not pleased with her; reference is made to her nerves being 'out of order', whilst her twenty-first birthday letter from her father tried to be jocular: 'I hope a rumour which Robin sends today of your having fainted is not true ... If you start your term's work with fainting, what will you be doing at the end of it?'

But for most of her time at university Flora was too happy to be ill. There were just two clouds. She missed Alice — 'I'm getting sick of writing stupid letters. I want to tell the things with my own sweet nigger lips.' And all the time that she was revelling in Newnham, Flora had to suppress her uneasy consciousness of Alice's deadly routine at Kingston. For Alice, as Flora only too well knew, was chained to the role of Eligible Young Lady at Home with Mother.

October 2nd 1892   Fearfully wet. Most of our mornings have
        been filled with mending. We had a dull sermon from a
        nervous curate. Annie very trying at Sunday School ...
December 26th 1892 I painted some mistletoe and holly. We
        had a dull Shakespeare reading of Henry VIII in the
        evening ...
January 6th 1893 We took a nice walk round the garden.
        Church, Sunday School, strumming. I sang Moody and
        Sankey hymns ...
May 17th 1893 I copied a photo of Rome in the morning
        under Aunt Anna's eye. We read Linnell's *Life* and
        played halma ...
May 20th 1893 I began some Scotch Songs and an
        Impromptu of Schubert's. I usually practise till 11 and
        then draw or read. There was a garden party at Mr
        Latham's where we met the people we meet everywhere.
        Mother began *Felix Holt*. I copied a photograph of
        Brussels ... (Excerpts from Alice Mayor's *Journal*.)

And so on and so on for weeks and months and years. In her
frustration, Alice secretly dreamed of becoming a concert
singer or of studying art in Rome, she attended lectures on
physiology, fantasised about adopting a poor child and
eventually drove herself to attend painting classes at the
Slade until some brutal sarcasm from her teacher, Tonks,
so shrivelled her confidence that she never went back. Flora
was afraid lest Alice be tempted to flee from Kingston into
matrimony: 'If that beast proposes to you *don't* like him
better than me, you *must not*.' But that beast did not propose. In retrospect, Flora was shocked by her own selfishness in relation to Alice during her Cambridge period:
'Fancy me having a *fourth* year.' But at the time, Flora's
zest for life had been an appetite which she simply
could not deny and her twin had had to be left behind.

    The second cloud, which grew greater as Flora's studies
drew to an end, was the uncertainty about her future once
she had gone down. Her uncle, Canon Robert Mayor of
Frating, had lost a great deal of the family money when a

bank failed in New Zealand. Flora's father wrote to her explaining that they would all now have to help:

There is no hurry about *you*, but it might be convenient if you had a place in the staff at Newnham offered to you after your degree. If you get a First class, or even a good Second, I should think they would be rather pleased to keep you on.

Flora had to stifle that oversanguine paternal ambition at once:

When I think of it, you know there's *absolutely* no chance of my being made a don up here . . . I don't get compliments about my history. I guess I'm going to do awfully badly. (Flora to Alice, 1895.)

Flora got a Third. Her father was sad but not reproachful: 'We are rather disappointed about Flora's third class, and it seems to have surprised them very much at Newnham, however she takes it sensibly, which is a comfort.'

   In fact Flora's poor degree result was a shattering blow to her self-esteem. She had started out so certain that she was remarkable, that 'Flora Macdonald Mayor' would be the name of a heroine in real life. So many people had agreed (or had seemed to agree) that she was special, yet here she was going out into the world with a third-class ticket — and one that she had, so to speak, printed for herself. At a stroke Flora learned what it meant to feel insecure and depressed, and in the first evidence of her secret ambition to become a writer, or an actress, or both, she wonders whether she is capable of becoming either:

. . . I am much exercised about my future . . . I am wondering whether I really am capable of writing or not. I feel sometimes I'm not really in the least clever and that it is futile thinking of anything even like research work, let alone writing my prophesied book. Now my dear girl think the problem seriously over. It's awful when one's self-complacency gets undermined. If only I *could* go on the stage, it's the one thing I feel sure of, that I am dramatic. Tho' I don't know if that means I could act . . .

I don't know *what* to do if father is set against the Stage. I
do want it and I feel more and more it's the thing I'm most
fitted for but if it really grieves him I can't do it. I want
awfully to talk to Mother and him about it. (Flora to Alice,
c. May 1896.)

The long debate within herself and with her family
about attempting a career on the stage had begun. (Flora
had, in fact, already confided this secret dream to her friend
Mary Sheepshanks. 'Miss Sheepshanks said you told them
you were probably going on the Stage,' wrote Alice, a little
jealous. 'I didn't know you were telling people yet.') It was,
in part, one way for Flora to deal with the 'Third-class'. If
she were deemed inadequate as a scholarly intellectual,
then she would become its polar opposite — a professional
actress. But no one in her immediate world as yet believed
that Flora either could or should do any such thing.

When Mary left Cambridge she had to make her own
way in the world with almost no contact with her family.
She immediately plunged into social work in one of the
most deprived parts of London. When Flora left Cambridge she had to return to the rose-coloured carpet of
Queensgate House, Kingston, and struggle against her
loving family's over-protectiveness, entreating their
permission to try her fortune in the world outside. Mary's
experience of higher education had left her determined to
be a radical interventionist in the world, but she was still far
from self-confident — she had no intimate, stable relationship in which she could feel rooted. Like her favourite
heroine, Lucy Snowe, Mary doubted whether she could
ever love or be loved.[14] And she did not want only to do
useful work in the world; she yearned to be happy. Flora
never had to suffer from such emotional self-doubt — her
bond with Alice alone ensured that. But she did go down
from Cambridge feeling intellectually more humble and
unsure. In just one way, however, Flora's Third Class
degree may have been a therapeutic wound. For she was
fired — as well as deeply hurt — by a supercilious remark

from her brother Henry, as reported to her by Alice in May, 1896: 'Oh, Flora cares about reading, does she?' — 'reading' in this case meaning intellectual seriousness. Ever after that it would never be enough for Flora to become an actress; she would have to prove herself a thinker and a writer as well.

3

OUT IN THE WORLD,
OR BACK AT HOME?
MARY AND FLORA, 1896–1901

By the time Mary Sheepshanks went down from Cambridge she had adopted her characteristic upright bearing, firm step and 'no nonsense' air. Her speech, always remarkable for its clarity and telling choice of words, had kept the strength of its downright Northern short 'a' whenever she said 'daft' or 'past' or 'working-class'. Mary was now to need all her toughness and exceptional height, for in October, 1895, at the age of twenty-three, she committed herself to working in the worst poverty blackspot in London — the borough of Southwark, with its 200 people per acre, where the ex-Newnhamite Alice Grüner had recently founded her Woman's University Settlement at 44 Nelson Square.[1]

On joining the Settlement, Mary began to walk the same Lambeth streets where Somerset Maugham was then going his rounds as a medical student to attend women in childbirth:

Up stinking alleys and into sinister courts where the police hesitated to penetrate but where your black bag protected you from harm. You were taken to grim houses, on each floor of which a couple of families lived, and shown into a stuffy room, ill-lit with a paraffin lamp, in which two or three women, the midwife, the mother, the 'lady as lives on the floor below' were standing round the bed on which the patient lay.[2]

These were the same streets then being preyed upon by Alf the 'ooligan, as he 'worked' his patch between the Elephant and Castle, Lambeth Walk and The Cut, thieving, fighting, passing false coin, mugging the occasional old shopkeeper, getting a reward for the occasional stray dog — 'they'll stray awright, even if you 'ave to pull their bleed'n 'eads 'arf off.'[3] And it was also in these streets in Lambeth, Southwark and Kennington in 1896 that hungry, ragged seven-year-old Charles Chaplin was trying to sell bunches of narcissus, before being picked up at night by the police, huddling near a watchman's fire.[4]

The University 'Settlement Movement' had first been pioneered by Canon Barnett at Toynbee Hall in reaction to an anonymous pamphlet, 'The Bitter Cry of Outcast London' in 1883.[5] That pamphlet had ended with the challenge: 'Will you venture to come with us and see for yourselves the ghastly reality?' Canon Barnett's response was that it was not enough for the most privileged and best-educated young people in Britain to 'come and see' the horrors of slum life; they must actually live — 'settle' — among the poorest in order to learn at first-hand about these people's struggle to survive. Only then might the young people begin some intelligent and effective efforts at real help. The 'Settlements' were emphatically not soup-kitchens or coal-and-blanket depots or any other such charitable headquarters for middle-class, religious 'slummers'. They were centres where young university-educated people went first to learn of life in poverty and then to share whatever knowledge and abilities they had with the poorest. Instead of hand-outs, they were offering themselves:

The Women's University Settlement sprang directly from the gratitude of women at finding themselves in what the Charter of one College calls 'a place of religion, learning and education' and from their determination to mark their gratitude by *sharing* their benefits with others not so fortunate.[6]

It was Alice Grüner's personal experience as Honorary Secretary of the Southwark Branch of the London Pupil-Teachers' Association that had convinced her that she 'would do more and better work if [she] lived a part of [her] time at least, amongst the people whose friend [she] wished to be.'[7] Inspired by Alice Grüner and Henrietta Barnett who both went and talked to Newnham students about conditions in Southwark, a joint committee was formed by Newnham and Girton, which the Oxford women's colleges then joined, and in 1887, the first Women's University Settlement was founded in Southwark.

The earliest activities at this Settlement included a Saturday morning 'school' for crowds of the very roughest local children. They were taught to play games and to make things, they were given Magic Lantern shows and a Christmas party with individual presents and a tree. Groups of pupil-teachers, aged fourteen to eighteen were taken to the National Gallery, to the Natural History and Science Museums and to the Zoo, and the young people were initiated into singing clubs, concerts, and amateur acting. For the older, married women, a successful branch of the Women's Co-operative Guild was inaugurated, while the young factory-girls were given a weekly Club night of their own.

One of the first women 'experts' in urban social work to be co-opted on to the Executive Committee of the Women's University Settlement was the eminent housing reformer, Octavia Hill.[8] At first she had been prejudiced against the whole scheme: 'for she believed so passionately in family life, that a collection of women, living together without family ties or domestic duties, seemed to her unnatural, if not positively undesirable.'[9] Nevertheless, Octavia Hill soon did give her support, won over by the Settlement's new Headworker, Margaret Sewall, another ex-Newnhamite and 'a very fine personality, able, clear-headed and warm-hearted.' (Mary Sheepshanks, *Autobiography*, ch. 4.) Not only Miss Sewall but also her young graduate apprentice social workers soon converted Octavia Hill: 'They are all very refined, highly cultivated ... and *very* young. They are so sweet and humble and keen to learn about things out of their ordinary line of experience.'[10] It is an endearing slant on Mary at this time to have her associated, for once in her life at least, with a group that was 'sweet and humble and *very* young' — for as a rule, Mary was taken to be a great deal older than she really was, an eternal Eldest Sister, always expected to shoulder the largest share of responsibility without a murmur.

It was soon recognised that these young women social workers needed serious training and that some of them, having no independent income, needed money. Octavia Hill set up a Scholarship Fund appeal, and in January 1896, Mary Sheepshanks was appointed to the Pfeiffer Scholarship. The Pfeiffer — 'only given to candidates who actually need the pecuniary help' — was renewed the following January. (Women's University Settlement Committee Minutes.) Evidently Mary was no longer being supported by her father.

Because late-Victorian England provided neither sickness nor unemployment benefits, neither old age pensions nor child allowances, whenever any poor family was suddenly stricken by some unforeseen blow, it had to turn this way and that in order to avoid the worst fate of all — the workhouse. Once such a family had appealed for help at the Nelson Square Settlement, a worker like Mary would be sent to visit their home, take notes of all the family circumstances and enter them on a family case work paper:

it was a good training in thoroughness and getting a good grasp of a problem before taking action. Any help decided on had to be adequate and really solve the problem. Sometimes however no help could do enough — a brave battle was fought, [but] in some cases there was shipwreck. (Mary Sheepshanks, *Autobiography*, ch. 4.)

Mary regularly visited the huge barrack Workhouse

School twice a week — 'I taught the girls embroidery and the boys negro songs just to liven things up a bit.' (Mary Sheepshanks *Autobiography*, ch. 4.) Mary also did 'property management' — collecting rent and seeing to necessary housing repairs in one street; she went School Board Visiting to check on absentee children; took sick and crippled children for hospital treatment; organised Girls' and Boys' evening clubs; and helped to run the children's country holiday fund. In 1899 a thousand Lambeth children were sent to the country. Mary also had to give classes to local pupil-teachers as well as teach at Morley College for Working Men and Women. And, as if all that were not enough, she had to visit, under Margaret Sewall's informed guidance, local infirmaries, hospitals, work-houses, district schools, labour homes and night shelters for the homeless. Finally, Mary also attended lectures on English Poor Law Relief and Administration, the Factory Acts, Bookkeeping, Labour and Wages and other aspects of contemporary sociology. It was, in fact, the women on the Executive Committee of the Women's University Settlement who pioneered the systematic training of the new profession of social work in Britain and whose classes later developed, in 1912, into the School of Sociology at the LSE.[11] As their founder, Alice Grüner, trenchantly put it, when speaking of the need for professional training:

It is a very current opinion that nothing but willingness is needed on the part of a worker among the Poor, and the pity of it is that, when at last a worker *is* brought to recognise that more than willingness is needed, he or she have bought their experience at the expense of those whom they wished to serve.[12]

This new sense of professionalism did not, however, discourage, let alone preclude the forming of friendships between helpers and helped. Far from promulgating a doctrine of 'non-involvement with the client', these women felt that the most important elements in our work are those which cannot be gauged or described, and I suppose that all workers amongst the poor, whether in Settlements or elsewhere, feel that it is in the recognition of real relationships with them as individuals that the true value of their work lies.[13]

One example of such 'real relationships with ... individuals' was their long-term case-work with the most vulnerable group of young people in England — the destitute, family-less girls who left their workhouse school at fourteen to go out into the poorest kind of domestic service where they were constantly tempted by the money to be made in prostitution. The Settlement workers made a point of keeping a watching brief on these girls, fitting them out with good clothes and visiting them regularly in their new work-place as a check against exploitation and loneliness. Sometimes the 'skivvy' and the woman graduate would become permanent friends.[14]

Mary Sheepshanks' two years' training at the Southwark Settlement gave her an unequalled education in seeing life through the eyes of 'the poor', for whom she came to feel an immense respect: 'There was no condescension, no 'de haut en bas'. Living amongst these people year in year out ... was a great experience.' (Mary Sheepshanks, *Autobiography*, ch. 4.)

During one of her visits to Queensgate House on her weekend 'off', Mary recounted to Flora Mayor some of her new, eye-opening experiences of 'the abyss' and communicated such a sense of excitement and passionate involvement that Flora and Alice Mayor also ventured to visit the Southwark Settlement. But neither of the Mayor twins was cut out for social service:

I went to a Miss Fowler who manages the Invalid Aid and she gave me two children to visit — one a three year-old paralytic boy, the other I hadn't time to go and see as the Mother of Albert (the baby) talked such a lot. She lives in a room about the size of the bath-room. I've never seen anyone so poor.

Happily she's a chatterer so she's easy enough to get on with.
I felt rather shy though I must say the Settlement people are
very nice but have *not* the faculty of making one at home and
one feels that they are frightfully critical. The basket-making
class was rather silly because there were too many helpers for
the children. I don't think I shall go again ... The children
are rather revolting I think on the whole. (Alice to Flora,
1896.)

Flora found the Settlement workers less intimidating:

I really don't think the Settlement people bad. Miss Bartlett
and another with projecting teeth and very short skirts came
and talked of their own accord. I do think M. Sharpley is
rather 'aughty and she looked so ugly too. That girl *has* gone
off in looks and dressing. Mrs Chappel was out at work and
the little boy at a crêche. The practical Dorothea missed her
train, so instead of drawing I played games with the children
in the Square — 'Nuts in May', 'Hunt the Slipper', 'Tig',
'Oranges and Lemons' with great fervour. The dominant
male mind was observed in Frank, a fiendish little cripple, do
you recollect him? He endeavoured to boss things entirely
and was certainly the sharpest of a very sharp set of children. I
squashed him however. He developed a G.P. eventually and
persisted in rubbing his dirty head against my dress which
rather transfixed me. (Flora to Alice, 1896.)

Even in the squalor of Southwark Flora could not do
without the tribute of a 'Grand Passion'. But even if Flora
and Alice had felt more than a passing interest in the
Alberts or the Franks, there would never have been any
question of their going to 'settle' in Southwark. The Rev. Dr
and Mrs Mayor had arranged to take both their daughters
on a tour of the churches and art galleries of Italy from
October to December 1896. But that Baedeker-guided tour
of Italy proved even less congenial and significant, at least
to Flora, than visiting the Southwark Settlement. Nothing
she ever wrote has less of herself in it than the journal she
kept, dutifully praising this church or that fresco 'very
much worn by time' in Padua, or Verona or Venice.

On their return to England, Flora and Alice resumed their familiar life of the cultivated English lady in Kingston-upon-Thames. Waited on by their servants each day, they had no house-keeping tasks, and Alice did not learn how to make a cup of cocoa until she was over fifty. The only permissible work for Alice and Flora was Sunday School teaching, coaching pupil teachers in French, organizing Church bazaars and rehearsing local children to give parish entertainments. In their free time away from these duties Alice painted or sketched or practised her music and Flora read and tried to write her first stories. But the most important function in their life as ladies was the paying of social calls. Sometimes their teatime talk would actually achieve 'that calm, quiet interchange of sentiments' which characterises true friendship. Just occasionally their dinner-table talk might even be scintillating:

Delightful party at the Lowes Dickinsons — I talked to Theodore Llewelyn Davies and to Walter Sickert ... Mary Sheepshanks appeared, very entertaining ... Theodore Llewelyn Davies and Melian Stawell came to dinner. Theodore exceedingly fascinating. He and Melian discussed metaphysics till our brains reeled. (Alice Mayor's *Journal* entries, June and November, 1900.)

But all too often the Mayor sisters' intercourse within the same narrow social group proved tedious to a degree:

Aunt Ina came to lunch — conversation languished so much we were thankful to untwist tangles of gimp ... We rather wondered how conversation on schools, foreign parts and the Congress could last us through the evening but luckily Tiddlywinks was thought of and we had a fine game over which everyone got excited. (Alice Mayor's *Journal*, September 1899.)

At the time of that game of Tiddleywinks Flora and Alice were twenty-seven years old. Theirs was an almost un-believably protracted childhood, but it was far from rare: 'A routine that is totally fulfilling for a child — a round of

pets and walks and aunts and bazaars — is not a rich
enough prospect for an intelligent energetic young
woman', Victoria Glendinning observed about Winnie
Seebohm.[15] Whereas Alice Mayor quite enjoyed this life of
'pottering', Flora could not bear it. Her exasperation at the
sheer inanity of it all erupted in a letter to Alice in 1897:

Thursday: We went to the Winter Gardens in the afternoon
and heard a concert — deadly dull orchestral things. Then
went shopping. Aunt Minnie [the aunt who had refused to
have Flora in the house when she was a student] went picking
up miserable little khaki hat pen wipers and pin cushions ...
Friday: was a deadly day. We were to have gone to a garden
party but it rained early in the afternoon so Aunt Minnie who
was glad of an excuse for getting out of it and pottering, said it
was too wet to go and we sat on campstools instead and
looked at a holly being transplanted in the rain. It is so
fearfully pottery ... The evening was too damp for sitting out
so we sat in and the light is so bad one could neither read nor
play.
Sunday: I am so fearfully glad you gave me the chance of going
on Monday, I really could not stand any more.

Some sort of low watermark was reached by Flora as she
sat on that campstool next to Aunt Minnie, watching a
holly being transplanted in the rain. It came to her that the
life which was now expected of her as a Victorian lady was
boring to the point of being death-in-life — literally '*deadly*'
dull. She would have to get away from Kingston — but
how?
Meanwhile, Mary Sheepshanks was experiencing a
deadly monotony of a different kind. She had moved, after
completing her two-year training as a social worker in
Southwark, to dingy lodgings in Stepney. Her work among
the people there, who seemed 'to be quite happy in poverty,
hunger, and dirt, enlivened with drink'[16] was dispiriting. So
little could be done by just one individual — and nothing at
all unless that individual first immersed herself, both body

and spirit, in the circumstances of those she was out to help. Octavia Hill wrote:

There is, in a court I know well, a great blank, high, bare, black wall which rises within a few feet of the back windows of a number of rooms inhabited by the poor. I have shown it to many ladies and gentlemen, and have said how cheerless it made the rooms. Some feel it and seem to realise what sitting opposite to it day after day would be. Some say it isn't so very dreary, and almost seem to add, 'Can you show us nothing worse?' Then I never do.[17]

Octavia Hill taught young social workers like Mary Sheep-shanks 'the sense of satisfaction in rendering a little fuller and gayer the somewhat same life of worthy working people.'[18] Mary did get some satisfaction; she learned to value the kindness and generosity that bind people to one another at times of crisis; she was grateful for the oppor-tunity to get on easy terms with people whom most members of her class did not know as people at all; occa-sionally she could even feel she had accomplished some-thing — 'sometimes help of some kind was possible and welcome.' (Mary Sheepshanks, *Autobiography*, ch. 4.) But it was all so inadequate and merely palliative; and the great, bare, black wall always remained.

It was as necessary for Mary Sheepshanks to get away occasionally from Stepney as it was for Flora Mayor to get away from Aunt Minnie's holly. Mary's escape route then, as later, was through friendships and travel. She went bicycling in springtime in Normandy and Brittany with her fellow social worker Olga d'Avigdor. She had never been to France and it is characteristic of Mary that the bicycle was hardly invented before she was not only off on it, but off to Europe. Mary's spectacles got broken early on and Olga's bicycle kept breaking down — 'But France is France.' Half a year later, having first taught herself Italian, Mary had two months in Florence and Rome with Olga's sister Sylvie d'Avigdor.

They were the first of my many Jewish friends, and, though most generalizations about race are fallacious, I venture to say that Jews are the most faithful of friends. [Those] two months in Italy stand out in my memory as amongst the most delightful and interesting of my life, and led me to take every opportunity of revisiting that heavenly country. (Mary Sheepshanks, *Autobiography*, ch. 4.)

The 'heavenly country' to which Flora Mayor was secretly trying to escape, meanwhile, was the tinsel and glitter of the late-Victorian theatre. Live theatre — embracing opera, pantomime, farce and music-hall 'variety' as well as 'straight' drama — was then the only form of entertainment in Britain.[19] As many as two hundred and fifty touring companies would be 'on the road' — or more probably on the train — at any one time.[20] The late 1890s marked a high point in the history of British Theatre. There were great Shakespearian productions by Irving and Ellen Terry and Forbes-Robertson; there was society drama such as Pinero's *Second Mrs. Tanqueray*; society farce in *The Importance of Being Ernest*; social self-criticism in a revival of *Caste*; and at the very end of the century, there was also the disturbing 'new' drama of Ibsen, Shaw and Yeats. The glamour of the stage had also reached its apogee during the decade after 1895. Whenever a Beerbohm Tree company went on tour, for instance, its leading lady, Constance Collier, recalled that:

we were very magnificent with a private train and the Royal Coach attached. I had the Queen's suite. We were met at stations by the Mayor and taken to formal banquets ... [At a Royal Command Performance] the whole dress-circle would be decorated with flowers and the auditorium ablaze with jewels.[21]

The star of stars in all this brilliance for every one of the thousands of stage-struck girls and women in Britain was Ellen Terry:

My dear child,

Ellen Terry is just sublime. Her gestures are so awfully
natural, and her voice thrills me to the marrowbone. Her
scene where Arthur is talking and she's lying on the ground is
perfectly splendid, also where she repudiates Mordred's offer
. . .

Oh, Ellen Terry in the last scene where she's asking any
one of the knights to fight for her is quite exquisite. (Alice
Mayor to Flora, 12 May 1895.)[22]

Ellen Terry, like her near-contemporary, Mrs Pankhurst, caused thousands of women to fall in love with her,
inspiring them to believe both in themselves and in the
women's cause. Her biographer has rightly called her 'the
Queen of Every Woman', for she embodied what all longed
to be — or to serve.[23] A few years later Alice Mayor reported
to Flora hearing Ellen Terry lecture on *Shakespeare's
Triumphant Women*: 'wonderful women, fearless, high-
spirited, resolute and intelligent — with far more moral
courage than men.'

During the late nineteenth century, increasing numbers
of women from well-educated and 'well-connected'
backgrounds aspired to emulate Ellen Terry by going on
the stage.[24] Nevertheless, there was still considerable social
and moral prejudice against a stage career for women like
Flora Mayor. Theatre life was insecure and even sordid;
only actresses and prostitutes then ever used make-up and
the unchaperoned young women would necessarily hear
bad language backstage and be thrown into undesirable
company. 'Would any of us wish our daughters to go on the
stage?' asked F.C. Burnand in the *Fortnightly Review* in 1885
— 'There can be but one answer to this: No!'

In the late 1890s as Flora Mayor scanned the columns of
the *Era* and the *Stage* each week, even her determinedly
high hopes were dashed as she read how very few openings
there were: 'Wanted, Lady to play Parthenia, Lady Teazle,
Queen (in *Richard III*) etc. Theatre Royal, Preston', and
how very many (five whole columns in all) young women

advertised themselves as 'Disengaged', pathetically quoting their favourable press notices from the past. Flora felt perplexed and prayed to be shown what to do. 'I do feel inclined to rough it but if it's all drudgery with no result of course it would not be in the least worth doing it ...' (Flora to Alice, 1896.)

In addition to all the general factors and conditions militating against her that she held in common with every other woman, Flora also had a host of opponents within her immediate family. Her mother was totally against the stage on snobbish grounds; her father was opposed on spiritual and moral grounds. Henry Mayor always doubted whether Flora was really as talented as she thought she was, while Alice was horrified at the thought of her Flora having to 'mix' with such awful people. Alice was also genuinely afraid for the effect of stage life on her twin's health — for Flora had already begun to have very serious attacks of asthma. Only Flora's eldest brother Robin was sympathetic and even encouraging, in his distant way:

I had an *awfully* nice talk with Robin today, dear boy he was charming. He said about my looks which I said I thought were a disadvantage for the stage 'Oh no you're all right when you're dressed up and when you're talking you're quite all right.' We talked about the Stage, he is certainly very keen. He recommends proposing Ben Greet for a year to Father as just for amateur acting. Again advised Ibsen as good for people with brains. (Flora to Alice, 1896.)

In February 1897, Flora grasped a chance to accompany an obscure theatre company on its Hastings 'run'. It is clear from her reports back to Alice that she was very far from being blinded by infatuation to the realities of theatre life:

The company arrived in detachments, very ordinary rather flashy-looking, shop-walking young men and pretty girls. The Leading Lady is charming-looking ... I feel horribly ugly beside them. There was one awful lady who crept along with a most terrible smile, very wicked-looking, a sort of Potiphar's

wife. The Ladies of the Company hate her and she tells
disgusting stories to the men. She was good-looking in a way
but very musty ...

The dressing rooms are rather horrid gloomy little holes,
no hot water or anything of that sort, a pot to act as a slop-pail
... Conversation in the dressing room is not inspiring, it is
mostly about what cleanser one uses and what lodgings one is
going to take in the next town. I have only heard one of them
say a single interesting thing about the acting, it is all
arrangements or make-up ... The play I think is rather a
questionable one. It really does seem to me rather immoral in
places, and the tone is low throughout. As to the acting none
of it was very bad and none very good ... These stage
experiences have been well worth getting — this is private of
course. (Flora to Alice, 1897.)

Despite having seen so little to impress her at Hastings,
Flora was still determined to break into the world of professional theatre. She haunted the theatrical agencies, she
exploited personal introductions through family friends to
a producer or an established actress, and she even paid to
be given walking-on parts as a 'lady extra'. Flora learned all
the sickness of 'hope deferred' and all the humiliation of
frequent rebuffs and rejection. Still she persisted, performing in amateur theatricals or in Shakespeare readings
in the Home Counties, hoping that sooner or later she
would be discovered as an outstanding actress of comedy
and that then the Mayor family would be reconciled by her
fame. Some friends of the family did believe in her, as
Alice's *Journal* reports: 'Mr Devonport laughed helplessly
at every word that issued from Flora's mouth ... Dr
Anderson said as he went out, pointing to Flora: "I have no
doubts now."'

But in December 1897, came a bombshell. The *Daily
Mail* ran the headline: 'Mr Clement Scott Denounces the
Stage'. Scott had been the theatre critic of the *Daily Telegraph* for thirty-seven years, and now, to general amaze-
ment, he turned upon the stage as a profession unfit for any

woman with pretensions to true gentility or morality — unless indeed she had been bred within a theatrical family and so built up immunizing antibodies. The *Daily Mail* selected some of Mr Scott's most challenging assertions to quote:

The freedom of life, of speech, of gesture, renders it ... impossible for a lady to remain a lady ... Nor do I see how a woman is to escape contamination in one form or another ... It is nearly impossible for a woman to lead a good life on the stage.

The complete text of Mr Scott's interview in answer to the question: 'Does the Theatre make for good?' in *Great Thoughts* had even worse to follow. All the Rev. Dr Mayor's and Mrs Mayor's most terrible suspicions were confirmed:

The theatre ... is emphatically *not* one of the forces that makes for righteousness ... If any one I loved ... insisted on going on the stage contrary to my advice I should be terrified for her future, and hopeless for the endurance of our affection or even friendship. For stage life ... has a tendency to deaden the finer feelings, to crush the inner nature of men and women and to substitute artificiality and hollowness for sincerity and truth. It is a good thing that the public knows so little of what goes on behind the scenes.

I speak ... to the hundreds of young people especially of the opposite sex, who have so unhealthy a craving for matters theatrical, and who enter upon the life with an absolute ignorance of all that is hidden by its glittering exterior.

It is nearly impossible for a woman to remain pure who adopts the stage as a profession. Everything is against her ... All I can say is that I marvel at any mother who allows her daughter to take up a theatrical career ... Nor do I see how a woman is to escape contamination in one form or another. Temptation surrounds her on every side; her prospects frequently depend upon the nature and extent of her compliances.

There, it was out — the 'Casting Couch'. To succeed, a young aspiring actress must agree to prostitute herself 'compliantly' to her actor-manager or theatrical agent. Scott tried to cover his tracks by saying that, of course, there were cases of women who managed to lead a 'good' life. But what everyone took to be his real message was his earnest entreaty:

No one is pure, no one is beyond temptation, and it is unwise to the last degree to expose a young girl to the inevitable consequences of a theatrical life ... Religion and the stage are now and must remain as widely separated as the poles themselves ...

Uproar followed. The Actors' Association protested; the actor-manager, Mr Wyndham, called Scott's diatribe 'the most foul, false and treacherous slander on our inner life.' The editor of the *Stage*, 6 January 1898, implied that Scott must be suffering from a breakdown connected with drink. Bernard Shaw looked on with glee, and then entered the ring himself:

Quite the best comedy of the season is the indignant protest which has broken out on all sides against Mr Clement Scott's now famous Great Thoughts interview ... Mr Scott ... told the truth ...[25]

Shaw delighted to point out that *great* actresses do not have to prostitute themselves, though 'their humbler colleagues generally do'; that actresses were working-women who should have no truck with such stupid pretensions as being thought a conventional 'lady'; that the three 'most admired, most respected the most unshamed and un-ashamed, the most publicly and privately honoured members of their profession' were all known to have committed adultery. And that in any case there were far more prostitutes outside the acting profession than within it — many of them girls who were being paid starvation wages by pillars of the Church!

Various Christian periodicals then entered the controversy. The *Christian Commonwealth* pointed out that after thirty-seven years' intimate acquaintance with the theatre, Mr Scott must have known what he was talking about and 'must have fearfully forcible reasons for his indictment.' The *Christian Million* felt that if Mr Scott was right then *all* theatre-going was wrong. And the *British Weekly* finally declared:

so long as women are exposed to such temptations and perils as Mr Clement Scott describes, no man who reverences woman as Christ reverenced her can possibly support the stage.

One might have expected that after such a public exposé of all the Mayors' private fears, Flora would have been forced by her parents to renounce any hope of ever becoming a professional actress. She did no such thing; but her struggle against the weight of their views was made very much harder.

From time to time during her vain assaults on the agents and actor-managers in the capital, Flora would call in for tea and sympathy with her friend Mary Sheepshanks in her lodgings in Stepney. Mary could always be relied upon for approval and encouragement in the matter of striking out independently and unconventionally, so Flora did not have to be at all defensive about the stage with her, but she did wish she could have reported a little more success. However, Mary did not depress Flora by claiming to be any more successful in life than she was. Flora could even feel that she was cheering Mary up by recounting her own inglorious struggle — 'Mary Sheepshanks was decidedly pleased to see me, I think.' (Flora to Alice, March 1897.) One bond between the two of them, in addition to their wish to achieve something in the world, was their shared sense that they were not a success with men. Men might find both women stimulating to talk to, but they did not invite them out. Marriage was far from being their great aim in life; nonetheless it was a sore point that neither of them could, at the age of twenty-five, feel confident of any man's passionate affection. Flora reported to Alice after one of these visits that Mary 'didn't seem to have been having a very gay time.' Very gay it may not have been, but it was soon to become very interesting, for Mary, in October 1897, left Stepney and joined her fortunes to those of Morley College for Working Men and Women.

Morley College had started life in the bowels of what had been a notoriously disorderly music hall called the Old Vic. Throughout the middle of the nineteenth century reluctant policemen had to be paid extra to patrol the Vic on Saturday nights, and a notice outside had read: 'Ladies without shoes and stockings not admitted to the dress-circle.' (Mary Sheepshanks, *Autobiography*, ch. 5.) Nevertheless, within the space of fourteen years, between 1880 and 1894, the Old Vic was transformed from a gin palace into a 'people's palace' where the poorest local inhabitants could, and did, enjoy classical music and science:

all coal-heaving London was in the gallery listening to *Souvenirs of Haydn* and *O Ciel, quanti Gioel* — the eager faces, with often the sparkling eyes as the only visible feature, were thrust forward to take in every note, like a row of quaint gargoyles hanging over the pit [as] the gallery of the Vic was reclaimed to civilization.[26]

The woman who had effected this extraordinary transformation was Octavia Hill's friend, the housing reformer, Emma Cons.[27] It was she who had first banned alcohol from the Vic's premises and then insisted that her new Temperance Music Hall should offer high culture and education. It was she who had kept the whole enterprise alive, despite constant imminent bankruptcy, in the belief that what was right *must* eventually triumph. And it was the local people themselves who had asked Emma Cons to organise more systematic teaching for them than that given through occasional illustrated scientific lectures on subjects such as the telephone. Gradually, in response to this appeal, Emma Cons instituted a part-time poly-technical evening college for working-class students under the same roof as the Old Vic. A few unused dressing-rooms were knocked into classrooms and soon nearly two hundred students were attending regular courses in elementary chemistry, electricity and physiology. The Morley Memorial College for Working Men and Women — named after Emma Cons' loyal financial backer, the late Samuel Morley — had come into existence. When, in 1888, Morley acquired its first purpose-built classrooms, they were erected under the stage, above the stage and behind the stage. There has never been an institution of further education like it.

From the first, Morley was a radical, innovative college. Its working-class students shared in its administration and curriculum development; deliberate emphasis was given to the humanities in order to counteract any tendency towards the merely utilitarian and technical, and there was real equality between men and women — women both serving on its council and acting as its chief administrators. 'In the early years the College owed much to the guidance and will-power of four outstanding women'[28] — Octavia Hill, Emma Cons, Caroline Martineau[29] — and Mary Sheepshanks. Thus the founding of Morley College was 'something of a landmark in the history of the women's movement, as well as in that of British adult education.'[30]

By 1900 the college prospectus offered the following classes:

Elementary Reading, Writing and Arithmetic; English Grammar and Composition; History and Literature; Mathematics; French, German, Spanish, Italian, Latin and Greek; Building Construction, Machine Construction, Botany, Physiology, Electricity and Magnetism, Heat, Light and Sound; Wood-carving, Drawing, Violin, Elocution and Singing; Dress-making, Cooking, Shorthand, Book-keeping and the Care of Horses.

Few of the students had previously received any secondary
education. Each class lasted for two hours, the first hour
being taken up by a lecture, the second by questions and
discussion. Most students entered for a three-year course
and wrote weekly papers. The fees were very low — usually
one shilling per term per course. The suggested course of
study would consist of several subjects at elementary level
in the first year (usually including English, mathematics, a
language and a science), leading to gradual specialisation
and advanced work in the second and third years. Certif-
icates were then awarded according to class work and
examination performance. From the first, the calibre of the
lectures was very high: Sir Frederick Black of the Admiralty
taught mathematics; Graham Wallas (later of the LSE)
lectured on Citizenship and the British Constitution;
Goldsworthy Lowes Dickinson and Mrs Bosanquet taught
ethics.

In 1900 the students' occupations were listed and found
to include amongs others:

172 Clerks, 39 Engineers, Fitters and Cleaners; 30 Shop
Assistants, 21 Compositors, 20 'Married', 20 'Work at Home',
19 Dressmakers, 13 Teachers, 13 Bookbinders, 13 Ware-
housemen, 11 Printers, 11 Photographic retouchers, 10
Carpenters, 9 Farriers, 11 Machinists and Needleworkers, 7
Tailors and Tailoresses, 6 Domestic Servants and, [shades of
Jude] 2 Stone-masons. [Even the humblest occupations were
represented] — Bricklayer, Buttonmaker, Cellarman,
Envelope-stamper, Hawker, Night Porter, Sugar Boiler,
Seaman, Stoker and Sanitary Attendant.

Morley's hours were from 6.30—10.30 p.m.

Very many of the students left home early in the morning by
the workman's train, came straight from work to their classes
and arrived home late, not having had any solid meal all day
... It was distinctly a school for tired people. (Mary
Sheepshanks, *Autobiography*, ch. 4.)

How had Mary Sheepshanks managed to convince the

interview committee that she would make a capable Vice-Principal of such a college? They had known her, as a teacher of history, on the voluntary college staff. They also knew from the Nelson Square Southwark Settlement just around the corner how she had acquitted herself as a social worker in two of the grimmest areas of London, Lambeth and Stepney. What they now wanted to know was: could she be relied on to stay, and was she tough enough to cope with the rougher side of the job? They asked Mary just three questions: had she sisters at home who could nurse her parents if necessary so that she would not have to be called away? To that Mary could answer blandly that she had *five* sisters — without going on to explain that nothing would have induced her to return home for long periods under any circumstances. Next she was asked whether she could tell when the lecturer on 'The Care of Horses' (a class popular among cab and van drivers and taught by a vet) was too drunk to teach? Yes, she assured them, she could. Finally, would she be able to stop a glove fight that was out of control in the gym? Mary's six feet height and her Guardsman's carriage convinced them; she was appointed. The committee had done rather better than they realised — for the 'semi-voluntary' stipend of £100 per year they had acquired not just a female 'chucker-out' of a Vice-Principal, but a *de facto*, highly competent Principal of the college for the next fourteen years.[31] Mary Sheep-shanks, no longer a pioneer woman social worker, was now a pioneer woman educational administrator — and one 'of great intellectual and administrative ability ... She possessed exceptional breadth of culture and determination of character — qualities which were soon in evidence at the College.'[32]

In retrospect, Mary felt that her responsibilities at Morley College had not been onerous enough, nor, in the long run, good for her:

It was a mistake to have taken an administrative post, and a light one at that, at such an early age. I ought to have been doing hard spade work and learning to be a good subordinate, a thing I never learnt. (Mary Sheepshanks, *Autobiography*, ch. 5.)

Not everyone would agree that the Morley College post was a particularly 'light' one. But Mary was right about her inability to be a good subordinate.

The following extracts from the college magazine for 1899 and 1900 give glimpses of Mary Sheepshanks in her new work:

December 2nd: New Students Welcomed. Miss Martineau was unfortunately prevented by her illness from being present in person, and the students were, therefore, welcomed by Miss Cons and Miss Sheepshanks.
Feb. 10th 1900: Miss Sheepshanks supported the Debating Society motion that women should have a greater share in Local Government. She gave details of the efficiency of women Poor Law Guardians, and the Motion was carried. Miss Sheepshanks was elected to the committee of the Morley Students' Convalescent Aid Society.
Dec. 1900: Miss Sheepshanks made out a strong case in favour of the Women's Gymnastic Class.

And so on. What Mary was also doing, as Alice Mayor noted, was securing her friends' services as tutors at Morley College whenever possible. So it is not surprising that the voluntary Latin tutor and examiner for 1897 should have been Miss Flora Mayor, or that it was Flora who introduced Mary to a man who was soon to become very important in both their lives — the young architect Ernest Shepherd.

Ernest Shepherd was a tall, thin, very 'gentleman-like' man, with kind, humorous brown eyes hidden behind glasses, a drooping moustache and an immense capacity for caring about other people's feelings. He had been orphaned as a young boy after his father's suicide, and he and his younger brother, Fritz and his two sisters, Gertrude and Daisy, had then been brought up by their mother's unmarried sister, Zoë Sinclair. Ernest Shepherd had been Henry Mayor's closest friend when they were both boys at Clifton College and, from that time on, all four of the young Shepherds were frequent visitors at the Mayors' home, while Flora and Alice would often call on Miss Sinclair and the Shepherds at 3 Warwick Square, SW1. Ernest Shepherd was a radical idealist concerning the social questions of the day and he was passionately eager to share his own love of music and art with people who had not had his opportunities to enjoy them. Flora knew what she was doing when she introduced Ernest Shepherd to Mary Sheepshanks and so she was not in the least surprised when, at the same time as beginning his post-graduate training as an architect in London, Ernest also began to give up many of his evenings and week-ends in order to teach the students at Morley College for nothing.

Ernest Shepherd was immensely popular there. His enthusiasm for church architecture and for conducting student excursions to local landmarks — in fact for every kind of antiquity — was infectious. He was a great 'joiner-in'. The Morley College magazine from 1899 to 1903 is studded with references to 'Mr E.B.S. Shepherd' leaping to his feet to lead the applause at a Lieder recital, or founding the highly successful Archaeological Society, or being given an umpteenth warm vote of thanks by his enthusiastic audience who 'felt above all that we had been made to think.' Ernest Shepherd was a born Adult Education Tutor, an absolute boon to Morley College — and also to Mary Sheepshanks.

But it was Flora Mayor with whom Ernest was secretly in love. He knew, however, that Flora still regarded him just as an extra brother whom she had known almost from child-hood, and he also knew that his 'prospects' were not good. He was without property, and, as yet, without a settled profession. All he could do was wait in the wings, en-courage Flora in her secret ambition to write serious fiction, worry over her increasingly desperate attempts to get a foothold in the London theatre — and pump Alice at every opportunity for news: 'The instant Ernest got a minute with me at the soirée he said with real eagerness, which certainly struck me: "Now I want to hear about Flora."' (Alice to Flora, c. 1898.)

Flora, meanwhile, was mildly in love with an unattainable, condescending young man — the literary editor and dramatist Rudolf Besier.[33]

Went to the Besiers. *Je ne crois pas que R. m'aime.* This put me in a state of absolute gloom. I got this idea I fancy from his not seeming very anxious to come down when I asked him when he was coming. He was very keen about my writing for The Royal which wanted stories awfully and he was sure I could do the style he wanted. There ought to be more sentiment; he thought I had very little sentiment or was cold, I forget which. (Flora to Alice, 1898/9.)

What gave Flora Mayor's life meaning during this frustrating period of the late 1890s, despite all the banality of Kingston's church bazaars and tea-parties, and despite her own failure to get into the theatre or to be fallen in love with by Rudolf Besier, was the writing of her first book. In *Mrs Hammond's Children* Flora was attempting something she did not think had ever been done before — or not in the way that she was trying to do it. She was writing a book for adults about the relationships between children. No one, in Flora's view, had yet captured the complexity of childhood, its bitter quarrels and crossness, its isolation and boredom as well as its moments of radiance, excitement and ridiculous fun.[34] In *Mrs Hammond's Children*, Flora Mayor wanted to do justice to the whole tragi-comedy of childhood. Above all, she wanted to remind adults that children's relationships with one another are much more like those between adults than we are inclined to remember.

There are eight Hammond children, aged between five and fourteen. They have kind, intelligent, liberal parents, a large, ramshackle house and garden, lots of books, a sympathetic, sensible nanny in charge in the nursery and plenty of freedom in which to play cricket, invent mock parliaments, write family newspapers and dress up for charades or their own elaborate costume romances. In other words, they bear a strong resemblance to the young Mayors. Nonetheless, *Mrs Hammond's Children* is not an idyll. The first chapter reveals the normal state of relations between children as being one of constant tension — a power struggle to decide who, minute by minute, shall dominate the rest.

'Oh, bosh!' ... 'Don't be so bossy' ... 'I shall tell nurse' ... 'Then you'll be a beastly little sneak' ... 'I'm the eldest' ... 'Oh rot — a girl having a sword!' ... 'You've got to shut up, Milly ... hold your jaw. It's my turn now.' ... 'I think this is a *stupid* story.' ... 'All right, I don't care.' ... 'I'm not a baby like the ... girls.'

Here are all the expressions of the jealous rivalry within every family: the pecking order according to age, sex, cleverness and each child's need to feel important in someone else's eyes. Without belonging to the Original Sin school of writers, for whom child-suffering is the punishment for child-sin, Flora Mayor does cast doubt on the concept of 'the normal, happy child.' 'Call no child happy,' Flora Mayor seems to be saying, 'until he or she has got through one day unscathed.' And each of her chapters shows a different member of the family discovering 'the loneliness of trouble.' Bob Hammond's eleventh birthday, for example, develops into one long series of disappointments and misery. He does not even shine at what is usually his best game — cricket — being caught out first ball. His elder brother, Lion, gloats at Bob's public humiliation:

'Hallo Ranji! well played, well played my son! You're too good for us' ...

    'Hallo, Ranji!' said Tommy [Bob's younger brother] dancing up at Bob and making a face of derision, 'caught out your first ball; what a lark!'

'You dry up, you little beast,' Bob said savagely.

And smashes his bat down on Tommy's face. For the first time in English literature the murderous hatred that children can feel for a brother or sister was expressed. Tommy's bleeding face dwindles into a bleeding nose; he recovers quickly, unlike Bob, who stumbles alone up to his room, 'dazed with misery' and crying. His one terror now is lest his elder brother Lion come up and find him in tears. But instead of Lion it is his sister Milly who finds Bob and flings herself upon him:

'rubbing her cheeks against any part of him she could find, his coat-collar, his hair, or his hot cheeks ... Bob felt one or two drops on his hand, and he was rather glad that somebody else should be crying too.

  'I like you better than Lion, Milly,' he said.

  'I shouldn't have liked to have had Lion, and I'm glad you came.'

  'I am glad you think so,' said Milly, 'I always thought you liked him best and I didn't like it.'

Their deliberately halting, very limited vocabulary admirably expresses the difficulty that the children have in talking about their feelings for each other. Such moments of emotional truth are the hall-mark of the best of Flora Mayor's writing. And for the first time in her fiction, Flora makes direct use of her unblinkered knowledge of herself, giving thirteen-year-old Milly Hammond some of her own most serious faults, including enviousness and a great disposition to show off:

'... [My father] is a very clever man, and writes very clever books. Perhaps you haven't read any of them; only *very* clever people read them mother says ...'

  'Yes, I've read some of your father's books,' said Mr. Hastings ... 'I think you're a very lucky girl to have such a father.'

  Milly was very much puzzled to know what to say, so she made the silliest answer possible under the circumstances. 'Perhaps he thinks he's very lucky to have such a daughter.' (*Mrs Hammond's Children*, 'The Bosom Friends'.)

Ernest Shepherd was delighted by Flora's capacity to mock herself:

The part I like best is where Milly shows off to the visitor at Mrs Norrey's party: I am so glad you have brought out the innate priggishness of children: I remember being atrociously priggish but thought I was peculiar in that; I am so glad to find that other children were the same. (Ernest to Flora, 1901.)

The two other stories in *Mrs Hammond's Children* which break new ground are *The Sirdar* and *A Foreign Cousin.* In *The Sirdar*, Milly's younger sister Polly, a passionate animal-lover, first adopts then forgets to look after an adored guinea-pig. Suddenly she races frantically across the garden, three days too late:

The hutch was quite bare, and the Sirdar lay on his side with his little paws stretched out.
    'I suppose he's gone to sleep,' said Polly, struggling at the wire; she could not open the door to-day. 'Sirdar,' she called out, 'my dear Sirdar, wake up!'

When the old gardener breaks it to her that her pet has starved to death — 'You feel 'is ribs, missy; why this 'ere's stickin' out quite sharp,' Polly cries so terribly that Ricketts says:

'You mustn't take it to 'eart, missy; it ain't as if 'e was a 'uman being.'
    'I like him better than all human beings though, except just father, and mother and Lion.'
Ricketts did not quite know how to go on after this.

In exploring Polly Hammond's first experience of guilt and grief, Flora Mayor shows how children manage to survive such things in precisely the same way as adults do — by postulating an after-life in which all is understood and forgiven, by ritual — for the Sirdar is granted a lavish funeral — and by planting a stone, suitably inscribed, to mark the spot. And far from smiling at Polly's grief, Flora Mayor feels

— and makes the reader feel — something like reverence for it.

A Foreign Cousin shows the Hammond children at their nastiest, ganging up on a resented intruder. German Maggie is treated like an Untouchable:

'She's not a bit like us,' said Milly ...
'Why on earth doesn't she go to India ... or stay in
Germany?' said Lion.
'I don't see why our Christmas should be spoiled. We can't
have strangers see my tragedy.'

— and the whole story becomes a painfully accurate study in the persecution of an alien.

There is also a great deal of comedy in *Mrs Hammond's Children* but the undercurrent of pain keeps breaking through. Quarrelling hurts; isolation hurts; bereavement, guilt and failure hurt. Some of that pain was derived from Flora's own childhood memories of Queensgate House, but she was also making use of the confidences of her friends Mary Sheepshanks and Melian Stawell, both of whom had had much more bitter experiences of childhood quarrels within large families, and of 'the loneliness of trouble', than she had had herself.

Some of the book's hard insistence on pain and transience may also have derived from the sorrow that was being experienced by the older generation of Mayor brothers and sisters in the late 1890s for several of them began to fall ill and die while Flora was writing *Mrs Hammond's Children*. Flora's Aunt Lizzie was the first to go, at the end of 1896, when she was seventy-four. Early in 1897 Aunt Charlotte died aged sixty-eight. A few months later, the second to youngest, Aunt Georgie, perhaps the most generally beloved member of the whole Mayor family, died of Bright's Disease. She was sixty-one.[35] Then the eldest Aunt, the redoubtable Anna, died in 1898, aged seventy-seven, soon to be followed by the eldest brother, Canon Robert Mayor of Frating. When Flora's father next went up to Hampstead to see his remaining sisters, one of them said, 'Let's all come and sit round the fire — there are so few of us left now.' The seven Mayor aunts are buried in West Hampstead Cemetery, under a cross inscribed: 'In Christ shall all be made alive.'

To be forced to meditate, as Flora Mayor was at this time, on the end of family life, had led her to reflect with a seriousness and a sadness that were new to her, also its beginnings. She does not devalue the children's feelings in her book merely because she and we know that such intensity will pass; instead she insists, as she will continue to do in her fiction, that emotional relationships — and only emotional relationships — are what human life is about.

Mrs Hammond's Children was rejected by several publishers as being suitable neither for children nor for adults, until at last it was brought out in September 1901 by a small firm called Johnson. Although another edition appeared in 1902, it did not make any impact and it remained, undeservedly, out of print for eighty years. Flora did not feel confident enough about the book to publish it under her own name. She adopted the pseudonym of 'Mary Strafford' — the same name that she was using to approach theatrical agents and actor-managers. And as a would-be actress, 'Mary Strafford' was discovering that the snubbing just went on and on:

Saturday. I went to the agent and found him out. Went on to Maud S. Rather depressed there. Maud advised me to give up acting if this was not successful. I suppose I am beginning to be a laughing stock. (Flora to Alice, late 1900.)

But in January 1901 the actress Mary Strafford was at last to be given her chance.

4

'MARY STRAFFORD', ACTRESS, AND 'MISS SHEEPSHANKS, THE VICE-PRINCIPAL', 1901–1903

Flora Mayor's 'career' as an actress could hardly have been less glorious. She graduated from non-speaking parts in Shakespeare to a very small role as comic crone with a third-class touring company unkindly christened 'Crummles and Co.' by her head-shaking family and friends. She did not follow her brother Robin's suggestion and seize the opportunity of acting in the 'New Drama' of Ibsen and Shaw[1] because she fiercely disagreed with much of what they had to say. Leonard Woolf has recorded his own huge elation in 1901 when, in *The Wild Duck*, Relling cries out 'Bosh!' to Molvik's unctuous 'The child is not dead but sleepeth':

[We] felt that Ibsen ... was saying 'Bosh!' to that vast system of cant and hypocrisy which made lies a vested interest, the vested interest of the 'establishment', of the monarchy, aristocracy, upper classes, suburban bourgeoisie, the Church, the Army, the stock exchange.[2]

But Flora could not say 'Bosh!' Remembering her parents and her seven Mayor aunts she could not reduce the whole nineteenth-century middle-class world-view to just one 'vast system of cant and hypocrisy.' As for Shaw, his *Mrs Warren's Profession*, published in *Plays Unpleasant* in 1898, was produced privately by the Stage Society in January 1902, but it would have been unthinkable for the

Newnham-educated Flora Mayor to have acted the
Newnham-educated Vivie Warren, daughter of a successful 'Madam'. Prostitutes, for Flora Mayor, were
'Unfortunates', terribly to be pitied — but to *connect* the
whole racket of prostitution, as Shaw did, with her own
intellectual, innocent world, was more than she was then
ready to face.[3]

Throughout 1900 Flora had suffered month after month
of fobbings-off by theatre agents and managers. Then, just
before Christmas, she did at last succeed in being promised
a part as a 'lady walker-on' with F.R. Benson's Shakespearian Company at the Lyric.[4] No pay at all for the first six
weeks, then 15/- to 25/- a week thereafter — not enough to
live on, without a subsidy from home. Flora was celebrat-
ing Christmas in Bristol with her parents and Henry — now
classics master at Clifton — when Benson's telegram came.

On Sunday, Dec. 30 I received a summons for rehearsal at 11
on Monday. Off I went. Everything was horrible. First
Mother and Father hated my travelling on Sunday and I
knew hated the whole business truly kind and sympathetic as
they were. I felt an odious hate. Alice did not like it either —
that was all vile. Minor disagreeables: pelting rain and raging
toothache.

> (Flora Mayor, unpublished *Stage Journal*
> January 1901 — April 1903.)

The only person in the world who really wished Flora
well in this adventure, besides Mary Sheepshanks, was
Blanche Smith, a much older ex-Newnhamite (and herself
a former actress), who wrote Flora the following advice:

Don't give up, however horrid it may be in detail or
disappointing on the whole ... Don't let people worry you
into giving up on account of health. Some of the best actors
and actresses are non-robust people: and there is *nothing* so
undermining to health as dullness and thwarted ambitions.
... Good Luck.

Flora's first professional appearance was as a lady of the household in *The Taming of the Shrew*:

We have to make a commotion at Petruchio's refusal to stay for the banquet ... When Petruchio draws his sword we all get terrified — one faints, another supports her, two jump up on the seats, I crouch and pray and cover my eyes, the men draw their swords, one falls wounded and the Lady ministers to him.

(Stage Journal.)

In addition, all the 'Walkers-on' had to invent appropriate background dialogue:

We kept up an animated flow of — 'Is Petruchio going to dine with us tonight? What is he talking of?' 'There must be some mistake'. 'The fellow's mad, stark mad!' 'Hullo, there's Kate asking him now, you'll see he'll give in to her' ... 'Oh poor father, he's getting it now. Here, let me go, let me go, I must draw my sword I tell you'.

(Stage Journal.)

In her next production, *The Merchant of Venice*, Flora had to throw flowers at the other extras during a tarantella — Benson, it seems, having vaguely associated Northern Italy with Southern Spain. Then came the highwater mark of Flora's 'Benson period' — *Coriolanus*, in which she was part of the angry Roman mob:

Mr Keats and I had a fine little fight for bread in the first scene. Mr Keats said I bashed in his front teeth but this was stopped — we were told we were pals. Mr A. told me my cursing was too like praying. There is no responsibility or worry about this, one comes in with everybody. I like it much better than the Tarantella ... it is most amusing to see the surging mass of men. Mr Weir said — Ah the governor's all right if you give him a good old Rugby scrum.

(Stage Journal.)

Flora's journal contains many vivid vignettes of backstage life, probably jotted down by her for future reference in her writing. She notes, for example, the anarchic confusion on stage itself just before the curtain goes up:

Mr Nicholas performing a *pas seul*, Mr Keats juggling, Mr Cole doing the Elysian Mysteries, some of the ladies doing the Lancers, Mr Shilly peeping through the curtain and any amount of managers and carpenters walking about the stage. Then there is the magic word 'clear' and everybody skips into position.

As for the dubious theatrical atmosphere backstage, so much feared by her family, Flora discovered that although blasphemy was popular, there was neither gross immorality nor any talk of it. All that she encountered was vulgarity and a certain amount of 'pawing':

The first day's manners of ladies and men struck me as a little unusual. Not quite our standard; some clasping and pawing went on. There is somebody Miss Wetherell calls 'Reggie darling'. [During the *Merchant of Venice* trial scene] the supers squeezed my hand which I suppose some people might have found rather agitating. There is a good deal more pawing and squeezing from the managers than one is used to but I really cannot honestly say I mind it much.

(*Stage Journal.*)

On her second day she had 'thought all the people beastly and felt quite degraded. It is odd how transient impressions are for I really don't think them at all beastly now and wonder why I disliked them so.' (*Stage Journal.*) The only person among her fellow actors who really intrigued Flora was the writer Arthur Machen who had recently joined Benson's Company in order to get material for his work.[5] He stood out from the rest as being humorous, courteous and cultivated. Flora liked him exceedingly. However, what Flora was most concerned about was, as always, what this new world thought of her. But 'comps' were much thinner on the ground than when she had been at Newnham:

I must put down my only attempt at a compliment. In what Vickie would call my big scene [in *Taming of the Shrew*] where we all show signs of terror the other praying lady was said to be too tragic but I was considered all right. Let us be content with very small crumbs.

(*Stage Journal.*)

When Benson took the trouble to say just a few words to her, Flora felt 'truly grateful'. Her looks — and what the theatre people thought of them — were a constant worry to her, now that she already had some grey hairs and new lines around her eyes replacing the 'exquisite complexion' and 'ideal beauty' she had so happily boasted about at Cambridge ten years before:

I don't seem to look much uglier than the others when I am made up, but I am sure they are all thinking how plain I am ... I think the dressing room does not at all admire my poor hair. I had rather a depressing conversation with Miss Hudson about my looks. She is absolutely truthful and evidently thinks me very ugly ... I'm sure I never shall be smart. Considering how much this profession depends on looks I felt plunged in rather deep gloom.

(*Stage Journal.*)

Flora's acting also gave her trouble. She humbly asked friends, relatives and fellow-'supers' to give her their criticism and they generously obliged:

Walk rolling and too careful. Attitude cramped, not free enough. Talked too much with Mr Woods. Walk too careful, hair rather untidy ... Too intent an expression: I [now] see the necessity for graceful movements always if possible and much clearer voice production than I have, slower, and louder and less jerky, also for ebb and flow and change of speed in talking.

(*Stage Journal.*)

Clearly one of Flora's problems was that she was trying too hard and the effect was one of constant and tense self-consciousness. There was a bad moment in *The Merchant of*

Venice rehearsals when Flora, who had repeatedly muffed her flower-throwing exit, was told by Benson apropos of the subsequent scene, 'Miss Strafford, I don't think we shall want you for this':

I don't deny this was a great blow to me and depressed me awfully ... I feel it's not a good earnest of things to come ... When I came back that evening I had a horrid feeling of hatred of the whole thing.

(*Stage Journal.*)

Ever after that incident Flora was haunted by anxiety lest she be 'chucked' from Benson's company at the end of the season. It was particularly comforting at such times to have Ernest Shepherd's whole-hearted affirmation and solicitude:

Ernest really was so very nice. He is such a true friend, so awfully sympathetic. He said several times how lucky Benson was to have me and '*Of course* they'll keep you, they'd be only too delighted to have you'.

(*Stage Journal.*)

But when the time came for the company to be split up, in April 1901, some to be disbanded and the other lucky ones to do a season at Stratford, Flora was not kept on. Flora, of course, felt 'very low', and acutely anxious because she had asked Benson to give her an audition before she left in order to advise her about her future prospects in the theatre:

I was kept on fearful tenterhooks, thinking every evening I was going to have my interview. I felt excruciatingly nervous, and it was quite a relief to find one was reprieved. One day Benson came to me and asked me to come next morning at 11.30 and 'Recite any little thing you know, just anything you like, get it ready for me'. ...

I wondered much what I should recite, and did 'And why I pray you, who might be your mother' ... I did not do it well and thought too much about gestures and consonants to act well.

He said at the end, 'Sit down.' Then a pause. 'I see you have had some training.'

I told him where. I asked him if he thought my recitation good. He said 'You ask me Miss Strafford — a difficult question — whether I think your recitation good.' Then there was a fearful pause which was embarrassing. I think he was too tired to get his words quick. It came out at length that he thought my recitation about the average, no certainly above the average of what he knew. To most people he said 'Give it up.' He certainly should not say that to me. As to whether I should go on, that was impossible to say. Things were so rotten from top to bottom of the profession, but there was no reason why I should not do very useful work.

He asked me if I had any other ambitions. I said writing.

He said 'I thought so, you have such a literary way of reciting and such an evident feeling for the passage.' He thought it would be better to stick to that. He thought I was too literary and analytical to act, lacked spontaneousness.

'The two geniuses of our company, Mr Weir and Miss Denzil, act by instinct, probably they could not talk about the parts they play. That is why Mr Weir fails sometimes.'

I said I thought I felt the things I acted. I think he said — 'That is not the same as making other people feel', but I am not sure.

'Have you heard actors oughtn't to have brains?'

I said from what one could see they often didn't.

He laughed and said he was afraid that was true. He thought there was some sense in the saying and then talked very interestingly about instinctive and intellectual acting, instancing Stephen Phillips as a type of the latter. He thought I ought to work out my own salvation and play big parts which he could not give me ...

I asked if I might ever come back to him.

He said certainly, he should be delighted. He talked a little about Shakespeare and we parted with much thanks and politeness on both sides.

(*Stage Journal.*)

Flora refused to accept Benson's advice that she should 'stick to' her writing instead of the stage. Their season finished on 9 April and on 10 April she went straight back to the theatrical agent in St George's Lane — without success.

So it was home again to the old round of Church bazaars, social calls or croquet in the afternoon, and reading, music, amateur dramatics and games of acrostics in the evening. The Mayor family was still quite unreconciled to Flora's persistence with 'that stage business', and when she had some pictures taken by a theatrical photographer to send around the agents — 'the results were very mature and bad-lottish, I hope they're not a forecast. Mother flung them across the room.' (*Stage Journal.*)

Flora was next called up to London for an interview with a theatrical agent who hinted that he might be able to get her a walk-on part in *The Sacrament of Judas*:

'But of course I have hundreds and hundreds of applications. Are you tall?'
I stood up.
'Ah, five foot ten I see.'
I corrected this — 'No five foot six, I'm afraid.'
'Oh, ah of course,' — in a very world-weary manner.
I fancy he thought I wanted to fling myself into his arms, but even if these people are not gentlemen, they ought to know when they are speaking to a lady.

(*Stage Journal.*)

Flora gave herself all the comfort she could with such reflections on her superior social standing, for that ungentlemanly agent, having promised to write, never did. Then she was granted an interview by the experienced actor, Arthur Paterson, who tried to put her off the theatre altogether by insisting that it was still not decent: Beerbohm Tree, George Alexander and Charles Wyndham, the three most important actor/managers of the day, all slept with their actresses.

He asked me if I should mind acting a part like Nell Gwyn. I said 'Not in the least', but that I should mind acting in plays I disapproved of like *The Gay Lord Quex* [by Arthur Pinero].

He said if that were so it made it almost hopeless for me to be an actress. That feeling of disapproval was one which no actress would appreciate. He illustrated this by his experience at the Playgoers' Club. If I refused a part the managers would all get to hear of it at once, and ostracise me. Art for art's sake, or perhaps money for money's sake, seems to be the managers' view.

(*Stage Journal.*)

Flora's self-respect might well have led her to wreck her chances — but that interesting moral conflict was anticipated unnecessarily, since in her case she was given no chances to wreck. Arthur Paterson proceeded to appraise Flora's face and figure out loud, summing her up as a still just about marketable commodity:

Good figure, ugly mouth. Striking eyes … When you first came in the room, I thought: 'No, she won't do.' Then when I'd talked to you a few minutes I thought: 'Yes, she will.' He thought my appearance was against me for seeing managers first off — 'You must make them talk to you and then you can do what you like with them.'

(*Stage Journal.*)

Flora merely commented, 'Quaint having all this from a man I had never seen before', whereas Alice was disgusted at having her *alter ego* and twin expose herself thus.

In September 1901, Flora had a walking-on part with Mrs Bandemann-Palmer's company in a now forgotten play called *Our Boys*. But then followed almost another year of frustration and rejection by the agents:

Whether being a lady is a help or a hindrance I never found out. I did everything I could think of; I went week after week to the wretched agent. I think going to the 'devaine' Mr Denton's aristocratic residence is the most odious experience I've ever had. It was situated in Maiden Lane, that haunt of falling and fallen actors. I used to see curious seedy, gaudily-dressed people very noisy and with very untidy artistic hair passing up and down, most on the same errand as myself I suppose. I found it the greatest struggle to work myself up to

going up the agent's stairs. I would walk up and down the
street trying to pump up sufficient indifference to go in and
look fearfully about lest there should be any old Bensonians
anywhere round. Once in, one mounted the stairs and came
into a shabby office hung with extremely vulgar photographs
of 'panto artistes'. There was always a crowd hanging about
in the room, on the landing, on the stairs, people pretending
to be cheerful and talking loudly and confidently as actors
always do to any acquaintances who turn up ...

After about half an hour Mr Denton would come wafting
in with a cigar in his mouth. We all made a dash at him and
the first who got him sometimes retired into a back room. The
door would be ajar and you would hear them gossiping
together. No one minded, as actors have no sense of time.
They have nothing to do all day and like lounging about with
a chance of seeing pals. I always took a book and sat in a
corner with my head bent so that people should not see, only
as I never wore spectacles on those occasions, I could not see
to read. At last my turn would come and I would get my
moment with Mr Denton ... He was handsome in the seedy,
fascinating actor style and supposed to be particularly
attractive. He did try once or twice to get me things but his
usual answer to my humble request was: 'No, dearie, nothing
today except panto and that wouldn't suit you, I know,'
laying a tender hand upon my shoulder ... No, going to the
agents was simply *beastly*.

Besides that I bought '*Era*', and constantly answered their
advertisements ... but I was always too funky to go on their
precious tours, I wonder what they would have been like ...

In my despair I thought about Ben Greet.

(*Stage Journal.*)

Ben Greet, 'a bulky, competent actor, with a floss of white
hair'[6] was a little like Benson. He too specialised for the
most part in Shakespeare and built up his own touring
repertory company. But first he would charge his would-be
actors to come and have drama classes under him and then
he would select those he wanted for one of his tours of
America. Flora decided to pay to join one of his classes for
the spring of 1902. Once again she found herself among a

motley lot of people, very few of whom she thought in the least talented, but all of whom were far nicer to get on with than the Bensonians.

Flora was cast as Sir Lionel O'Triggers in *The Rivals* and her Irish brogue was greatly admired. She asked Greet if he would give her a part in his touring company sometime, and he said certainly he would. So she was 'extremely wild' when she discovered that he had asked two of the other girls to go to America instead of her. Greet then asked Flora if she would like a part in *Sherlock Holmes*; they were to start rehearsing the next morning. When she turned up, however, everyone else's name was called but not Flora's. There had been a muddle, she was told. 'But you promised to give me something if I had ability,' Flora was reduced to wailing to Mr Greet's secretary. She went up to London the next day and the next, only to be told at last that they would not have her because she had refused to play the piano — her piano playing had never been as good as Alice's.

It was mean of Greet because he had never said there would be piano-playing. I was frightfully disappointed, I don't think I have ever minded anything so much ... tears stood in my eyes ... I managed to dodge people and went somewhere up into Maiden Lane, looked at a shop window and howled.

(*Stage Journal.*)

It was Flora's Third Class Degree all over again, but worse. 'I thought the whole thing had been a waste of time and everybody thought better than me.' (Flora to Alice, July 1902.)

In the autumn of 1902 Flora did 'walk on' in Laurence Housman's *Bethlehem* produced by Gordon Craig[7] and designed by Edith Craig.[8] And in January 1903, she began the last episode of her stage career — her first and only provincial tour, in Hall Caine's *The Eternal City*, adapted for the stage by Beerbohm Tree. Flora had got her chance by continuing to besiege the agents. Desperation had toughened her and no modest disclaimers about her piano-playing or anything else should jeopardise her chances now:

At one time it seemed absolutely all over and I was in despair. Then Topham sent for me. Arrangements were going on for *The Eternal City*. Part after part seemed filling up and there was apparently nothing for me. There was an organ wanted and a harp. Who could play them? I said I couldn't, but at last as I saw opportunity going I felt I must make a supreme effort and I caught Mr Topham and said I might. This was extremely rash, when I think of 5 or 6 lessons at Montmirail twelve years ago. However of course they didn't know that. Upon this I was welcomed as an acquisition, given a pass to His Majesty's and told to observe the part of Francesca and see how I should like it.

I went to His Majesty's and can say with truth I never saw anything so despicably dull as *The Eternal City*. My part was tiny, but I saw in it germs of character and the other small parts seemed to have no character at all. The rehearsals went on at 3, Bedford St. At the first one there again seemed a mistake about my part; however I went firmly to Mr Topham, settled it with him, got the part from Collins the stage-manager and stuck to it ...

I was in for a rather curious time over the organ. Of course it was a kind of American creature with all sorts of dodges of which I had no idea. I was requested to begin pianissimo. I began to play and the organ roared. I pushed in stop after stop but it roared still louder. Collins came up decidedly cross: 'I thought you said you could play the organ.' With great presence of mind I declared the organ must be out of order and was strongly backed by a Mr Jenkins, a foolish old thing who knew no more of organs than I. This excuse managed very well and then Foster and Collins came after the rehearsal and muddled about with it, pulling out everything, just the sort of thing men love. I was a good deal worried about the organ, wondering how *I should* get on. However next day I went up early and practised and gradually things came right, though I found it difficult to control the creature first of all ...

(*Stage Journal.*)

Flora soon discovered all the exhaustion, discomfort and the insecurity that are involved in 'touring'.[9] Her first dress rehearsal went on until half-past one in the morning:

... I felt quite drunk with weariness as we walked home and found it hard to get along straight. When we arrived home the fire was out and our poor bread and milk stone cold. This was a vile climax and I thought it splendid of Mrs Symons [Flora's fellow theatrical lodger] and me not to lose our tempers. We had to share a bed but I was too shaky to care.

(Stage Journal.)

At first the primitive squalor of backstage life had come as a dreadful revelation to Flora:

I was absolutely flabbergasted when I saw Gravesend. The back artistes' regions were cellars that smelt horribly. Drainage appears to be nonexistent in provincial theatres, also ventilation and lighting. None of the theatres I went to were really, properly equipped behind the scenes. Cambridge which is supposed to be the ideal had quite atrocious gas and one broken chair to sit down on. Most theatres provide no seat and it is a great exception if there is one looking-glass in *one* dressing room ... The floor and walls of everywhere behind were filthy. In *front* things were different. The box office would be brilliantly clean. Theatres, unfortunately, being neither shops nor factories, are not inspected.

(Stage Journal.)

Most worrying of all was the humiliating business of actually finding lodgings for the night in each new town that they visited:

In Bromley we tramped all over the place bags in hand hunting high and low. The good ones seemed snapped up. One I liked but it was too expensive for Mrs S.; another was horribly dirty. At a third a woman slammed the door in our face and said she wasn't going to have no more professionals. At last we came to a nice-looking house with a clean woman. We asked for rooms and she asked if we were professionals. We owned the sad fact and she said she was sorry she had had such a dreadful experience with pantomime people she was never going to take any again.

'You *look* quiet,' she remarked doubtfully.

Mrs Symons assured her we were. 'I am a married woman and this lady is a clergyman's daughter, I think you would have nothing to complain of.' I said how tired we were and how we had tramped all over the town. Mrs Symons thought this quite the wrong tactics. The woman went to consult her husband, and he advised: 'Try them, *poor* things if they're so tired you can't do better than *try* them' and so it was arranged.

(Stage Journal.)

When the 'theatricals' weren't loafing, they were staggering under their luggage running to catch a train:

It was awfully heavy work carrying the bags and latterly I took to engaging boys which was thought self indulgent I fancy. Theatricals are really rather plucky about that sort of thing. It is their great virtue. They carry enormous packages. And they grumble marvellously little over the discomforts and the smells. For one thing they are used to them as they come from a class rather unaccustomed to decencies, still I do admire that. We usually had a rush to the station, there would be a great struggle at the last moment forcing bacon and cakes into one's bag, so as to get one's money's worth; quite a good thing to do of course, only it was vile having the butter in one's pocket.

(Stage Journal.)

Every so often Flora would stop being the vagrant actress 'Mary Strafford' and turn again into Miss Flora Mayor, the scholar's daughter, as she paid a duty visit to some local church dignitary who was an old family friend during the company's stop at Cambridge or at Kettering. Her hosts were not told what else she was doing in Cambridge or Kettering. At such times Flora must have felt she really was leading a double life and it is understandable that she should have written at the end of her journal: 'Now that it's all over it seems so dreamlike to think one ever was on the stage.'

Flora never indulged in any illusions about the ludicrousness of her own tiny rôles in *The Eternal City*:

In the second scene I appeared as an old peasant woman. I wore an ancient hockey skirt ... rubbed two reddish grease paints on to produce an Italian complexion and crabbled blue and purple lines on with those vile grease-paint pencils to represent wrinkles, and roughed up my eyebrows the wrong way. The light is so atrocious in dressing rooms that I never could see much what I was doing and I emerged a wild object. Alice said I looked exactly like a monkey ... My next job was playing the organ and a curious quartet in deshabillé would assemble, one girl in a dressing jacket, his Holiness wrapped in a towel, another man rubbing his make-up off, I accompanied them in a Latin hymn to the Virgin ... and then everybody assembled as rabble to start a revolution ... I thought I was most conscientious in my joy, hatred, amusement and horror. However Collins [the manager] blamed us for spoiling his big scene. He declared we made him laugh.

'And you're the worst of the lot,' said he to me. 'I don't know what it is, you've got such a funny face. It's funny enough off, but when you're made up, it's a regular comedian's face. When I look at you I begin to laugh.'

(*Stage Journal.*)

Once Flora's letters began to arrive home, candidly reporting the rackety people, the crazy hours and the disgusting drains, the Mayor family's opposition to Flora's stage career intensified. Alice, in particular, began to remonstrate with her more and more fiercely:

I do think your life sounds so detestable, it makes me quite depressed to think of you being on an equality with these beastly people ... *how* you can stand it — it seems to me such an utter waste of time and everything else and of course it will make your hair greyer. I knew it would ... now it comes across me how *loathsome* it is ... Henry has written to Aunt Fanny about it. He thinks it's a pity you've gone in for it as he doesn't think you're cut out for a great actress and that you had a real gift for writing. But he doesn't think you'll get

demoralized by it ... I must tell you of a talk I've been having
with Robin about you — he showed me your letter and
thought the descriptions very well written. Couldn't
understand how you could stand these people though he did
not think your letters enthusiastic ... He then began
inexorably reckoning up years and thought you were going on
too late to go through the grind; he didn't think age mattered
a bit if you were in a good position but it was too late to work
right up. He thought it would be absolutely useless to do any
more touring and would probably spoil your acting — he
thought it was the rarest thing for successful and good acting
to go together. He thinks it very curious for you to be so keen.
I don't think he's a bit keen on you doing it now. I expect
you'll hate reading this ... but do face it and see how hopeless
it is. I for one shall do something drastic if you don't. Now
that Robin's sympathy is quite alienated don't you feel off it?
(Alice to Flora, January 1903.)

But there was a doggedness in Flora which made it next
to impossible for her to admit either to herself or to her
family that she was 'off it', even when she did feel low. The
one positive aspect of her inglorious stage career was that at
least she had survived it. She had proved to herself that she
did have grit and stamina, having endured, she felt, more
snubs and worse squalor than any other girl of her class
would have tolerated. There had been times when she had
broken down and cried, but she had never sunk to quarrelling with her fractious companions, and she had not run
away. But in another respect the experience had not been
good for her. Flora's secret judgements on her fellow-
troupers — only confided to her journal or to Alice — had
become increasingly uncharitable in order to compensate
for her own battered self-esteem. 'X' was 'very vulgar and
Cockney', 'Y' was 'vain and flirtatious', 'Z', 'self-centred
and bourgeois and can no more act than a cow', 'R' was
'feeble and babyish, like all actors', 'S' 'exceedingly spiteful
and a liar', and 'T' 'dirty and common with a perfect
passion for stuffiness'. Desmond MacCarthy has written in

a 1920's review of a London production of *The Cherry Orchard* that 'Nothing chills sympathy so much as consciousness of superiority.'[10] The chilling of Flora's capacity for sympathy due to 'Mary Strafford's' demoralizing failures as an actress threatened to damage the potential novelist, Flora Mayor. Her unsuccess in the theatre was an irritant sore for years to come, a memory that she had to lie to herself about and sentimentalise in retrospect. Much of her later writing about the stage[11] is vitiated by an all too obvious egotism that idealised herself and patronised all the rest. It would take Flora several years to master this defensiveness and to regain her exceptional capacity for large-hearted imaginative sympathy as a writer.

While Flora Mayor was looking like a monkey in *The Eternal City*, Mary Sheepshanks was struggling to run Morley College. The period 1898-1903 was a particularly difficult one for Morley. In 1898 the Borough Polytechnic had opened less than a mile away causing Morley to abandon its own technical courses and limit the subjects it offered to the humanities and to commerce. Simultaneously, the London School Board expanded its own free evening classes and recreational offerings, with the result that Morley lost many students: 'in the mid-nineties the membership had risen to more than eleven hundred students, but by 1902 it was down in the seven hundreds'.[12] In 1899 further demoralisation and confusion had resulted when the London District Auditor successfully challenged the financing of post-elementary education from the rates. There was a general crisis in educational advance, affecting children and adult students alike — as many as five thousand children were estimated to be walking the streets of Lambeth in 1900 without any schooling at all. Mary had to take up the cudgels on behalf of the educational value of Morley almost single-handed. The college Principal, Caroline Martineau, had become terminally ill in 1899, and so Mary, at the age of twenty-seven, was left to steer the

college administration through some very troubled meetings, against a general background of diminished confidence in education. Mary made it her business to inject
renewed vitality into Morley over this difficult period.

From the first, she took a special interest in the women
students, perceiving that they were much less confident,
physically, verbally, socially and intellectually, than were
the men. Mary did all she could to encourage the Women's
Gymnastic Club, the Cycling Club, and women's participation in college debates. In 1901 she encouraged more
informality and less self-consciousness about dress by
passing a new rule allowing the women to remove their hats
in college. Evening dress was forbidden in order to prevent
dressing up 'and so keep the place open to the poorest'.[13]
There was also a significant and moving entry in the *Morley
College Magazine* for December 1901. Mary Sheepshanks
had recognised that many of the women were simply too
tired after their long day out at work to commit themselves
to a whole course of study in the humanities. But she could
not bear them to be deprived of literature and social history
altogether. Therefore she instituted the experiment of
single lectures specifically aimed at interesting such
women. Mary herself gave one lecture on her old favourite,
Charlotte Brontë, and she organised others on the
Women's Co-operative Guild, on 'Heroines', and on Jane
Austen.

By October 1902, Morley College's student members
were picking up again and 'Miss Sheepshanks' was formally thanked for all her efforts — 'Not only was she a hard
worker herself, but even more important, she had the
power of bringing fresh ideas into the College work and of
finding persons to help carry out those ideas.'[14] Among the
persons 'found' by Mary at the turn of the century were the
pianist Miss Geissler-Schubert to play chamber music, the
Misses Meinertzhagen to play Haydn quartets, and
Mary's own 'significant other' from her Newnham days,
the imposing classical scholar, Melian Stawell, to lecture

on Ibsen, and the Greeks. And, of course, her own and Flora's great friend, Ernest Shepherd, continued his good work, taking parties of Morley students to the Public Records Office and to the Rolls Chapel, conducting them over St Saviour's Church, Southwark, and writing articles for the *Morley College Magazine* on every kind of antiquity dear to his heart, from monumental church brasses to European armour.

Morley College gave a great deal in warmth and responsiveness to those who gave themselves to it, but it also demanded a great deal. Mary appreciated the liveliness of the place but everyone clearly expected her to participate in all their activities seven nights a week:

Almost every evening some of the students were to be seen in the Common Room, often planning and working for one or other of the Clubs, especially the Field Club, the Photographic Society and the French Club; but as often in eager discussion of scientific, political or social questions. There was a happy absence of class feeling or sex prejudice. Everyone was taken on their merits and often put through their paces by astute questioning ...

There was a pleasant social side in the College. Saturday and sometimes Sunday excursions were made, in winter to museums or city Churches, in summer to not too distant country. Many of the students were keen naturalists, and the Field Club collected botanical specimens, books were produced from pockets and flowers or pondlife identified. Some branch of nature study was a favourite subject for Saturday evening lectures.

But, Mary adds:

from my own personal point of view there were serious drawbacks to my work there. I earned very little money, there were no avenues to promotion and, worst of all, the work being in the evenings cut me off from London social life. I had many friends and many invitations and could have had a gay time, but evening work made it impossible. One evening a week I had free, and I then went out to dinner with perhaps a party to follow. Week-ends too had often to be sacrificed to Saturday evening fixtures at the College. (Mary Sheepshanks, *Autobiography*, ch. 6.)

Despite this demanding commitment, Mary did manage to establish a stimulating home of her own at the turn of the century. For almost twenty years, between 1899 and 1919, Mary had the lease of a small Georgian house, 1 Barton Street, behind Westminster Abbey. And it was there, in what had recently been slum property with ineradicable bugs scampering behind its wooden panelling, that Mary set up house with a succession of woman friends.

Mary always needed to romanticise her friends. Thus her first protégée was Clotilde Brewster, the young daughter of a misalliance between a German aristocrat and a rich, expatriate American philosopher and aesthete, Henry Brewster. Clotilde's father was the great friend and lover of the composer Ethel Smyth whose overpowering presence would also occasionally descend on 1 Barton Street. Mary described Ethel Smyth as the most dynamic being she had ever met. Clotilde herself was a very cosmopolitan and sophisticated young student of architecture who had just been expelled from Newnham for smoking. Mary aways warmed to someone whom she thought had been given a rough ride. When Clotilde married in 1903, her place in the house at Barton Street was taken by a succession of other interesting young women, including the Quaker granddaughters of John Bright, Hilda Clark the doctor and Alice Clark the first secretary of the L.S.E., Blanche Smith, a failed actress and author — and friend of Flora Mayor — and Gertrude Sandilands, Irene Cooper Willis and Emily Leaf, all of whom were later to become prominent Suffragists. Mary and her friends

were usually three in number, and each had a bedroom and sittingroom and shared the dining-room. We had a cook and a housemaid. Many years later one of my lodger friends introducing me to someone said, 'I lived with Mary, and she *did* make us comfortable and *did* feed us well.' It was easy in those days. (Mary Sheepshanks, *Autobiography*, ch. 7.)

Barton Street at that time had something of the character of a village; Adeline and Ralph Vaughan Williams lived there, as did Bertrand Russell's greatest friends, Crompton and Theodore Llewelyn Davies and, just a few streets away, was Ernest Shepherd at 3 Warwick Square. Mary made strenuous efforts throughout this period to keep her friendships alive in the face of her commitments at Morley College. So desperate was she at times to get right away and to enjoy herself — with the nascent Bloomsbury Group, amongst other friends — that she would set off in a cab at 10.30 p.m. after classes were over and arrive at one of the Sangers' Friday Nights, or late on Thursday evening at the Stephens' in Gordon Square, just when her hosts were hoping that their guests would soon leave. Mary also helped to run an informal Sunday Walks Club with some of her old Cambridge friends, among them George Trevelyan, Hilton Young and Desmond MacCarthy:

We went by train to one station, walked across country, ate a sandwich lunch and had tea at an inn before taking the train at another station, and so home again. In spite of the enthusiasm with which people joined, it too often happened that they were lured away by luncheon invitations or other attractions and failed to turn up; so that it was several times my lot to arrive at the appointed station and find myself left alone for a solitary tramp. (Mary Sheepshanks, *Autobiography*, ch. 7.)

This self-conscious spinsterish isolation on Mary's part could also be detected at work. Instead of having a separate office, Mary simply had her own desk in the Morley College Common Room — but she could not find the right way to be on the easy terms with the students that she yearned for and so she was driven to make a formal entreaty to be treated more informally: 'Miss Sheepshanks encouraged the students to come freely to the desk in the Common Room ... they were not to suppose that in so doing they would be disturbing her in other work.'[15] When Flora Mayor visited Mary at the Morley College Soirée in October 1903, she was struck by 'how little Mary seemed the centre of things. None of the Morley people were talking to her at all.' Mary's bespectacled, severe and somewhat unexpressive features as well as her unbending posture made her not easy to approach. All her life she lacked Flora's attractiveness and magnetism — and knew she did.

For all Mary's complaints about her lack of social life, she did keep in regular touch with her friends, including Flora Mayor. Flora's *Stage Journal* records several visits that she paid to Mary at Barton Street during her Benson days:

Went to M. Sheepshanks to coach Morleyites in *Pygmalion and Galatea*. Told her about the stage. She was sure I would let the whole thing out to everybody. Was laughing about my lack of all grandeurs. Teaching, Writing, Historical Research, Acting — she thought me an odd mixture. She told me some amusing scandal about royalty.

On another occasion when Flora suddenly felt very sick after a matinée of *As You Like It*, she again sought refuge with Mary Sheepshanks and sent word that she was too ill to take part in that evening's performance.

Alice Mayor's journal also gives many glimpses of Mary Sheepshanks during her visits to Queensgate House:

25 March 1899:   M. Sheepshanks came, much more benignant that when I last saw her but with an increased way of bringing out private information in a very public manner.

24 Sept. 1899: M. Sheepshanks biked over, most company and suave [sic].

17 March 1900:   M. Sheepshanks came. Very attractive for a short time but one gets to want to avoid her later she's so cynical.

4 June 1900:   M. Sheepshanks appeared — very entertaining
  and quite amiable — talked about the stinginess of rich
  people — Miss Pease ordering for them both a coffee for
  one. Also of the self-absorption of most people.
26 April 1901:   Lunch with M. Sheepshanks. Blanche Smith
  was there and they both became most pessimistic about
  the Transvaal War.
11 May 1901:   M. Sheepshanks came with a great deal of
  thrilling Society gossip.
20 Feb. 1902:   M. Sheepshanks and Mr Wood came to
  dinner. Mary talked in her usual cynical style and secured
  Mr Wood's services for the College.

On one particularly memorable day, Mary was invited
down to Queensgate House at the same time as their
mutual friend Ernest Shepherd:

23 June 1900: Mary Sheepshanks came to lunch looking very
pretty. We met Ernest and Earp and went on the river, most
successful and most cheerful tea. Ernest was very lively,
possibly owing to Mary. Mary talked a good deal about Mr
Fountain's engagement. (Alice's journal.)

Two weeks later, on Friday 6 July 1900, Alice went to visit
Ernest's sister Gertrude — 'We talked about Mary Sheepshanks and Ernest with some apprehension.' (Alice's
journal.)

Ernest, however, had no thoughts of proposing to Mary
Sheepshanks, greatly though he esteemed her work at
Morley and stimulating though he found her. His thoughts
were still all on Flora, but his prospects, even well after
1900, were not good. 'Looked in on Ernest in his office.
Miss Sinclair [Ernest's aunt] talked sadly about Ernest's
not getting on.' (Alice's journal, January 1902.) Flora's
father was moved to suggest to Ernest that he should
become a clergyman. (Alice's journal, July 1902.) But
Ernest could not take that way out because he had no religious faith.

In the meantime the gifted classical scholar, Frank Earp,
another old friend of the family, had fallen in love with

Alice. He proposed to her — 'I live for the times I see you' —
but Alice did not love him, and she rejected him.

When Flora finally set off on her gruelling, farcical
Eternal City tour, in January 1903, Ernest Shepherd
decided that he must take drastic action. He applied for
work abroad. There was one possible post going in South
Africa and there was also a position vacant on the Archi-
tectural Survey of India. Early in March 1903, he was told
that he had been appointed to go to India. And on 19
March 1903, Ernest wrote to Flora, addressing his letter to
'Miss Mary Strafford' at the theatre, Macclesfield, saying 'I
should greatly like to see you.'

Flora was just then at a very low ebb, both physically and
emotionally. She had recently admitted to Alice: 'I do miss
home and you and I miss no-one *loving* me and I miss not
being my own self and not being with people who can
sympathize with things I like.' When the company got to
Macclesfield, Flora was unwell with a heavy period and felt
very faint; she took some whisky and then felt drunk. On
getting to the theatre she found Ernest Shepherd's letter
asking to see her:

I was too ill to think properly but I managed to send the wire
off telling him to come. It did not strike me first what the
probable meaning was. When it did I tried to put it out of my
head ...
    I had hardly come back to these dismal Macclesfield
lodgings when Ernest came ... and from his extreme
nervousness and stammerings and his looking so awfully ill I
felt sure what was up. I said would he come out and have tea
at a hotel, our lodgings were so horrid. As soon as we got
outside he began.
    'Do you think I look different?'
    I said 'I think you look ill.'
Then he told me of India and he said 'Now you must know
what I want to say?'
Of course I said No I didn't.
Then with much stammering he said, would I go with him?

I said 'Yes, I think I should'. And then immediately afterwards felt I couldn't. I said I did not know if I could leave you. He is as nice as can be. If I don't like the thought of India I am to stop in England and he will come over but that would be too unfair. Still, what am I to do without you? ... I don't think I feel in love, in fact it is all so horribly oppressive and exciting ... I do feel giving up the Stage awfully, I suppose you can't understand it —

Being kissed is so odd.

Darling,
    Goodbye.
(Flora to Alice, 24-25 March 1903.)

On that same afternoon of Ernest's proposal, 24 March 1903, Mary Sheepshanks featured prominently in the newly engaged couple's first conversation. Each had to tell the other whether there was anyone else whom they had ever thought of marrying. Ernest said he had always thought Flora the nicest girl he knew. Flora then challenged him point-blank about Mary Sheepshanks. She asked if he had ever proposed to Mary, to which he responded emphatically with a 'Never *near* that.' Flora said she knew that both Alice and her mother had noticed how greatly Ernest had taken to Mary, but she herself had felt Ernest could never really fall in love with her.

As for Alice, her first thought on receiving Flora's garbled account of getting engaged was that Flora had gone mad. It was all so sudden and so incoherent. But her second reaction was happiness on Flora's behalf — though desolation for herself. Never again would she see her twin in the depths of depression at not being loved or worrying herself silly about her grey hairs and her wrinkles. And marriage would get Flora off the stage. But the prospect of losing Flora, and to a country as distant as India, was more than hard.

Flora's own reaction, after she had got over her initial numb shock, was that Ernest's proposal was a kind of deliverance:

I feel God has done so much more than I deserve ... I do *so* hope I shall be worthy of it and not nasty ... I think these things coming at a hoary age [she was thirty] makes one not so set up. As for the Stage it is curious how uninteresting it seems now that I am not sticking to it and the privations seem much more disagreeable. It is very odd to think all that bother for engagements is over and that I shall read the *Sketch* and the *Era* without a qualm. Providence has arranged things in such a delightful way. It could not have been nicer for me. I should have found it so horribly hard chucking the stage without this, and most painful going on with all of you protesting. (Flora to Alice, March 1903.)

Ernest had rescued Flora from a situation that was becoming intolerable.

5

'FLORA SHEPHERD',
MARCH–OCTOBER 1903

The *Eternal City* tour had to go on, with Flora in it, for a little longer. Ernest had to content himself with trying to catch her up at Lincoln, or Grantham or Kidderminster, or, failing that, with thinking over dinner: 'Flora must be having her egg now.' (Alice to Flora, March 1903.)

Whenever two people love, there is usually one who loves more and one who loves less. At this period in their lives it was Ernest who loved more — if only because Flora was still divided between her old allegiance to Alice and her new one to Ernest. But it was characteristic of Ernest's exceptional sensitivity that he also should have been aware of Alice and of what she was suffering:

How can you forgive me, Alice, for what I have done? I know from my dearest what a cruel blow it must be to you; and I can't do anything to make it less; save only if I may say that I love her all the better for the love she bears to you ...

Believe me that I shall never be jealous of you: it would be impossible with her; however close the relations between you, even if it be sometimes to my own exclusion I shall not complain nor think myself wronged ... don't be too hard on me. (24 March 1903.)

Hitherto it had always been Alice's rôle to take care of her identical twin — even mother her — 'she looks after my health and my happiness and thinks for me, I can't tell you'

(Flora to Ernest), and now Alice had to relinquish that rôle and even to rejoice that she was giving place to Ernest: 'She has written to me in wild ecstasies of joy, she has wanted this for a long time' (Flora to Ernest). But to Ernest himself Alice did admit:

I do think the conventional view of marriage is very hard to put up with — no-one seems to think Flora will or will have any right to feel her parting with me at all, and Ernest dear it is a *real* comfort to me to feel that you do understand and sympathize with us both ... sympathy is the most important thing in the world I think.

Ernest doted on Flora. He was loyal to her gallant if inglorious attempt to become a professional actress: 'Poor Mary Strafford; dearest I don't feel a bit inclined to laugh about her; she was really a very promising young woman ...' And he also counted himself at the head of those who recognised Flora Mayor's potential as a writer: 'Don't imagine that I fail to appreciate her literary gift. I would back myself to come out top in an examination on *Mrs Hammond.*' (Ernest to Mrs Irwin, Clifton College, April 1903.)

Early on in their correspondence after Ernest and Flora became engaged, there appears an interesting letter from Ernest concerning Mary Sheepshanks:

I called on Mary Sheepshanks to-day and told her about ourselves; you know I said I should; if I had not told her myself I should have felt a sneak the next time I met her. Of course I did not expect her to care one way or the other and I don't think she did; but she spoke very nicely, and was pleased that I had come to tell her; so though it was very awkward, embarrassing and hateful I am very glad I did it: I hope you think I did right.

Two days later, Ernest was immensely relieved to hear again from Flora,

because a horrible thought flashed across me this evening that

I had not had a letter because of what I did about Mary
Sheepshanks. (N.B. I have never called her Mary — though it
is a much prettier name than Flora — poor dear — or got
anywhere near it); but I have dismissed the thought and am
not worrying. (Ernest to Flora, March 1903.)

Why should it have been so 'very awkward, embarrassing
and hateful' to tell Mary about his engagement to Flora? A
week before Ernest sailed for India, Mary, Flora and Ernest
found themselves together in Winchester where Ernest was
fulfilling his promise to the Morley College students to
guide them over the ancient city.

The Archaeological Society met on April 17 to take a formal
farewell of Mr Shepherd, and marked the occasion by
presenting him with a silver inkstand as a token of
appreciation ... The great esteem in which Mr Shepherd is
held personally was shown by the large number of members
who attended to wish him well in his new sphere and
happiness in his approaching marriage ... Miss Sheepshanks
presented the testimonial.[1]

But Ernest was to find himself in a much more complex
emotional entanglement. At first both Alice Mayor and
Ernest's 'Auntie' (who had reared all the orphaned
Shepherd children as her own) made heroic efforts to affirm
the future marriage of Ernest and Flora. But soon cracks
began to show. First 'Auntie' broke down at the prospect of
losing her favourite adopted son to 'another woman'.
Ernest blamed himself — in his self-absorbed happiness he
must have been insensitive to Auntie's needs. Flora
commented: 'It was just like you to say it was all your fault
when I think it was simply human nature for her to mind a
little about your engagement.' But in that same letter Flora
herself set up a second difficult situation for Ernest:

Dearest, I do so hope you won't mind, I am showing your
letters to Alice. You see she has always been in the habit of
opening, reading, losing and forgetting the contents of my
letters before I have seen them, it would seem so odd to stop it

now. If you do mind say at once and I will not show them any more; I had a struggle but I thought I would do it at the risk of your minding. Alice must not feel anything is coming between us.

Ernest responded like a saint:

Yes I can truly say dearest I am glad you have shown my letters to Alice; it is quite unconventional for which I don't care a scrap; but I see that if you didn't show them it might be the beginning of what you dreaded; and anything is better than that; but dearest please don't, either of you let Auntie know of it; I have not shown your letters to her.

Despite all their real fellow-feeling for her, Alice soon began to imagine that Flora, in particular, was not sympathetic enough. On 4 April, Alice went to Canterbury to wait for Flora:

How I counted the hours ...
Sunday 5th: An evening walk by myself in the precincts, a dreary evening. I felt riled with Flora as I thought she didn't mind leaving.
Monday 6th: Flora came. As soon as we got upstairs I told her what I had been feeling and we wept and then all got right. (Alice's journal, 1903.)

Flora had repeatedly to reassure her twin sister that she *did* mind their parting. She even promised Alice that she would postpone joining Ernest in India for at least six months more. But that did not please Auntie. How could Flora hesitate, even for a split second, between the claims of a mere sister and those of 'her boy'? Auntie thought Alice should stop being so selfish and release Flora immediately. Not surprisingly, then, on the last day before Ernest left England there was a most painful public scene between Flora, Alice and Auntie. After it was all over, Ernest, loyal and supportive, as ever, wrote to Flora:

My dearest,
    I cannot tell you how sorry I am about what passed

between you and Auntie this afternoon: it was hard my darling that these words should have come just now, though you knew that some time or another they would have to be borne. I have absolute confidence in you my dearest and know that you are doing and always will do what you think to be right; it is a matter between you and me and provided we are agreed no one else however dear to either of us has any right to interfere. And my darling I won't think for one moment that you are being selfish; nor will I think it of Alice nor presume to judge her; what you decide my darling is enough for me; give me half or a quarter of your love and I shall think it more than I deserve ...

I know you felt most for Alice dearest; but don't don't be hard on Auntie; you see it isn't likely she should see with our eyes: and we are trying a difficult task which others will think mistaken and impossible, will say that you must give up Alice or me. But my darling we know too that it is difficult: only we have confidence that we have love enough to carry it through; we'll try at any rate to make a good fight for it ... Don't harden your heart towards Auntie my dearest, and in time I believe you will come to love each other ... I think it is quite likely she will learn that Alice and you are not the same as most sisters ... And remember darling we haven't yet learnt to feel as she does; perhaps we never shall; but we can feel for her and make the allowances that a noble and fervent character deserves.

Goodnight my darling: goodbye — for we shall only see each other tomorrow amongst others.

Flora received that letter after Ernest had already waved to her from the boat at Dover, looking tall and thin and white with strain, despite his encouraging, loving smile. She wrote to him at once:

Dear

Your letter was like yourself. I think there is hardly anybody in the world ... who would be what you are about Alice. It makes me love you more and more. The way to my heart is through Alice really I suppose. Dearest I cannot measure affection or say anything of how much I love, but I think you can trust me. I have had some suffering already through loving you and Alice and I expect there will be more, I know there must be, but Alice and I both feel it is worth it. I think it is the best thing in the world to have you two loving me and I you, I would not have it otherwise for anything, whatever pain there may be. I wrote to Auntie but I have not sent the letter, I think it was rather sore. I will write another ... I do love her already and I hope we shall get closer ... You know I shall make lots of mistakes but I think I shall mean well ... Goodbye my darling don't *worry* about things and be morbid ...

In her next letter Flora struggled to spell out to herself as well as to Ernest just what it was she was asking of them both, or rather of all three of them:

I have been trying to think out the whole thing ... As far as I can see if people feel like Alice and I do to one another, if they marry at all they *must* try and keep the feeling just the same. I mean that not only do I want to, but that it would be wrong if I did not. I think there is no doubt that is right, as far as Alice and I are concerned. But then darling when I think of you I see that Auntie is right. It *is* hard on you, I suppose, to have Alice as well. I wonder if you realized things were going to be like this. I could not explain straight off at Macclesfield, I simply was incapable of so doing, but perhaps all this time I have been taking an unfair advantage of you. Have I been behaving badly to you? Are Alice and I taking advantage of you to get things out of you which we have no right to ask? But then when I think of Alice's side, she must anyhow lose my presence, even if we keep the same together in mind, so that I cannot anyhow see that she is selfish. The selfish person is I who want to have both of you. I do pray to be able to act for the best and both you and Alice do everything you can to help me.

On 1 May 1903, Flora went up to lunch with Mary Sheepshanks.

Mary was nice, gentler and less pessimistic than usual. She spoke nicely of you, said you were the most considerate person she knew. I liked that of her. (Flora to Ernest.)

It was not only Mary who was becoming 'gentler'. Flora herself, under the influence of loving and being loved by Ernest Shepherd, was becoming a more tender person and much less the superior 'hanging judge' that she had been in danger of becoming during her stage days. She was beginning to bear out Shelley's theory of the 'Epipsyche' — that our true love is he or she who brings to life in us our real/ ideal self. Flora found herself confessing the existence of her earlier judgemental, hyper-critical self to Ernest:

You know Alice and I are both morbidly analytical and critical, too much so I think, and when I was first engaged I found all my critical faculties strained to their utmost about you, specially at Manchester. I hated wanting to criticise, but I felt all the time I was doing it. Dearest I think it shows I care for you that though I looked so hard, I could not find anything. You know I am morbid particularly when I am tired ... The critical spirit has gone to sleep now. (13 May 1903.)

Will you care about me as much when you really know me, when you see my bad faults that you don't suspect and that I should hate to tell you of, though I shall tell you of them? Alice knows me through and through and loves me, but then her character is very like mine. (3 July 1903.)

Besides writing introspective letters to Ernest, Flora spent the months of their separation and engagement in getting her trousseau ready and in paying farewell visits to all the people who had meant most to her in her life. She visited her old nurse Hannah, the three surviving Mayor Aunts in Hampstead, Uncle John and her Cambridge friends at Newnham and Madame de Salis of Neuchâtel and the Moravian School at Montmirail. There were long visits to Grote cousins in Norfolk, to Ernest's sisters and to Auntie ('If she will care for me, I am sure I shall care for her'), and to Ernest Shepherd's cousin, Kitty Howard, daughter of Canon Howard of Weekley, Northamptonshire. Mary Sheepshanks was also invited down to dinner at Queensgate House, together with Mr Marvin, with whom 'she ought to get on because they are both so zealous for the poor.' But the most precious long last visit of all was to Mary Walton at the Manor House, Shelford, near Cambridge. Mary Walton, the unmarried niece of a mathematician of Trinity College, had known and loved Flora and Alice since they were young children, and they in turn were devoted to her. Their relationship had something in it of kindred-spirited mother and daughters — indeed Mary had once told Alice that if she had ever had children she would have liked them to be like her and Flora. Now it was time for Ernest Shepherd to get to know Mary Walton too, if only through Flora's letters:

Shelford is a second home; we have stayed every year for eleven years — we are quite different to Mary than ordinary friends ... Nothing is allowed to be fished or shot, so they have numbers of birds and beasts about — rooks, jays, kingfishers, voles, owls — Mr Carr the nice rector calls Little Shelford the land of Goshen because no ordinary plagues and troubles can come to it ... We know Shelford rather as you know Weekley ... Mary Walton is delightful — she is years older than us, getting on for 50, but I don't feel the smallest difference in generation with her. She is not at all clever or intellectual — but she is a dear — so generous in her appreciation of others and tender-hearted. (30 July 1903.)

Despite Alice's and Mrs Mayor's demurs, Flora was also very loyal in keeping in touch with her former companions on the stage — she visited backstage at the Comedy Theatre — 'It was so funny to get into that loud larky atmosphere again. I do like it, how sad that I should, but it does amuse me so.' (Flora to Ernest.) She also kept track of her fellow-troupers, Miss Atkins, Mr Ayliff, Mrs Moss and Mrs Symons, writing to them, visiting them and even having some of them to tea. When she heard how many of her old *Eternal City* company had now fallen on bad times — 'I felt heartily glad to be out of it.'

As for her writing, it was during these months that Flora was putting together the latter part of her *Stage Journal*— 'it is rather interesting but I suppose it would be a little scurrilous for publication' — she was giving pupil-teachers lessons in economics, literature and French; as well as struggling each week to keep order among unruly hordes of Sunday School boys — her *bête noire* — and she even helped an old Kingston friend to escort a troupe of factory girls on their annual outing — 'Miss Young really *loves* these wild girls — that seems very strange to me' (Flora to Ernest, 31 July 1903). In addition, of course, there were the usual church bazaars and parish entertainments. But in the interstices of all these disparate social activities Flora knew that her one essential role was to stay close to Alice each day and hour that they still had left together. Indeed, what she was now doing was to lead Alice's usual life with her, week by week, rather than her own. From choice, not necessity, the thirty-year-old sisters still shared a bedroom. Nevertheless, Alice still felt that she was about to be deserted. On 17 August, having written Frank Earp her final letter of rejection, she told a friend that home was her greatest interest — 'I said Flora is the person I care most for.' The next day:

Flora and I were reading our old letters and I said I thought she was unfeeling. She went on reading, then I caught her and pulled her down beside me and we both lay and cried. (Alice's journal, 1903.)

On the 4 September, Alice was reading *Récit d'une Soeur* in bed.

I talked to Flora about it and said how when I was alone I often thought about her going out to India and wondered how she could do it. She said she thought she could never make it up to me and said she'd rather I should be happy and forget her a little than be too dull when she goes. *Nous avons beaucoup pleuré mais c'était mieux de le dire.*

Flora did not tell Ernest the whole truth about how distressed and reproachful Alice was concerning their marriage; she merely reported in general terms — 'of course we have often wept bitterly about India, you would know we should', and then drifted off into fantasies about the most perfect thing of all would be if they could all three settle down in England together, some time.

Ernest Shepherd, meanwhile, was suffering from double culture-shock for he was being exposed simultaneously to the strangeness of India and of Anglo-India. India itself first repelled, then frightened, then enchanted him and with his usual candour, Ernest expressed all his reactions and worries and moods, however discreditable he felt them to be, to Flora:

Agra, the hotel, the natives, everything are *absolutely extraordinary* ... the verandah is crowded with natives, punkah coolies and so on who squat and lie about all over the place. There is *no privacy* of any kind. (13 May.) ... India is the most muddling place out so far as I can see. (16 May.) My darling what you say about the Indian servants is really most amusing: they in your power indeed: do you understand that this is their country, that the language spoken is theirs; and that in all these matters you are entirely dependent on their information? That it rests with them whether you get good meat or bad, cheap or dear — there is nothing fixed and nothing definitely known to the European. (13 June.) ... Delhi — I believe I am getting to like India — The lovely bright sun and clear air, the beautiful views of the country through the arches of the mosque quadrangle. (2 August.)

But the British Imperialists were more difficult to like:

Anything more vapid, futile and insipid than Hill Station Society it is impossible to conceive. We had a gorgeous picnic — lobster and champagne, woman dressed up to the nines of course. At first we talked more or less sensibly; but after two or three hours it degenerated hopelessly: we had to hold hands and guess thoughts and do everything that from the depth of my soul I most deeply abhor ... The men are

unutterably *dull* — they never talk of anything but sport and
bridge; and are intensely competitive about tennis ... it is
remarkable that these people with all their immense
friendliness seem in no hurry at all to show you their real
selves ... I don't know anybody — never shall know anybody
as far as I can see; everyone is so exceedingly reserved: they
are so amongst themselves too: it isn't only with me. (11 July.)

If leisure in the company of the Anglo-Indians was less than
enlivening, Ernest's official post also created problems. He
had been appointed to supervise the restoration of ancient
monuments and buildings for the Archaeological Survey of
India, but he had reckoned without the Viceroy, Lord
Curzon, and his subordinate, Marshall, from whom he had
to take his instructions:

Marshall has the most *awful* notions concerning restoration
... he wants to make all the old buildings spick and span,
entirely destroying their remarkable character: and the worst
of it is these are not his own ideas but the Viceroy's which he
faithfully echoes. I simply don't know what to do. Perhaps I
have already spoken out too freely ... I am a government
servant and until I am better established I must I suppose
keep quiet and carry out work which I think a desecration.
Marshall is neither a real scholar nor a real artist and simply
devotes himself to licking the Viceroy's boots ... (16 May)

... my position is really very awkward; here is Marshall
representing the government of India giving me all sorts of
silly instructions, and on the other hand the local government
which I may offend by carrying them out. (12 July.)

Behind all Ernest's reactions both to India and to Anglo-
India lay his constant worried self-questioning: what
would Flora make of the peculiar life out there? How could
he ask her to leave everyone and everything she loved just
for him? The climate was so overpowering and she was not
strong. They would have to be separated for several months
of the year — and what on earth would his poor Flora find to
do, stuck up in a hill-station, marooned among the clothes-

and-protocol obsessed Anglo-Indians? If Ernest were feeling well and India was looking beautiful, he would dare to make hopeful suggestions:

My own plan is this; each district as I think ought to be taken in order, and examined, its buildings mapped and described. Now if government would allow me to work like that it seems to me we might be together all right; for having taken the train to the centre of our district we could then have tents I think and carry about our own servants and our own cows etc. You have no idea how horrid it is living in anything but your own house out here; and not healthy either ... There are some tents I believe at Lucknow which we could use. (21 June.)

Flora responded to this startling suggestion of tent and cows very pluckily:

Dearest ... I am looking forward to the Camping, though I think it will be rough and messy and the travelling too. You see I have the virtues of my defects. I don't mind mess and shoddiness ... I do want to see the untouched native part of India and I shall be awfully disappointed if we don't get plenty of that ... I might manage sometimes to stay with Missionaries when you are away and do some teaching or something for them. I should like that you know ... Don't look on me as a *tender flower*, darling. I saw Mr Durrant the other day and he said I looked a good person for India, being thin and pale, that was the wiry lasting sort ... I think together we shall enjoy the fun of it all, — even if it is not fun, — *Allons, courage, l'amour attend à la maison* as one of my French songs remarks ...
    Do not be sad about me, your own for *whatever* turns up,
       Flora.
Remember I really am tough. (18 and 23 July.)

... I do not in the least mind travelling alone ... Travelling is not the sort of thing I do funk. Really when you have interviewed theatrical agents, you feel like a lion about most things — (24 September.)

Ernest felt heartened and more in love with her than ever:

My dearest ... I know you are a brick at standing discomfort
... I think your notion of taking up some teaching work when
you are at Naini Tal is most excellent; it would give you
employment and interest and all sorts of good things ... I had
thought you'd find it so utterly dull and objectless [in the
Hills]; I can't think why it didn't occur to me before. India is
a great place for education by women and I foresee quite a
career for you; you would be able to get pay if you wanted it
too I expect, but grubber of annas as I am, we shan't reckon
on that. (2 August.)

However, there were other times, particularly when he
was weakened by a bout of fever or stricken by the loneliness and frustration of his work, when Ernest felt over-
whelmed by depression and anxiety. And once again Flora
rose to the occasion:

I would *much* rather know even if you do get horribly
depressed ... mind you don't hide things ... You see, having
experienced that kind of depression I can sympathize ...
depression is like physical pain — you can have vast crowds of
people round you knowing you have got it, but that does not
drive it away. It is a most odious form of illness and I think it
must be treated like that. I don't know if you find sudden
acute fits come on — that's what I had ... Isn't homesickness
awful darling? ... I'm sure depression is the very last thing I
should ever blame anybody for ... (23 July and 30 July 1903.)

At such times Flora would set herself to force Ernest to
smile:

Fritz [Ernest's brother] sketched me. I said I don't mind
whether it's like, only make me a type of English beauty. He
seemed quite agreeable and said: 'What type?' So I said that
didn't matter so long as it was a type. The sketch came out
exactly like a rather unattractive pig, so I conclude he selected
the pig type for me ... He is going to have another shot ...
    Dearest, you *won't* become Anglo-Indian about the
Natives, *will you, please* don't. Wait till I come, and we can
become Anglo-Indians together.

Flora wrote long letters once a week, Ernest wrote short letters every day. They discussed their friends — 'Didn't I always tell you Mary Sheepshanks was a fine character' (Ernest to Flora, 26 May). 'Henry dislikes particularly your friend Theodore Llewelyn Davies, though I like him as you know' (Flora to Ernest, 18 September). They argued with each other about art, music and literature. Ernest was shocked at Flora's lack of awe before Greek sculpture and Beethoven, Flora was shocked at Ernest remaining unmoved by Lamb's *Letters*, or *The Mill on the Floss*. But each was happily confident of converting the other to a more proper view of things in a very short time: 'As soon as I get a piano I'll *make* you admire Beethoven — head and shoulders above every musician that ever lived — save Bach I suppose' (Ernest to Flora, 30 September). Flora did share Ernest's reverence for John Stuart Mill and she also revealed to him her secret ambition to draw a convincing portrait of a man in fiction, able, as she said, to stand beside Charlotte Brontë's M. Paul Emmanuel, or Mrs Gaskell's Dr Gibson or George Eliot's Tom Tulliver — 'I *should* like to do a decent man, but I know they will all be prigs bless them.' References to *Mrs Hammond's Children* form a *leitmotif* throughout Ernest's whole correspondence. When he was on board ship he lent the book to any likely fellow-passenger and listened eagerly for their praise. Once ashore he told Flora that it was not photographs of her but 'Your letters and *Mrs Hammond's Children* that bring you before me', and when in hospital in Simla, 'I have just been cheering myself up by reading Mrs Hammond's Children' (23 September). Another bond was their humanist perspective on Christianity. It is significant that the one book Flora sent out to Ernest in India was the eighteenth-century rationalist philosopher d'Holbach's *Ecce Homo* and Ernest endorsed every word. Ernest had assumed, understandably, that Flora, as her parents' daughter, would have been a devout Christian — but she energetically denied being anything so straightforward:

Me religious, or as having the gift of faith, no indeed, no I have no possible right to claim that; but I can understand what people mean by it now, which I used not to do at all, and I can earnestly wish to have it, which I used not to either. (24 September 1903.)

But for the most part Ernest and Flora wrote about what they meant to each other — particularly what Flora meant to Ernest. Flora, predictably, asked Ernest whether he found her beautiful, and he, candid as ever, said 'No'.

God forgive me if I was brutal; but you know dearest you would have it out of me: am I making it worse again? Anyhow you have *charm* — and that is what all these excellent dames are utterly without. And my own darling you have everything else in the world that I *most love and honour*: all I feel is that you are a thousand times too good for me and for India. (13 June.)

In reply, Flora said she did know that she could build her whole life on Ernest:

I can't imagine anything happening that would shake my trust in you. I remember so well when we said goodbye in the drawing-room at Warwick Square: you said: 'I shall never forget you, never think less of you.' I don't believe you would, however much I might deserve it. I hope you trust me. (30 July.)

Ernest Shepherd, Flora knew, was a very rare man — capable not only of feeling but also of expressing his feelings. There is an interesting letter from Flora to Ernest in which she criticises the emotional inhibitedness and mask of flippancy then generally fashionable among the English intelligentsia:

The Sanger[3] dinner parties are always amusing but I think the people are getting sillier. They *are* so affected about never saying what they mean, and pretending everything is a joke … George Trevelyan[4] was specially bad in that way and poured forth sparkles unceasingly. They are all ashamed of showing they have any feeling. Frank Earp would say it was a

Cambridge fault and so it is. I do feel thankful darling you are not like George Trevelyan ... Robin [Flora's brother] is a dear but I wish he had a little more feeling. It is there I am sure and would come out in times of trouble, but I wish he had a little more for everyday. I think feeling may get rusty for want of use. (3 July 1903.)

Given the six-week interval before Ernest's and Flora's letters could reach one another there were some inevitable misunderstandings. The most important topic on which they found themselves at cross-purposes was the date and place of their marriage. Ernest suggested January in Bombay, whilst Flora had the brainwave that they should wait until March to marry in Egypt. Her idea was that this would enable her parents to accompany her so far but no farther. Since both the Mayor parents were now in their mid-seventies, Flora could not contemplate the risk entailed in dragging them both out all the way to Bombay. However, although he loyally tried to do as she asked, Ernest soon discovered that it was out of the question for him to obtain leave in order to go to Egypt in March. But it took weeks to convince Flora. Moreover, the inevitable time-lag caused their moods to be at cross-purposes; by the time Ernest received Flora's loving sympathy for his depression, he was no longer feeling depressed, merely ashamed of himself for having inflicted his depression on her. But then, just as Flora's letters got more and more sanguine — optimistic to the point of thoughtlessness — about their future together (and together with Alice) Ernest again fell ill with a mysterious fever and was once more the prey of bitter black depression. On 22 October 1903, two days after Flora's thirty-first birthday, he died. Flora wrote the following account of how she learned that she had lost him:

Thursday October 22nd, 1903
    I was in bed feeling seedy. Mary Walton ... had been with us and had just gone after a tender talk of our coming parting.

Then about 4 o'clock Mother came in and said she wanted to say something to me ... Mother said: Did I feel well? She said it very tenderly and I saw she was crying. I thought she was overcome thinking of India. I said, 'Yes darling, quite well.' Then I seemed to know there was something. I said: 'Is there any bad news? Is it about Ernest?' Mother showed me Mr Marshall's telegram: 'Regret to say Mr Shepherd's condition very critical. Please inform Miss Mayor.' ... I wrote a letter —

'My dear, dearest, I have just got Mr Marshall's telegram telling me about you. I feel in a maze and can't think of anything. Darling if God spares you to me I shall come out at once, for you must not be alone. My own darling I must tell you how I love you, and I can't find any words. Then I think of your love for me and of our goodbye in Warwick Square and my last sight of you at Dover. In your last letter you said I was not to "absent me from felicity". I did not feel anxious only sorry for the dull time for you. And now all this three weeks I don't know what has been happening. Have you been all the while keeping back from me how ill you were? If I knew what it was, I might bear it better. Oh this horrible India.

It's no good darling, I *can't* write a long letter till I know more. Only you don't know how I wish I was out with you and doing something for you, and here I can do nothing and know absolutely nothing ...

Goodbye dear darling, God be with you and take care of you,

      Your own Flora.

I kept turning over those words 'very critical' wondering what ray of hope could be got from them and how I did pray all that long long day ...

In the morning, Friday, the 23rd there was no more news and I began to hope a little. I thought I would go out to India that evening if I could ... I went up at once to Warwick Square. As I got near I thought they might have a message and the blinds might be down. I was relieved beyond measure that they were up. Gertrude opened the door. I said was there any news? She said 'No', and I felt *so relieved.* I began crying rather hysterically and I think we got more cheerful together. Then there was a ring. Gertrude went to the door. I heard a boy saying 'Telegram for Miss Sinclair'. Gertrude took it. Of course we both guessed. The one hope had been there would be no wire. She opened it, looked at it, and nodded to me. She couldn't speak. We went into the library. I sat down on the sofa and she knelt by me just saying over and over again sobbing, 'My darling, my darling' ... I was quite blank and dazed ... Marshall's telegram said: 'Deeply regret Mr Shepherd died yesterday, funeral today.' I read it over and over but it really didn't convey anything ... I don't know how long we stayed in the Library. Daisy came in and Gertrude told her and then Auntie. She went upstairs alone first of all, then she came down crying rather hysterically. She said 'Poor child, this is cruel, it's cruel.' Then Mother and Alice came. Gertrude went out and told them. I heard Mother's exclamation of horror. Then I went out. Alice said 'You *must* let us comfort you.' I don't know what I felt — miles away from everything I think. We went back — oh it was such a radiant Autumn day. Alice and I came upstairs and Mother told Father. He knocked at our door and Alice said to me 'Here's Father!' He came up and kissed me very tenderly. I don't know how the afternoon passed. Robin was coming in the evening and I wanted to tell him myself ... When he came he said 'What is it Flora?' I said: 'I've got something to tell you. Ernest is dead'. He turned away and I said 'You *must* comfort me.' He came back and seized me in his arms and carried me somehow to the sofa. Then he kept saying 'Oh Flora, oh my dear Flora'. I was so much touched, so *very much* for ... he is cold and reserved and I thought the coldness was growing ...[5]

It emerged that Ernest had been suffering not only from malaria but also from an undiagnosed acute enteric disorder. The shock to Flora was so sudden and so appalling that at first she simply could not grasp it. But soon the rest of the world confirmed that Ernest had indeed died, by sending her their letters of condolence to Queensgate House. Each writer struggled to express his or her sense that Ernest Shepherd was a truly irreplaceable man:

So trusty a friend, so pleasant a companion, so modest and unselfish. What he was to you, you alone know.[6]

What I like to think of most is that he lived a noble life; I think his long continued industry, and his unstinting work for Morley, when he was pining for work for himself and not getting it, were grand.[7]

He had that real distinction of personality which is so rare.[8]

You speak of the tender way he wrote of me in one of his letters, that was one of his distinguishing characteristics, his tenderness and care of those weaker than himself ... Why are the best people so often taken away? How many have asked that question![9]

At any rate we both know that he was the best, most unselfish and most upright of anyone we have known.[10]

He was so truly good Dear Flora all is well with him.[11]

I can't realize that it is not yet a month — it seems such a long time. Did Flora tell you that she showed me two letters? I *am* so grateful to her, and I can't tell you how much I appreciated reading them. They were a revelation to me, not only in that I had never before seen letters from a man engaged to be married, but also that such things could be expressed so freely and so beautifully ...[12]

But among the letters that arrived week by week at Queensgate House were also the three last letters from Ernest himself. Flora read and re-read this at the time of his death:

September 30th
Now dearest you'll begin I am sure to think me unsympathetic: you are living at home you see with all those who are the most attached to you, and as a result you are inclined to be in a constant bath of feeling and sentiment; and then you go and see your women friends and find the same

thing ... I on the other hand am out here alone seeing nothing but men and very few of them and of course never anybody for whom I entertain a real affection: so *my* emotional side is gradually being dessicated at the same time that yours is being beautifully watered; and indeed I'm awfully afraid lest you'll find me rather dry and dull when you come out: but I think you'll cure that all right. In the meantime dearest what all this is leading up to is that I think you have been misled by your emotional state concerning this scheme of coming out in March. The argument I take it is this: 'I don't think father and mother ought to take a long voyage so I shall fix my passage at such a hot and unhealthy time that they won't be able to come.' Well now seriously this is a piece of extravagance; you must try and settle the matter in a commonsense way and not by wild impulses of this sort. What would be the result of coming in March? The heat in the Red Sea would be extreme and you would arrive in Bombay a rag ... we should go straight up to Naini Tal where I should leave you ... and not see you again for the next month and a half. Well I don't think that's a very satisfactory plan ...

No my dearest you must please look at the matter in a commonsense way and do your best to induce your mother to do the same: and you must realise clearly these things. (1) that the Egyptian scheme is definitely knocked on the head, and (2) that January is the *very latest* time that you can come this cold season and that it lies absolutely between that and the following October ...

Now darling I fear you'll think this very hard and dry: but I explained at the beginning that I am inclined to be rather hard and dry ... Whatever you decide darling I shall be satisfied with — except passages made in March or similar extravagances ...

As to writing to Alice dearest I'll try when I get better: at present I find it quite as much as I can manage to write to you and Auntie and Gertrude: and you must remember darling it is you I hope to marry, not Alice; — and though I can't help being fond of her since I am fond of you it must be and ought to be through you as it were that I know her and she knows me: I think here too you're carried into sentiment a little

extravagant — or is it that dessicating process which I confess
has been going on within me? ...

I have said several things in this letter that I'm dreadfully
afraid you may think hard and cruel: I do hope you won't;
only darling you must be sensible: remember that a tropical
climate isn't a thing to play with; if you come in January I
shall be *very, very* glad: if you don't come till October I shan't
complain; remember there is *no intermediate time.*

Next day, 1 October, Ernest added:

Dearest, After sleeping over my letter I feel I can't let it go
without a postscript. I'm afraid from such expressions as 'a
bath of emotion and sentiment' you'll think that I'm scoffing
at the love and affection of home and friends: yes darling it
does seem like that. Only I wasn't really. I was only pointing
out the great differences in the influences that have been
acting on you and me in the last five months. No, the
immense amount of true love and affection that has been
given to you and Alice and which you give back again is I
know the most precious thing, and it is because you are so
sweet that you have it: but I think it makes things all the
harder for you just now darling.

My letter is meant to help you darling; and it is also meant
— this I stick to — to warn you against following the dictates of
feeling *too blindly*, and not giving enough weight to common
prudence. Dearest I hope my letter won't hurt you.

That was hard enough to cope with, especially 'it is you I
hope to marry, not Alice', when there was no longer any
chance of explaining and trying to come to a better understanding with one another. But Ernest's next letter, which
Flora received the Monday after learning of his death, was
worse:

October 4th
My dearest,

I keep wondering whether you'll have thought my last
letter harsh and severe. I do hope not; it wasn't meant to be
anyhow; please forgive me if you found it so ... I meant to say
dearest, but forgot it, that I quite see what a generous impulse

it was that made you think of coming in March; it was just like you to want to sacrifice yourself; but then I don't quite see the fun of your being sacrificed. I wish I knew how you felt my darling about coming by yourself or with comparative strangers; would you hate it *very* much, you have never said anything about it. I shall be so glad darling when the matter comes to some final settlement ...

October 7th, Walker Hospital, Simla
Don't be alarmed at this address; I'm not worse, in fact I think I'm decidedly better; but when I went to see the Doctor on Monday he said I wasn't getting on a bit and looked the picture of misery — which I thought a gross libel — and therefore I'd better go into hospital and take vigorous measures to get well, which seemed sensible ... Dearest I have your letter of this week and enjoyed it very much; only one thing darling rather horrified me; you said that low rooms were *snugger* than high ones — think, think of anybody wanting to be *snug* in India — *snug*, the word is so exquisitely inappropriate I cannot help saying it over to myself. And then darling I can't think why you are so keen about coming in March: I am sure it's a very bad plan: don't you see that it would mean our being separated at once; you don't seem to mind that darling a bit — to me it seems simply horrid. Who is this Tabor who advises it: I am afraid it is wrong dearest but I feel jealous of all these strangers and their advice ...

Why, why did you fix all your hopes on that Egyptian scheme which was hopeless from the first as everyone said? Well I must stop now darling. I feel as if this letter had turned sour somehow: put it down to my state of health ...

'You don't seem to mind that darling a bit' — when Flora first read that reproachful sentence several days after learning of Ernest's death, she wrote, 'It was the most wretched moment of my life.'[13] If only Ernest had still been alive — 'I might have been extravagant and wired again — we could have settled it all, — but that that should have come when there was no possibility of telling [you] ...'[14] In that one moment Flora felt all the virtue to have gone out of her — convicted at last of the worst sin in her own canon — unlovingness. 'I felt I couldn't forgive myself. I thought I must have been so horrible.'[15] In her extremity Flora turned not to Alice nor to her brothers nor to her parents, but to Auntie. She cabled her, asking her to come down to Queensgate House. No one but Auntie, who as Flora knew, had loved Ernest totally all his life, could talk to Flora now and convince her that it had not been any real doubt of her on Ernest's part — only the fever speaking. Somehow Auntie got Flora through the rest of that day and the following night. There followed six more grim days and nights — 'Oh I was miserable — I thought you felt against me and that you thought I didn't love you and felt doubtful of me and sore.'[16]

'You have to be beaten and broken by things,' Virginia Woolf once told the young Stephen Spender, 'before you can write about them.'[17] Those seven days and nights were when Flora Mayor was 'beaten and broken.' On the eighth day, which was the following Monday, Ernest's last letter arrived, written on his deathbed:

My darling,
    Here she's only going to get a little scrap of a letter again: it is a shame and I am sorry. Only this fever has turned out a wee bit more serious than I thought . . .
    Your letter not come — what a nuisance: but it won't be lost never fear, they always come to hand. You'll think me very careless darling but I've been so helpless all alone with this fever.
    Marshall's a bore; such a 'manager' like Mrs Elton, riles me so; at the end of this week all friends except Marshall will have gone — alas. I feel like nothing else than a great helpless baby.
    Don't be anxious dearest; not particularly bad and getting better; writing due to bed, otherwise all right.
    Love darling again and again — Ever your own Ernest.

'Your dear last letter', Flora called it.
    The lady superintendent of Walker Hospital, Simla also

wrote to Flora by the same mail, enclosing a lock of Ernest's hair:

He was conscious up to the last, but very, very weak of course. Just at the end I asked him if he had any message for you, and he said 'Tell her I have never forgotten her', and his last words were 'Best Beloved'. I send you some of his hair which we cut off for you. He looked so peaceful and he was taken to his last resting-place surrounded by friends and exquisite flowers. Forgive a complete stranger saying so, but oh! his love for you was so true and ever-present with him, and I want you to feel this and to know his last thoughts were yours.[18]

At first Flora wanted to die too. Although no one could comfort her, their yearning to comfort her and their need for her to go on living did gradually enable her to live.

... remember your tender kind folks about you, who have loved you all your days and put that decent outward face upon it which will be a little consoling to them and in the end help you.[19]

Flora's seventy-five-year-old father forced himself to sit down and write to her hesitant, heartfelt words of meditation on earthly love which, as he believed, gives us promise of a Resurrection in the next life and inspiration to re-consecrate ourselves in this. He ended:

I hope, my dearest Flora, that it may be given to you, as it was to your Aunt Georgie,[20] to live such a simple, natural, and yet heavenly life, overflowing with sympathy for all who need sympathy, and yet losing nothing of your innate courage and enterprize, so that you may be enabled to comfort and strengthen others with the comfort taught you by God, and may feel, as the years go on, that your life has been no wasted one, but full of highest blessing to yourself and to others.
So prays your sorrowing and affectionate father.

An agnostic Newnham friend wrote rather differently:

Dearest Flora,
I heard from Alice Gardner[21] today. I can't invent one

single word or thought of consolation, and I can't pretend.
Try not to mourn too terribly . . .

Many of us stumble along without meeting the one co-
soul; to have known that there was such an one, and what life
could hold, can't have been a thing to crush and blight you
utterly and for ever: I mean somehow or other you must live
upon the riches you have got within you.

But damn my moralizing, it's easy for me you'll think.
Yours affectionately, Mary Bateson.[22]

Friend after friend reached out to Flora, offering her not
just their words but their homes to stay in for a while, and
fifty-year-old Mary Walton offered still more in what was
perhaps the most heartfelt letter of all:

My poor darling Flora,

What can I say to comfort you in this terrible blow that has
befallen you. I learnt it in a note from your Uncle, and am
utterly grieved for you, my poor child. Dearest, you know how
I love you; I feel as if, had it been possible, I would willingly
have given my own life instead of the one that has gone, to
spare you this sorrow. At first I know that nothing can
comfort in such a sorrow, but I think of you night and day my
darling Flora . . .

Mary.

What Alice's fierce pity and minute-by-minute care for her
meant to Flora's survival can only be imagined. In later life
Flora would confide to their closest friends that it had been
Alice who had made it possible for her to take up her life
again, and even enjoy it.

In all these ways, having cast her emotional bread upon
the waters in her thirty-one years of life, Flora now found it
being given back to her a thousandfold. The undermost
support of all came from the memory of Ernest himself,
whose unique worth Flora only began to realise after she
had lost him. Gropingly, Flora tried to express for herself
the new meaning of the previous nine months in her *Grief
Journal.* That unpublished journal, which Flora wrote
under the name 'Flora Shepherd' — ('I put your dear name

which now I can never use here . . . If you knew how I long to
have it') — is a heart-rending document. It consists of
eighty-six hand-written pages, the first seventy-six of which
were written between November 1903 and October 1904,
the last ten pages containing entries dated 1905, 1907, 1908,
1912 and 1913. The journal is actually written to Ernest.
Only by doing that apparently mad thing of writing, month
by month, to the dead, did Flora Mayor save herself from
actual madness. 'The thought of you near me pulls me
along.' The journal contains some of the most powerful
prose that she wrote. There is no evidence that Flora ever
showed her *Grief Journal* to Alice; it was the one thing she
shared with Ernest alone.

I have realized our love so much more. Darling, I did love you
before, but in a calm, easy-going sort of way, and now I feel
what poets say about love. Tennyson says in *In Memoriam* that
death brings out all the love that would have ripened with the
progress of years, and that's how it happened with me . . .

Darling I think I have not got a very deep or intense or loving
nature, I don't think my love is much worth getting, but such
as it is you've got it. Take it, and somehow make it worth
having . . .

I have been re-reading my letters [to you]. Self-satisfied, I
think, not worthy to tie your letters' shoes; never mind dearest
you would have loathed them grovelling . . .

You loved *me*, you *love* me. 'Your joy no man taketh from you
— and no man can take it can they? . . .

People have worse troubles than ours darling, lovers who
cease to love you, lovers who aren't worth loving . . . But
loving goes not by deserts.

I remember your kisses and your solemn tender way of saying
you would always love me. I can hear that serious voice of
yours and a kind of emphatic shake of your head which made

me trust you ... Those words 'Best Beloved' will always be a comfort to me. Love *is* better than anything else. Goodness and love are the eternal things.

Lover, husband, friend. I shall think of you as all three.

Do you realize each day we get a step nearer? That comforts me so much; — another day off.

Goodnight my darling.

6

PICKING UP THE PIECES —
FLORA AND MARY, 1904–1907

One cannot recover from an irreparable loss, but one can survive it. Flora Mayor made a weary, disciplined effort to survive. Her chronic bronchial asthma, aggravated by the emotional shock of Ernest's death, literally affected her heart. Alice took Flora off to Bordighera on the Riviera for the January, February and March of 1904 and there Flora was treated for what was very nearly a complete physical and nervous breakdown. Medical research had not yet discovered the non-toxic drugs which now make asthma more tolerable by controlling the earliest stages of an attack and so nothing

'is so painful to witness [wrote a contemporary specialist] ... as that hard struggle for breath in the more severe attacks. Unable or unwilling to speak, a prey to the terror of a threatening asphyxia, the patients answer only in mono-syllables the questions that may be put to them. ... They assume all kinds of postures ... and tug and strain — but all in vain. The incessant cough which torments them makes no impression upon the impediment ...

The patients groan or even scream under the pain from the prolonged forcible contractions of their fatigued muscles, and point to the insertions of the diaphragm as the seat of their greatest distress.[1]

In their anxiety to relieve such torment, doctors had

recourse to medication which was at best counter-productive and at worst addictive and acutely toxic. Berkart himself recommended paraldehyde to induce sleep, potassium iodide or ammonium chloride or a weak infusion of ipecacuanha to induce vomiting, and injections of diphtheria anti-toxin, arsenic and morphia;[2] other specialists recommended strychnine. Adrenalin, opium and heroin were also commonly prescribed. Flora commented, 'One feels much worse while undergoing a cure.' At Bordighera she was injected daily with phosphates — 'I always dislike the shock of being dug into by a needle and Alice has continual alarms about the needle which gets out of order without provocation.' (Flora to her mother, January 1904.) Ever since her Newnham days Flora had been far from robust, but now, in addition to her asthma, she also suffered from sick headaches, fainting fits, a 'jumpy' heart and period pains so abnormally acute and incapacitating that she had to lie in bed for days at a time unable even to write a note to Alice. The medical remedy was rest, rest and more rest. For whole months at a time during the years after Ernest's death when she was not actually undergoing a 'cure' at some spa or seaside nursing home, Flora still had to lead the life of a complete invalid. Her regimen: stay in bed till 12; half-hour walk; rest till 3; half-hour walk if not raining; rest 4-6; bed at 9; one visitor allowed for half-an-hour morning and afternoon. It was like watching Aunt Minnie's holly in the rain once more — death-in-life.

Every chronic illness is frustrating and dispiriting, but asthma has an additional complication all its own. Because an attack may be triggered off by some intense nervous excitement, asthma has long been thought to have a nervous rather than a physiological *cause* — in other words, the asthmatic is not simply born with narrow bronchi, he or she is psychologically responsible for the asthma and is induced to feel guilty for having a 'nervy', hysterical, valetudinarian personality.[3] Flora knew that Ernest's Auntie and sisters and even her own Alice and Henry sometimes suspected her of choosing her invalidism and of surrendering to nervous debility — 'I feel rather low, people thinking I've been ill so long, — you do, you know, and Henry does.' (Flora to Alice, 1905-6)

One way of enduring extreme emotional and physical suffering is to accept it, Job-like, as a God-sent testing-time for the soul. Flora did not find it easy to accept either Ernest's death or her own very poor health as God-sent. In the end, however, she did so accept them. The crucial question for Flora was whether or not she could believe in Ernest's immortality and their eventual reunion. From the first she was divided between the consciousness of her need to believe and her recognition that that need was not a valid reason for belief: 'Am I believing this because I want it? The worst reason for belief, Huxley says, do you remember, the reason I know why *you* would never believe.' (*Grief Journal*, 1904.) Yet if the need to believe is not a self-validating reason, what other evidence for immortality is there, since all empirical knowledge stops short at the grave-mouth? As Dr Johnson, one of Flora's most cherished mentors, wrote:

Reason deserts us at the brink of the grave, and can give no further intelligence ... Let hope therefore dictate, what revelation does not confute, that the union of souls may still remain ... (*Idler*, no. 41.)

Flora struggled to go on hoping, in the very teeth of doubt:

I can't know and I never never shall ... I read books, and ask people whose judgement I believe in but after all they are only men; they don't know any more than me... I have been reading St John again to see ... I cannot make out what I do believe. I want it so much — for that very reason I question it ... I don't think I love Him in the least ... I feel very unhappy and faithless tonight and you seem so far from me... I think and think and I never come any nearer and I don't see how anybody can ... Oh *why, why*? And yet I hate to question. It would be so unspeakably terrible if you had been snatched by a blind fate... I remember saying I thought men were irreligious because they felt no need for God. You said that was a poor reason for being religious, so it is, but it's my reason. (*Grief Journal*, 1904.)

The very act of writing the *Grief Journal* to Ernest was an act of faith that communication between the living and the dead was still possible — at least for as long as the living cannot live without it. Sometimes Flora would doubt even that: 'I cheat myself by writing to you. I think one has no faith.' At other times there would be some desperate shadow of hope that she could still reach him, and he her:

I have this fond but baseless hope — a kind of Watts's despairing hope that you know, — that in some inexplicable, mysterious, miraculous way you know. I have just enough glimmering of hope to make me go on writing the more. Darling if you had lost me you would have none at all. You had the honest intellect which discards everything there isn't proof for, while I manage, or try to manage, to take myself in. (*Grief Journal*, 1904.)

Time and again Flora would be assaulted by a sense of utter desolation:

Oh the meaning of the whole thing, what is it? ... You are in Eternity now and you can say nothing ... And I can only have finite thoughts about you. (*Grief Journal*, 1904.)

But gradually the other note, that of hoping against hope, of believing without any possibility of proof or even of evidence that 'all shall be well and all shall be well and all manner of things shall be well',[4] did become stronger. On 23 March 1904, the first anniversary of their engagement day, Flora was able to write: 'Into God's gracious keeping I commit you.' Two years later she affirmed, still very uncertainly, 'I think the existence of God does mean a lot more to me than it did.' Then, in 1907, she had something akin to a mystical experience:

Last Sunday somehow I realized how all the generations were
united in God and that we were in communion with them ...
It is so confusing and overwhelming, we must trust in God.
Sometimes I do seem to see the meaning of it all in a flash,
then it passes. (*Grief Journal.*)

The final entry in Flora's *Grief Journal* is dated 20 March
1913:

It is just ten years ago since our engagement. I am forty. You
seem so young, thirty-one. I always love best your letter to
Alice and the one about Alice to me. Help me if you can to
cure my faults and make me more tender, you are so much
much more unselfish. Each year brings us nearer.

It was Flora's overpowering need to believe that one man
was immortal and that she should be reunited with him,
which converted her from semi-sceptical liberal humanism
to a belief in the supernatural and the superhuman:[5]

You must be the first object I open my eyes to — you mean
so much more to me [than Christ]; is that blasphemous? No.
Christ will understand. (*Grief Journal.*)

Human love was all the evidence that Flora had for the
existence of Divine love, and Divine love, in sheer pity, must
grant humans immortality: 'We can't be given love just for
a few years and then for it all to be as nothing. It would be
too senseless.' (*Grief Journal.*) The passage in Bach's B
Minor Mass — *Et Expecto Resurrectionem Mortuorum et Vitam
Venturi Saeculi* (And I look for the resurrection of the dead
and the life of the world to come) — became Flora's
favourite music; its first three words to go on her grave.

In April 1904 Flora's brother Henry, then classics master at
Clifton College, Bristol, suggested that he and she should
set up house together in Clifton, giving her a new,
independent and yet sheltered existence. Alice could box
and cox with her whenever they wished and the sisters
could have regular reunions each month either in Clifton or

at Queensgate House. When she and Alice were apart they could (and did) write to each other every day. At first all went well. Flora entered into setting up house at 43 Canynge Square with some spirit: 'I like being monarch of all I survey ... Today I bought two kitchen chairs second-hand, beautifully cheap ... and fire-irons and a coal-scuttle. How I adore shopping.' (Letter to Alice, 1904.) At the age of thirty-one she gave her first dinner party — 'I was so funky before the dinner, quite dentisty, but I managed with consummate skill ... I didn't find the rising and taking the ladies away difficult.' (Letters to Alice, 1904.)

But work was the only effective therapy, and work was hard to find. Flora's recurrent invalidism made it out of the question for her to take up a regular teaching post. She did do some private coaching and occasional reviewing, she was made secretary of the local Newnham Association where she read papers, she was on the committee of the Charity Organization, she studied Italian and musical Harmony — and she also tried to write — 'although the excitement of writing is so tiring.' First Flora tried writing about her life on the stage. In April 1905, she published a long article called *Life in a Touring Company* 'By One Who Has Tried', in the *Queen, The Lady's Newspaper*. And in 1905-6 she wrote three rather less nostalgic one-act plays about the actress's life off-stage, only one of which was ever publicly performed.[6] By far the most interesting of these one-acters is *Going Downhill*, in which Flora reveals the darker side of her own character, and sketches an all-too possible scenario for herself if she had not had either Ernest Shepherd or her asthma, but had continued with her unsuccessful struggle to become an actress — and 'gone downhill'. Nell Marsden is thirty-five (Flora's own age when she wrote the play) and is first seen in her dingy 'digs' looking into the fire and smoking:

She is handsome and fascinating, with a power of drawing out people by means of a delightfully sympathetic manner, which she has practised so long that it has become quite easy and natural ... Unlike most people, she has too much humour. She does not take either life or herself seriously enough, which may be one reason why she has always failed. (Flora's stage directions.)

At the end of the play, having rejected her chance of marriage, Nell is left as she was found at the start, sitting alone, smoking and looking into the fire with allusions to whisky and 'settling down at the bottom of the Thames' the only hints as to her probable end. Nell's part includes some strangely resonant lines:

'I was a nice child. Why doesn't one stay nice?'

'I really am attractive, above the average ... and I'm the one out in the cold.'

'I had rather a nice brother once, but he couldn't do with me'.

'I'm not the right sort for helping, I always relapse.'

Nell Marsden's compulsion to fascinate everyone by *acting* the interested, sympathetic listener and her secret envy of the happiness of ordinary, less interesting people, these were, Flora Mayor knew, her own particular kinds of nastiness — all that she meant when she called herself 'horrid':

I prayed so much we might be less critical and more generous about other people's happiness. It is *far* our worse fault. (Flora to Alice, soon after Ernest's death, November 1903.)

I think being ashamed of yourself is worse than anything. ... I want not to be worldly and self-seeking and self-centred and thinking a great deal of myself. ... Sometimes I seem to fall back horribly and care about [popularity] again. ... I'm so horrid, but loving goes not by deserts. ... Help me to be more tender. (*Grief Journal* entries, 1904, 1905, 1906, 1907 and 1913.)

In addition to writing these three not very successful plays Flora spent the years 1905-8 trying to write a detailed evocation of childhood, to be called *Reminiscences*, which she finally decided was a failure. The manuscript has not survived. Other depressing factors, beside this impasse with her writing and the constant wearisome frustration of her bad health, were the strain caused by her brother Henry's extreme reserve — 'Rather silent meals lately. What *did* we do without Rab [the dog]?' — and the sheer grey boredom of her ladylike Clifton routine:

What on earth am I to do all day? ... I feel that the salt has gone out of things, the whole prospect seems perfectly grey, nor do the things which have given me most pleasure please me at all — particularly human intercourse which always used to be the thing I liked best. I was saying to Alice how strange it is in a way how calmly one acquiesces to change. Up to the afternoon of Thursday Oct 22 when Mr Marshall's telegram came, I instinctively put happiness as what I was aiming for and expecting as my right in life. Since then I have also quite instinctively given up expecting it and also aiming for it; it seems absurd to aim for it when I see no prospect of getting it. That means ... really my whole outlook on life is changed, and yet here one goes on outwardly absolutely the same, one eats, sleeps, drives, walks, shops, reads, talks, writes letters, is philanthropic. I do all the ordinary things, I laugh and make jokes and enjoy other people's jokes ... and yet inside one is so altered. (*Grief Journal*, 1904.)

Flora had no children and now never would have. She had written to Ernest in the *Grief Journal*, November 1903: 'It is *so* bitter to me I have not your name, but far, far bitterer that we have no baby.' Her life was indeed 'perfectly grey': her writing was going badly, some of the people at Clifton were not just dull, they were 'aggressively conventional', she took country walks around Clifton without enthusiasm — 'How it would bore me to live in the country' — and she even got irritable with Alice:

Perhaps I was suffering from the boredom of life. I do
sometimes. Life is so very different from what I expected. I
with over average powers lead a more *petite vie* and run a
house rather less well than the ordinary fool and so *volent* by
my best years. (Letter to Alice, c. 1908.)

There was a terrible temptation for Flora to pass secret,
bitterly negative judgements on everyone around her —
especially on those of her contemporaries who were having
children or enjoying greater worldly success than she.[7] The
very loss of her chance of marriage entailed yet another
'failure' in the eyes of the world for which Flora had to
compensate. Whatever the reason, there was a real danger
that she would pass straight from protracted and over-
protected youth at thirty, to premature crabbed middle-
age at thirty-one.

Flora was not alone in learning the corrosive effects of
unhappiness at this time. The psychological destructiveness of loss of hope was also being felt, and all too keenly, by
Mary. Hitherto, Mary has had to be seen from the outside,
partly because she was such a 'doer', and partly because
her own record of her life, written in extreme old age,
stresses public social issues, ideas, events and places
instead of her own feelings. But the life of Mary's heart went
on every day nevertheless, and underneath that tall
stalwart, forbidding exterior it is still possible to detect the
isolated, unhappy child in the Anfield Vicarage, the fierce-
spirited schoolgirl in Liverpool and the pioneer woman
student, social worker and educationist who had a great
capacity for admiring others but a very insecure opinion of
herself.

Recently four letters have come to light, written in 1905
by Mary to her friend Bertrand Russell which reveal much
more of her usually concealed emotional life. These letters
focus on Mary's unhappy love for Theodore Llewelyn
Davies.[8] Theodore and Crompton Llewelyn Davies lived

together in a house in Barton Street, Westminster, exactly opposite that of Mary Sheepshanks. There was much coming and going between the two houses and Mary lent the men her own home when they wished to hold meetings on Land Tax Reform.[9] She and Theodore had many friends in common — including the Sangers, the Trevelyans, the Russells, Ernest Shepherd and the Mayors, Ralph and Adeline Vaughan Williams and Goldie and May Lowes Dickinson. Alice Mayor had been prone to describe Theodore Davies in her letters and journals over the years as 'moody', but there is a more friendly glimpse of Theodore at one of Mary's parties in a letter from Alice to Flora:

Mary had arranged everything so well for her party — candle-light, mysterious and becoming and people sitting in the garden. I hardly spoke to Theodore Davies. May Dickinson was amused to hear Mary arranging with Theodore to come to breakfast.

That was in June 1905. At the end of July Theodore's body was found drowned in a pool near Kirkby Lonsdale. 'It was supposed that he must have hit his head on a rock in diving.'[10] In the sentence preceding his description of Theodore's death, Bertrand Russell had written:

I never knew but one woman who would not have been delighted to marry Theodore. She, of course, was the only woman he wished to marry.[11]

But that woman, Meg Booth, the very beautiful daughter of the social investigator Charles Booth, loved his brother, Crompton.[12] And Crompton, as Theodore almost certainly knew, loved her. Theodore and Crompton 'had been always together, they shared everything, and Theodore was as careful of Crompton and as tender with him as any mother could have been.'[13] Some months after Theodore's death, Crompton proposed to Meg Booth but she refused him.

Where Mary came in to all this pitiful emotional tangle, was, alas for her, nowhere: she had merely loved Theodore Davies without any glimmer of an illusion that he loved her in return. Flora had had to go through the pain of losing someone who had loved her and then feeling that she had not loved him enough while he was still alive — 'I think I have not got a very deep or intense or loving nature ... I'm so horrid — I wonder how you could have cared for me.' (*Grief Journal.*) But Mary Sheepshanks had to experience the opposite pain of knowing that she had never been loved by the man whom she loved. And since he did not love her, she could not love herself. When Flora was bereaved, she was supported by her sense of closeness to Ernest, by her struggled-for faith in their eventual reunion and by the sympathy of her whole world. When Mary lost Theodore Davies she had no consoling sense that he had ever felt particularly close to her, no faith that their souls would survive to meet again, and no one on earth to confide in, or from whom she could seek sympathy — except for Bertrand Russell, who was much more Crompton and Theodore's friend than he was hers. Mary had first met Russell when they were fellow-students at Cambridge and their shared attachment to the Llewelyn Davies brothers had brought them together frequently in the years that followed. Mary wrote to Bertrand Russell:

The days are naturally long, and the present is dreary when there is nothing happy to look back on, or forward to. ... I feel sorry that I did not ask you to tell me more about Theodore. I have been wanting to, but hardly dare, and there is so much of him that you knew and that I should like to hear; but in some ways it may be better to wait, and a better opportunity may come later. I can't hear about him from anyone else. (August and September 1905.)

On 6 November 1905, Mary wrote Russell a long pain-filled confession that she felt she was an emotional failure in life:

Dear Bertie,

May I add several things to what we talked about? You are the only person to whom I have told everything and as you are so kind as to let me talk about myself I am taking full advantage. I know it is not very heroic, but if I keep everything to myself it gets so much worse, and I get so much worse, that you must try to forgive my inflicting it on you ... I am very miserable, and as you are really the only person to talk about it, I do give you a good deal, but it is not really quite typical ... As far as I can, I think I do occupy myself about other people and try to help them, and when I spoke as if I didn't think other people's troubles mattered so much, that only represented wicked moments of despair ... But, it does seem to me as inevitable and as justifiable that one should want affection, as that one should want air and food, not as a reward, but because life is unbearable without. To the ordinary sort of woman like me with no particular talent or ambition, it is absolutely the only thing that matters. And this autumn I have felt so deserted. You are almost the only person who has been to see me or written to me ... The fact is I have a fair number of acquaintances, and hardly any friends. Everyone else seems to have their life full of people and interests, and I have failed to fill mine. I know I have no right to complain, but it is dismal and depressing and work is cold comfort. I know that everything you say about the necessity of self-repression is true, I am afraid I have got a great deal to do. It is dreadful to feel such a desperate love of life and not the courage to give it up ... I am very grateful to you for letting me once complain long and loudly. I don't think I shall want to again.

Mary was almost suicidally wretched, and she was also sharply aware that misery was having a bad effect on her:

I am afraid I am more bitter and sour and unamiable than ever, but I must not be, I know it is horrid and inexcusable, and it is useless to be angry with life and envious of other people. (September 1905.)

For a time after Theodore Davies' death Mary Sheepshanks did in fact become a byword in her own circle for
being a bitter, self-pitying depressive. Alice reported to
Flora a revealing tête-à-tête she had had with Lady Young[14]
on the subject of Mary:

she said she was very fond of her [Mary] indeed but felt she
wanted to be very well and strong for her. I said I was very
sorry for her. She said she was as far as her disposition went
though she felt everyone could fight against that [i.e.
depression], but she thought she had a great many things in
her life. I said I thought it was hard on her not being first with
anyone. She said almost every woman had to put up with
that — 'I suppose you think all wives are first with their
husbands but they're not and then things change, one is first
with one's children for a little but one must make up one's
mind to that changing.' I then told her about our relationship
as I didn't wish her to think I was pining for a husband. So
she said, 'Well, that relationship comes from unselfishness on
both sides. Mary has very nice sisters, she might have it with
one of them. Mary ought to get real happiness out of her work
— you must get out of yourself and be happy. I should like to
give Mary a nice husband but I know she'd best him in a
week and she wants to be set on a pinnacle and be adored
which is simply bad for people.' I said it was Mary's paganism
made her unhappy. She said she thought Mary had got her
views from George Trevelyan ...

Flora's reply was critical of Lady Young and loyally defensive of Mary:

I *knew* you'd get on to Mary Sheepshanks with Lady Young. I
think it was not very nice of her to run her down so. I should
have thought it untrue though very interesting that most
women have to put up with not being first. I should have
thought most wives were first as far as people were concerned
— the men might put their work before them but that's a
different thing. I mean it might be a poor first but still it
would be a first ... I don't think our relationship comes from
unselfishness. You can't get a close intimate relationship
because you want it. I don't see that Mary can get it out of

her sisters. It is very unfortunate Mary isn't happy in her work. Of course I agree the experiment of marrying Mary would be rash ... I wonder if I like Lady Young.

Flora herself then had a tête-à-tête about Mary with Dora Sanger, which she, in turn, reported to Alice:

Dora said: 'feel I've behaved badly to her, I know she felt Theodore's death very much.' Dora thought Mary was losing her attractiveness and said that somebody else had said so too. She thought her without pity. I stood up for Mary. I prayed beforehand not to say [critical] things and I think I was careful ... I said to Dora I wished Mary Sheepshanks would marry. She said: 'Yes, but that wasn't always a remedy by any means.'

Another friend, Charlotte Wollaston, went out of her way to criticise Mary to Alice Mayor for bragging about all the distinguished people she knew — 'You could tell Mary wasn't a lady.' But Alice commented sympathetically: 'Mary Sheepshanks is probably passing through an awful time. Her going out always hung on a thread rather like mine, and she's now in a backwater as well as feeling miserable.' Virginia Woolf was less sympathetic:

[Mary Sheepshanks] deluged me till 1.30 in the morning with the most vapid and melancholy revelations — imagine 17 Sheepshanks in a Liverpool slum, and Mary (so she says) the brightest of the lot.[15]

Thus when they were in their mid-thirties both Flora and Mary found themselves in the same hard situation of having lost their chance of what ordinary happiness there is in marriage and parenthood; their work, they felt, was going badly, and they were both in danger of degenerating into the stereotype of the 'frustrated spinster' — 'I feel so much older now, years older' (Flora Mayor, *Grief Journal*) — sucked under by eddies of self-pity, and an envious anger that they tried to conceal.

But in the event, neither Flora nor Mary *was* sucked

under. Both women had the resilience and stamina to survive with their greatest work still many years ahead of them.

Flora, of course, was immeasurably helped by her memories of Ernest and by the devotion of her whole family:

I've had a very nice talk with Henry tonight, in which the darling has been expanding ... I am writing so badly, I feel too full of it to write. I feel we ought to thank God *again* and *again* for our family. What have we done to deserve to belong to such people as we do, people we can honour from the bottom of our hearts? God has given me that, and you, my own girl, and Ernest and numbers of people have *no-one.* I think we do try to be nice to them all, but I mean to try still harder. I kissed the old thing and called him dear. I feel so *very* glad he should have been able to speak. Oh I *do* hope he'll marry. I do feel rather torn to pieces about it all. (Flora to Alice, 1907.)

Mary never had that sort of feeling for any of her family, much less for them all. But she did have a less stable, sub-stitute family of extraordinarily gifted friends.[16] If Bertrand Russell was the man to whom Mary felt closest after Theodore Davies' death, the woman to whom she then felt most drawn was the poignantly beautiful Virginia Woolf. Mary met her when the latter was recovering from her first attempt to commit suicide and whether or not Mary intended the offer of work at Morley College as therapy, it did, in fact, do Virginia considerable good.[17] For Mary's part, although she always maintained a strictly profes-sional and even critical stance towards this novice tutor,[18] she later confessed that Virginia had exercised 'an irresist-ible charm' over her. Mary found herself confiding in Virginia a great deal more than in retrospect she would have wished. Their relationship did not last, for both Virginia Woolf and Bertrand Russell, as Mary wrote in her eighties, had the habit of dropping former friends about whom they no longer felt curious, 'down an oubliette'.

Neither family nor friends, however, were sufficient to save Flora and Mary from sinking periodically into a slough of despond. Both women needed something outside themselves to live for, and, fortunately for them, they found it. Their private crises, during the years 1904-1907, coincided with the gathering momentum of a great social revolution — the struggle of British women to be granted equal citizenship. Many women in Britain at the beginning of the twentieth century felt challenged to prove themselves rational, effective human beings, and neither Mary nor Flora contemplated escaping into a permanent 'decline' just then.

7

MARY, FLORA AND 'THE SUFFRAGE',
1908–1913

To the working-class socialist, Hannah Mitchell, the women's struggle for the vote was quite simply 'the greatest experience' of her life: it 'seemed like the quest of the Holy Grail.'[1] To Mary Stocks, later Baroness Stocks, Principal of Westfield College, then a schoolgirl of sixteen, it was 'a great adventure ... an unforgettable experience to see the great women of an older generation at work.'[2] For the publicist and preacher Maude Royden:

> To work for the enfranchisement of women was a tremendous experience, a tremendous education ... The struggle both absorbed and widened my life. It gave me a sympathy — and I believe an understanding which linked me to all disfranchised persons and nations.[3]

To the historian, Ray Strachey, the women's movement was not a cause, it was *The Cause*. What the women Suffragists were after, she said, was not to acquire power as a right in itself and in so doing to triumph over men at last, but to acquire power solely as 'an extended means to do good in the world.'[4] Idealism and comradeship crossed class barriers and brought an unprecedented purposefulness and zest into countless women's lives:

> the ever-recurring crises seemed to have a glamour greater than the light of common day. The meetings which multiplied in halls and drawing-rooms, in schools and

145

chapels, at street corners, and on village greens, did not seem like the dull and solemn stuff of politics; they were missionary meetings, filled with the fervour of a gospel, and each one brought new enthusiasts to the ranks.[5]

There were great rallies in the Albert Hall and Trafalgar Square addressed by spell-binders like Mrs Pankhurst — and even those who could not follow her into the ways of militancy were spell-bound.[6] There were great processions, many thousand strong, with gay woven banners and the new women university graduates in their colourful academic robes. There was not just one suffrage newspaper but nearly a dozen, including the *Common Cause*, the *Englishwoman*, the *Church of England League for Women's Suffrage, Votes for Women*, and the paper of the Women's Freedom League. Plays and novels were written by women for women about the cause, the most notable being Elizabeth Robins' *The Convert*[7] with its idolisation of Christobel Pankhurst as the irrepressible perky little Ernestine Blunt. Soon more and more groups were affiliated to the movement:

There was the Actresses' Suffrage League, and the Artists' Suffrage League; the Catholic Women's Suffrage Society, the Church League for Women's Suffrage, and the Conservative and Unionist Women's Franchise Association; the Free Church League, and the Friends' League, the Jewish League, the London Graduates' League, and the Scottish Universities' Women's Suffrage Union, and so on.[8]

And that was not counting the Women's Co-operative Guild or the 67,000 strong women textile workers' union in the North.[9]

Jane Harrison, Emily Davies, Ellen Terry, Melian Stawell and Margaret Llewelyn Davies were all declared Suffragists. Even Virginia Woolf, despite her shrinking from any exhibition of mass-feeling and her protective reflex of fastidious mockery, now felt impelled to write to her Greek teacher, Janet Case, on 1 January 1910:

Would it be any use if I spent an afternoon or two weekly in
addressing envelopes for the Adult Suffragists ... I could
neither do sums or argue, or speak, but I could do the
humbler work if that is any good. You impressed me so much
the other night with the wrongness of the present state of
affairs that I feel that action is necessary. Your position
seemed to me intolerable. The only way to better it is to do
something I suppose.[10]

Both Mary and Flora were suffragists. It was Dr Hilda
Clark, Quaker granddaughter of John Bright, who converted Mary to taking an active part in the campaign. Not
that Mary had needed much converting. She had championed the less privileged women students of Morley for
years. And in 1907 she introduced there the innovation of
'At Homes' for women students only, to give the women an
opportunity to discuss subjects relating to women, and
simply to meet one another socially because:

Working women as a rule work longer hours than men and
for less wages, and moreover have home duties in addition ...
when they do attend a class they are apt to go straight home
afterwards, nothing analogous to the men's billiard and
smoking rooms being available for them ... In a mixed
college there is a tendency for women to fall into the
background.[11]

Mary also encouraged college debates and guest lectures
on the Women's Suffrage question — one notable occasion
being the debate led by Christabel Pankhurst in April 1907.
It took courage for the Debating Society to invite Christabel
to speak at an official Morley College meeting since she was
already a notorious national figure, having been imprisoned in October 1906, for spitting at a police officer.
Something of the flavour of Christabel Pankhurst's style
and her leaning towards 'separate development' for
women can be seen in this report of her speech at Morley:

We are absolutely determined to have our way, and to have
our say in the government of affairs. We are going to develop

on our own lines and listen to the pleadings of our inner nature. We shall think our own thoughts and strengthen our own intelligence. We want the abolition of sex in the choice of legislative power as well as privilege. For the present we want the woman to have what the men have. When the men have adult suffrage, then we shall want the same ... We have only to look back to such characters as Joan of Arc, the revolutionary movement in Russia, the Boer women and the like to see who can do the dangerous work.[12]

Mary Sheepshanks wound up the debate, supporting the motion for women's enfranchisement on two grounds: (1) that the vote would benefit women, (2) that it would benefit the state. The motion was carried.

In April 1909, Mary invited forty women students to an 'At Home' in the college library, where Amber Reeves (the original of Wells' Ann Veronica) addressed them on the positive social consequences of women's enfranchisement in her native New Zealand. And in 1913, Mary's last 'At Home' concentrated on the current efforts of the Fabian Society to raise the wages of low-paid women workers.

But educating Morley students in the suffrage question was not enough. Mary soon found herself spending an increasing amount of her spare time canvassing from door to door, and speaking at public meetings up and down the country. Her friend, Bertrand Russell, a convinced and passionate advocate of women's equality, has left a vivid account of what was then entailed in working publicly for women's suffrage — good-natured banter was not the worst one had to fear from non-sympathisers:

It must be quite impossible for younger people to imagine the bitterness of the opposition to women's equality. When, in later years, I campaigned against the first world war, the popular opposition that I encountered was not comparable to that which the suffragists met in 1907. The crowd would shout derisive remarks: to women, 'Go home and mind the baby'; to me, 'Does your mother know you're out?' no matter what the man's age. Rotten eggs were aimed at me and hit my wife. At my first meeting rats were let loose to frighten the ladies, and ladies who were in the plot screamed in pretended terror with a view to disgracing their sex.[13]

Mary Sheepshanks was more fortunate. She and Philippa Fawcett, the brilliant Newnham mathematician, found large, friendly audiences at Louth in Lincolnshire and at Bicester in Oxfordshire. But at Bicester they did have an incident:

While we were out at a meeting some young men, sons of neighbouring squires, broke into our bed-rooms and made hay of them. A few days later I had friends to dinner in London, including Jos. Wedgewood, who had previously rescued me and a friend from an angry election crowd in the Potteries. He took up the matter in the House of Commons, and the Home Secretary undertook to look into it ... The father of one of the young men offered an apology — provided I would not say I had received one.

Mary, however, insisted on having an unqualified apology — 'and as it was made known that, unless an apology was forthcoming, the names would be given in Parliament, a proper one was made.'[14] Mary's comment on this incident was that the boorish behaviour had, of course, been 'provoked by the violent tactics of the Suffragettes.' Her attitude to the Suffragettes, like that of many of her fellow Suffragists, was ambivalent. She disliked their methods, having an aversion to violence, but she greatly admired their individual acts of bravery and doubted whether she could have shown similar courage herself.

Meanwhile Flora, confined for much of the time to her sickbed at Clifton, had to content herself with prodding Alice for more details about the suffrage movement in London — 'remember I'm interested'. The first reference to 'the Suffrage' in Alice's letters occurs in 1905 and the most frequent allusions occur between 1907 and 1908. Alice told Miss Emily Davies (founder of Girton) that though she herself tended towards indifference, she had a sister who was 'keen'. Just how much more ardent Flora was than Alice can be seen from the following letter:

I saw the little Kenny again, [i.e. the Suffragette Annie Kenny, the Lancashire mill-worker in the W.S.P.U.] to whom I feel quite warmhearted. She again implored me to join her, but I would have none of her, chiefly for your sake you stupid ass. I thought about that text Whosoever loves Mother or sister etc. cannot be my disciple and I think it is rather cowardly of me when I do feel it is right and important. (Flora to Alice, 1907.)

In other words Flora was very tempted to join 'the Pank-hurst lot.' Alice promptly took care to tell Flora everything that she was discovering about the Suffragettes' excesses:

Emily [Leaf]'s cousin Miss Coles is *rabid* about suffrage and she actually hinted that *perhaps* the Suffragettes might take to bomb-throwing. I shall not tell this to *anyone*. Emily thinks Mrs Despard and Mrs Cobden Sanderson getting almost irresponsible through the strain of the one idea, rather sad. ... Yes, the bomb woman gave her address the S.P.U. place. (April 1908 and July 1908.)

Flora retorted: 'I feel just as keen on Suffrage. Why should one fool make any difference to me?'

There are also references in the Mayor letters to a propagandist suffrage play by Flora's old friend, Blanche Smith, in which Flora bitterly regretted she was not strong enough to take part. And even that redoubtable Tory dowager, Flora's mother, agreed to attend a suffrage tea. Flora was pleased. In Flora's case, the suffrage campaign had to be waged, not in front of coarse hostile strangers at public meetings, but in the face of amused and con-descending friends and relations within her own drawing-room. So many decent people in Flora's set, including her own brother Henry, believed in the intellectual inferiority of women. If pressed, they would actually say that they believed women had been created for the sake of giving men restful relief — 'the harem idea' in Flora's words. And precisely because such views were so abhorrent to her it was difficult to counter them in a measured, convincing way. Flora became particularly upset when even Alice said she agreed with men that beauty in a wife was a reward for goodness in a husband. Flora burst out:

It is the most ridiculous uncivilized idea I ever heard of. It is the fact of really nice men holding such odious views about women which is the one excuse of the Pankhurst lot. It seems to me such a thoroughly harem idea. How could you enjoy it? You mustn't mind me putting it very strongly, duckie. Think of Ernest's views about beauty. You *mustn't* like these views darling.

Flora had a long, searching talk with her brother, Henry, on the subject:

I said 'You find women very puzzling don't you?' He said 'Yes' — it was so difficult to find topics in common ...
I said I thought he thought women inferior intellectually. He said 'No, not inferior but different.' He thought that most women had an instinct for family life that men had not and it was a pity to leave that for the things men could do. I said of course as things were [a reference to the surplus female population then in Britain] women had to work and that teaching girls could only be done by women and I thought a woman's mental health suffered and through that her family suffered if she hadn't outside interests. He said he thought the modern sort of woman less restful. He instanced Mrs Russell as very unrestful. He thought men and women having the same interests created rather than lessened the barrier. I said women were bound to work and that [though] their relationship with men had not been taken into consideration when [they] became working women, on the face of it, it seemed to me it ought to be a great help in the real relationship of the sexes, though I thought it likely that the absence of leisure in women's lives might destroy their charm. He said that there was little enough of that in the world and we could ill spare it.
I said I doubted if there had really been more in olden

times. Then we had to stop. (Undated letter from Flora to Alice, c. 1908.)

Flora commented on that very 'illuminating' conversation with Henry that, although she had been very glad to have had it, it was not satisfactory:

Henry, while meaning to be perfectly fair-minded about women does really want to restrict them to the old-fashioned life which I think proved satisfactory when there was much more to be done in the household — when I think it was in many ways a very good life — but now that is gone and can't come back and women must have something more. And I do feel that looking round and comparing old and the new, the new [women] are much more livable with and wide-minded and less likely to take offence. I am very sorry Henry doesn't approve the modern type ... (by modern I mean the [Newnham] Collegy sort) because I do think take its average it is a much higher one — much nicer about servants, to take one instance ... Robin's view of women is a much more satisfactory one.

It was in conversations such as that one between Flora and Henry, multiplied a thousand times over in drawing-rooms and at dinner-tables up and down the country that 'The Woman Question' was then being aired by the British middle class.

Flora felt herself caught between opposing half-truths — that of the traditional world in which woman's only role was that of home-maker, and that of the 'moderns' in which women were to be the new enlightened law-givers, wiping for ever the tears from all eyes. She herself had found it so impossible to breathe as the conventional, nineteenth-century, leisured daughter-of-the-house, that she had chosen instead to expose herself to the humiliation and failure of the theatrical agency in Denton Street. But no political vote could ever bring Ernest back from the dead, nor could it free the writer's creative power within her. Flora's final position on the suffrage question was that the denial to women of the right to vote was a positive evil but

Mrs Mayor with Flora and Alice aged about six (Flora on her right)

The Sheepshanks family c. 1892. Mary, aged twenty, at the rear

Flora Mayor aged about eighteen

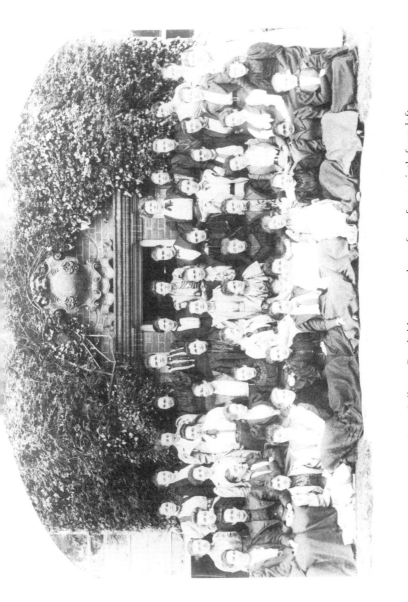

Mary Sheepshanks at Newnham College, Cambridge, second row from front, sixth from left.

Mrs Sidgwick, Principal of Newnham College when Flora and Mary were students

Flora Mayor at about twenty-five, as an amateur actress

Ernest Shepherd, aged thirty, the last portrait

Flora aged thirty, at the time of her engagement

MISS SHEEPSHANKS' AT HOME.

ON Saturday, March 15th, Miss Sheepshanks entertained the Women Students of the College and the guests began to assemble at about 6.30 p.m. Mrs. Anstruther and Mrs. Buxton came in for a while and the throng soon included the Members of the Greek Play classes. The last to arrive were the Gymnasium teams. A wave of sound surged up the stairs and they had to make their appearance amid resounding applause, for it had been a momentous day, and they brought with them a Silver Cup won in a competition at the Alexandra House.

Several people wished to know how Miss Sheepshanks intended to employ the coming year and learnt that during the first month or so the Vice-Principal was to lecture on the "Women's Movement" in French and German in various towns of Europe. As this goes to press, post cards now on the notice board in the Common Room mention Paris, Zurich, Vienna, Munich, Constance, Berlin and Prague, as some of the towns already visited. The following extracts from a letter dated May 23rd, will be of interest :—

From *Morley College Magazine,* 1913

Jane Addams in old age, surrounded by immigrant children in Hull House, Chicago

Die modernen
Kriegsmethoden
und
der Schutz der
Zivilbevölkerung

Kathe Kollwitz poster for
Frankfurt Conference on
Modern Warfare and the
Protection of Civilians, 1929,
organised by Mary Sheepshanks

Flora Mayor aged fifty-two,
photographed for *Vogue,* 1924

Mary Sheepshanks in 1940

that the granting of it would not be an all-solving good.

While Flora was restricted by her chronic ill-health to a frustratingly narrow life in Clifton, the Woman Question was leading Mary out into an ever wider world. In 1908 Mary attended the International Woman's Suffrage Association Congress in Holland and by 1913 she had become such a recognised activist in the cause that she was invited to undertake a lecture tour of Western and Central Europe, beginning in Brussels and ending up in Budapest. To do this, Mary asked for a year's leave from Morley. Her farewell took the characteristic form of a party for the women students, given by herself to celebrate the success of Morley's Women's Gymnastic Class which had recently vanquished the British College of Physical Education. Mary had first asked a representative from the Fabian Society to come and distribute questionnaires to the women worker-students present concerning their low wages and then she explained that she herself was now taking a year off. She would be lecturing nearly every day with long journeys between Brussels, Paris, Vienna and Warsaw, finishing with various towns in Hungary. She would have to speak either in French or German on different aspects of the women's movement — including local government and industrial conditions, and altering the substance of her talks according to the different organisations inviting her — sociological societies, free-thinkers, temperance movements, educational institutions, as well as suffrage groups.

Preparing the stuff has been pretty hard work and I am doubtful whether I shall be able to speak without reading it as I do in English. I feel nervous and anxious now it comes to the point. (Mary Sheepshanks to Bertrand Russell, March 1913.)

Once on the Continent Mary found herself usually having to lecture in a hall where the audience sat at little tables drinking beer — but this, she found, had its good side, since she could feel that if they didn't like her speech at least they could enjoy their beer.

What I found exhausting was adjourning after the lecture to a café where eating, drinking and eager discussion went on far into the night. What I enjoyed was the cordiality; members of the audience coming up to be introduced and inviting me to meet their husbands or wives, calling on me next day and being generally jolly. (Mary Sheepshanks, *Autobiography*, ch. 8.)

Mary, now aged forty, still had her deprived child's yearning for 'a jolly time.' Her letters to Bertrand Russell, written during this tour, are an invaluable historical record of the Women's Movement in Europe just before the First World War. It is significant that Mary also reports on European views on free-thinking and free love to Russell, knowing those to be two of his most cherished causes, in addition to feminism, at this period:

train near Lübeck, 26 April 1913

Dear Bertie,
    ... the suffrage movement is very little supported in Germany, nearly all the men are dead against and nearly all the women indifferent. Much less interest is taken in politics altogether, and also the men are more brutal and coarse and self-indulgent and domineering. The women are not quite so effaced as they were but their present claims seem rather more material, better clothes, etc. The keenest and most intelligent are generally teachers and Jewesses, the ordinary girls and married women are tepid and timid. Immense capital is made by the press and 'antis' of the Suffragettes [i.e. in Britain] and obviously their outrages injure the cause and alienate numbers of moderates. Many women do a lot of social ameliorative work, but they think suffrage too extreme.
    Most of the suffragists are advanced in politics, either *fortschrittliche Volkspartei* or *Social Demokraten.* It is considered a damning thing to say it is 'international' and 'socialist'.
    In *Munich* I had a row. Augspurg and Heymann the two most extreme women in Germany[15] are mad keen on the

Suffragettes and stipulated that I should not attack them. I
said not one word against them, but they passed over all I
said and made passionate speeches in favour of the 'gettes',
and sent a telegram to Mrs Pankhurst. I thought it unfair in
connection with my lecture and likely to injure the cause, so I
put a disclaimer in the paper, simply saying I had nothing to
do with the telegram. They are annoyed. I am sorry, because
though they are tiresome they are keener than any other
women I have met here and abler and I really like them
better. We had a *huge* meeting, and the sense of the majority
was against them. All the people I met in Munich and
elsewhere say they injure the cause by their extremeness, but
really German men are exasperating and would infuriate one.

Constanz and Freiburg: the work was being done by very
keen school teachers, simple and earnest and so poor but
idealists, I loved them.

Stuttgart: we had an enormous meeting, members of the
Landtag and people from Ulm, Tübingen and Heidelberg; 30
new members joined and they collected a good sum. I met no
one very impressive and stayed with Mrs Lindemann, whom I
used to like, but whom I now like much less as she is selfish
and unkind to her servants, and so smugly self satisfied ...

At *Bonn* the audience was dull, benevolent persons with
narrow ideas, no discussion, the only nice people a teacher
and nurse.

Then I had a delightful time in Brussels, the nicest people
since Vienna. Awfully nice women in the movement, married
society women, cultivated and charming, and awfully
interesting men. I thought I should hate Belgians because of
the Congo, but those I met were A1 ... The next day I met
the leader of the Catholic Democrats, who is working hard for
suffrage — I couldn't help mistrusting his motives, but fear it
is true that women have nothing to hope for from any party's
sense of justice, only from its interest ... They find it very
difficult to get [suffrage] workers everywhere, the girls aren't
allowed to, and no one else has time and in Germany they
can't get money.

In Belgium all the people I met were rich and could get
money. One delightful middle-aged woman, Léonie la
Fontaine was jolly and extreme, and founded the movement.

She wants free love and all the rest, and is rich enough to say so. She has suffragette leanings and a twinkle in her eyes. Jane Brigode the president is a dear, a good mother and all the rest, but no genius or dash. So far I haven't met imposing personalities except Augspurg and Heymann, but I have hopes of Berlin, where all the leaders are ...

Dortmund: dull, *Hannover*: nice, stayed with two Jewish widows, charming, cultured and advanced, rich but the daughter learning a trade, a lot of nice sympathetic talk; ... the secretary also a poor Jewish teacher, happily married but in favour of free love.

Kiel: my hostess a cultivated cosmopolitan *Dame*, very liberal views about marriage but thinks the Scandinavians take it too lightly ... We had a horrid meeting, very full, and 2/3 enemies, all the speakers opposed us and in a gross and offensive way — they wanted 'no Englishwomen', *Sie sind ja nicht verheiratet, lernen Sie den Weg zum Männerherz!* [You're not even married — just try to get a man yourself!] — and these were *Oberlehrer* [senior school teachers] and so on. Unluckily the women's speaker didn't turn up and I find controversy difficult in a strange tongue ... However I began to answer and was then interrupted by a previous speaker and so put off that I couldn't go on. I can only hope that the tone of the antagonists will disgust the women enough. The contempt and beastliness ought to rouse them if they have a spark. I pity those who are awake enough to resent it. They jeered at the other woman for being a Jewess and had rounds of applause from students and others. They wanted to remain *echt deutsch*, no international nonsense, — I gathered they were ultra Conservative ... The suffrage women were boiling with rage ...

Mary was very vulnerable to such sexual insults, as well as being quick to resent anti-Semitic insults to her Jewish friends. Nevertheless, she continued doggedly with her lecture tour:

Berlin: I think certainly there are young and fresh people in the German suffrage movement but they seem to be few and what I wanted to add for your information concerns the bad political split which is tearing the suffragists to pieces and of which I had evidence in nearly every meeting. The suffragists' constitution since 1907 claims by Clause 3 — Universal, secret direct suffrage. Lately many local committees have rebelled against this as being too radical, being far in advance of what the men have and as identifying women's suffrage with the Social Demokraten and keeping out more moderate and Conservative women. The Committee at Weimar therefore recommended the abrogation of Clause 3 and thereupon Minna Cauer (national leader in Berlin) resigned and now the battle rages fiercely ... In Berlin we had a huge meeting and a fierce discussion roused by a Soc. Dem. woman who attacked the army ...

In *Gera*, in the little principality of Reuss, I stayed with a dear little doctor of the best sort, poor and idealistic, really a heavenly man, with a horrid stuffy, evil flat where he works 16 hours a day.

Then *Prague* which was an experience in many ways ... Unluckily I had a horrid time there personally which spoils the association, but I learnt a lot that was interesting. The standing feud of the Czechs and Germans makes it very uncomfortable if one only speaks German (as I did). There are 500,000 Czechs to 40,000 Germans and the latter have a bad time. The Czechs gain ground and are triumphant — they purposely misdirect one if one speaks German. I suppose they have had great provocation from the Germans in the past and still complain that Germans push the Czechs off the pavement in the main street in Prague at noon[16] ... A Viennese Excellenz told me that in Prague he always looked about for a well dressed man and addressed him in French — but, as I told him, that was not good advice for a lady.[17]

Mary's letter to Russell continues:

What I have heard of German oppression and bullying lately is dreadful ...

In *Gorlitz* ... my lecture was arranged by a wonderful man who is really persecuted for his free-thinking views. He was accused of blasphemy but acquitted, but they have deprived him of the right to teach ... He told me revolting stories of oppression, e.g. how now many innocent men are in prison on trumped up charges to prevent their taking part in the Prussian Landtag elections, and how a poor workman was imprisoned for saying: 'In my opinion the Church is a stupefying Institution' — *Verdummungs-Anstalt.*

Vienna: Austrian women are not allowed to belong to political parties, so Police permission had to be obtained for my lecture and a uniformed official sat on the platform. First he announced that there could be no discussion after my lecture, but at the end he got up and went away and said we might amuse ourselves — 'Ladies, I will now leave you and hope that what follows will not endanger the State!' A good example of *Absolutismus, gemildert durch Schlamperei* — A *Times* correspondent who was present told me that if in Germany they had said there was to be no discussion, that would have been that . . .

Kalisz (Russian Poland) Here the conditions are too depressing and distressing I had better not write about them. I admire and like all I see of the Poles, who make heroic efforts to ameliorate social conditions . . . This town has 60,000 inhabitants, no drainage, and no water supply, the same is true of Lodz, which has 400,000 inhabitants (my speech there was forbidden). Telegrams somehow don't arrive and in a thousand ways one is aware of what it all involves . . . People don't have spare rooms in Eastern Europe. One rolls up in a quilt and sleeps on the sofa, which is wholesome discipline of course, but water is unknown.

Posen (German Poland) the way things go in Posen is awful, the Germans seem to be mere brutal oppressors for all their culture. Polish women are infinitely wider awake than Germans — they really have the divine spark.

Russian Poland — including Cracow and Warsaw. After all I am not being allowed to speak, even in private circles.[18]

In a letter to Morley students and staff, 25 May 1914, Mary amplified on the situation:

In Russian Poland classes for workmen are forbidden, friendly societies are forbidden, any gathering of 10 persons is forbidden unless special police permission is obtained. One priest was imprisoned for preaching temperance, because the government has the brandy monopoly, another was arrested for possessing a typewriter — and in spite of everything the Poles struggle to educate and uplift their nation... They ask me why England takes up the cause of every other oppressed nationality except Poland, and the only reasons I know are:- that we have no money interests in Poland and that we fear Russia too much.[19]

Mary herself found the political atmosphere personally oppressive:

When I borrowed some quite harmless book [in Warsaw], a child warned me to wrap it up before going into the street or it might be confiscated. When I walked with my hosts in the park, they looked nervously over their shoulders.[20]

What dark shadows are cast by these letters written by Mary Sheepshanks in the spring of 1913 — rival nationalisms, and imperialism, militarism, authoritarianism, anti-Semitism and the secret police. Nostalgia has gilded our collective image of Europe before the First World War. Out of that same Europe came the War.

Her lecture tour had proved an immensely stimulating political experience for Mary and it came to a fitting climax at the International Women's Suffrage Association Congress in Budapest in June 1913. There the most important event was Mary's first meeting with Jane Addams — the champion of the exploited immigrants in American cities, supporter of unionising underpaid labour, pioneer of equality for the American Negro and the emancipation of women, and in 1931, laureate of the Nobel Peace Prize. Mary called Jane Addams quite simply: 'the finest human being I have ever known.'[21] They were to work together for the rest of Jane Addams' life.

The other notable event at the congress for Mary was that she was offered and accepted the post of Secretary of the International Women's Suffrage Alliance, running its new Headquarters in London and editing its monthly paper, *Ius Suffragii* (The Law of Suffrage).

Ius Suffragii was an extraordinary phenomenon, too little

known even to this day. A single copy, costing 4d. or 4
marks or 4 francs, published in English and French, would
include reports on women's issues from countries as
disparate and as distant from one another as Argentina,
Armenia, Australia, Austria, Belgium, Bohemia, Bulgaria,
Canada, China, Cuba, Denmark, Egypt, Finland, France,
Germany, Great Britain, Hawaii, Iceland, Ireland, Italy,
Japan, Netherlands, New Zealand, Norway, Philippines,
Romania, Russia, South Africa, Sweden, Switzerland,
Turkey and the USA. The topics included agriculture, care
of children, divorce, economic conditions, education,
illegitimacy, the legal position of women, liquor restriction,
maternity assistance, the peace movement, prostitution,
and war relief, as well as the progress of suffrage itself.

Mary was responsible for collecting, analysing and
summarising all this material from all over the world:

All presidents and correspondents are urged to send all
important news to the International Headquarters at once.
The cost of telegraphing when necessary, will be refunded...
If news is unavoidably delayed beyond the 25th of each
month, correspondents are requested to let the Editor know
and space will be reserved for their reports... Translators are
now wanted for Czech, Polish, Icelandic, Norwegian and
Danish — Please communicate with Miss Sheepshanks. (15
November 1913.)

Mary was just forty-one. She worked for very little money,
but with complete ardour, endorsing Maude Royden's
affirmation of the idealistic humanism in feminism:

For peace and against prostitution, alcoholism and the neglect
of children... Women will be moved by the hope of moral
reforms, or they will not be moved at all. (July, 1913.)

While Mary Sheepshanks was reaching out to help
establish a world-wide network for the emancipation of
women, Flora Mayor was turning more and more inwards.
She too had brooded on 'The Woman Question' all her life,
but she deliberately decided to write her first novel about

an uninspiring, 'superfluous' woman. Flora distilled into the 144 pages of *The Third Miss Symons* all the experience and observation and reflection of her forty years so far.

8

THE THIRD MISS SYMONS (1913):
FEMINIST TRACT OR HUMAN TRAGEDY?

By 1913 the English spinster — of whom by then there were over a million — was regarded as a problem:

The Empire gave men an identity, a silent pride ... But Spinsters had to face the fact that they were a nuisance to everybody, because there was no provision for them to be independent of a man's help in an economy set up by males for males.[1]

Throughout the second half of the nineteenth century many great British spinsters, including Florence Nightingale, the educational reformers Dorothea Beale and Emily Davies, the workhouse reformer Louisa Twining, the housing reformers Octavia Hill and Emma Cons and the shopworkers' champion Margaret Bondfield, had all worked heroically in order that Britain might become a more humane society.[2] But among their contemporaries there was a whole submerged population of spinsters generally regarded as *un*heroic. On 23 November 1911, the first number of the *Freewoman* printed a powerful anonymous article, 'The Spinster' by 'One', which expressed the pain of such women, their self-hatred and their longing to rebel:

See how she is made and from what ... in babyhood she begins with her dolls. Why do not the parents of a prospective spinster give her a gun or an engine? If society is going to have spinsters, it should train spinsters. In girlhood she is ushered into an atmosphere charged with sex-distinctions and sex-insinuations. She is educated on a literature saturated with these ... She is ready to marry, ripe to marry, needing marriage ... It is there where there is a smattering of education and little interest to fill in the time that the spinsters' numbers rally and increase. It is here that Society ... turns round arbitrarily on one in four and says Thou Shalt Not ...

Is it all because a man did not turn up at the right time? Well, partly yes and partly no. Not *any* man; *any* man was not what she had been led to expect. She had in fact, been specifically warned against *any* man. It was the right man she was expecting, HER man. The spinster, both wretch and culprit, is the failure, and she closes her teeth down and says nothing ... Then mind and body begin. *They* get their pound of flesh, and the innermost Ego of the soul, the Dweller behind the mind, stands at bay to meet their baiting. Day by day, year by year, the baiting goes on. To what end — for what temporal or final good is all this? ... To whom and for what?

In her barrenness and repressed misery, says this anony-mous writer, the spinster has made herself the repressive censor of British civilisation — 'She has become our social Nemesis ... at once the injured and the injuring.'[3]

More spinsters at once wrote to the *Freewoman*, either confirming or trying to rebut that first writer's anguish. The Suffragists' main paper — the *Common Cause* — was sym-pathetic but uneasy — 'To harp on the one string of sex will jar the nerves of readers in the long run. One article of the type of 'The Spinster' would be stimulating; but five or six give the impression of an obsession.'[4] Then young Rebecca West joined in:

... the spinster question is really an urgent matter. Today there are hundreds and thousands of spinsters all over the country, produced for the most part by educational systems. Hence you have a large population deprived of the possibility of wifehood and motherhood. The only people to whom such a deprivation could be of any value are artists. But then, again, a spinster is usually a sentimentalist, and therefore incapable of art. So what is the good of all these spinsters?[5]

The forty-year-old spinster, Flora Mayor, was writing *The Third Miss Symons* at that very moment and proving Rebecca West wrong. But the latter's contemptuous dislike was generally shared. In literature, the spinster was treated either with sentimentality or else as a butt for cruelty. For example, Herbert Wales' novel *The Spinster* (1912), is sentimental, giving its grey-eyed heroine of thirty-seven both a single night of forbidden passion and then a devoted brother to rescue her from starvation in the streets. Examples of authorial cruelty are the six Miss Huxtables — sterile in spirit as well as in body — in Granville-Barker's *The Madras House* (1912) and E.M. Forster's Charlotte Bartlett in *A Room with a View* (1908) and Harriet Herriton in *Where Angels Fear to Tread* (1905). It has been suggested that the brutal over-reaction to the militant Suffragettes (many of whom, of course, were spinsters) between 1907 and 1913, was rooted in the contemporary fear, amounting to hatred, of such women on the march.

When, in 1913, Flora Mayor took an unattractive, aggressive-tempered spinster for her first heroine, she was deliberately focusing on the most disturbing and least inspiring facet of 'The Woman Question' — the *unwanted* woman question — a source of embarrassment, as well as of indignation, to feminists, and of ridicule, contempt or fear to everyone else. What Flora Mayor put into her Henrietta Symons was all her understanding of the nine-teenth century's failure to satisfy the legitimate aspirations of an ordinary unmarried middle-class girl. Flora's sources, besides her reading of nineteenth-century litera-ture, were her own relations, her quiet observation of acquaintances at Continental spas, the confidences of her intimate friends — and herself.

Flora knew that her own seven Mayor Aunts had been

saved from going the way of Henrietta Symons by their educated brains, their work, their religious faith and their lifelong devotion to one another. They were the models, not for her Miss Symons, but for all the happier spinsters in the book whom Henrietta Symons tried but failed to emulate — Henrietta's busily affectionate great-aunt, her bright-eyed old teacher lapping up lectures on Aristotle, the philanthropic parish-workers, or the nice cheerful elderly ladies on the Continent who 'made little encampments in the wilderness, so that ... unfortunates might gather round them, and almost feel they had got a home.' (*The Third Miss Symons*, ch. 10.) The two Mayor Aunts who still survived in 1913 might have safely read *The Third Miss Symons* without feeling that they or their dead sisters were being satirised.

But even within Flora Mayor's extended family there were others much more like Henrietta Symons in her decline — selfish, bad-tempered, domineering Cousin Selina, for instance, or feeble, easily intimidated Essie on the Sterling/Grote side. And there was no shortage of querulous elderly ladies, among Flora's acquaintances, always taking offence in hotel dining-rooms abroad or at parish bazaars in Kingston. But most revealing of all, and perhaps what had inspired Flora most, were the confidences of her unmarried friends. Flora's letters to Alice contain scores of reports and comments on such confidences. Both Melian Stawell and Mary Sheepshanks had told her how they had grown up feeling isolated and unloved within their respective huge families. Other women friends had told her, often in tears, how they had never once been spoken to by their Victorian parents as though they were fellow-adults, although they were now nearly forty, and how they had never been given the chance to meet a man, or even to talk with one alone. They had been forbidden to leave the claims of home to find work outside and they felt that any talent they had ever possessed had now atrophied with disuse. Over and over again it

emerged that the one great relationship of their lives had
been with a woman teacher or a sister or woman friend now
dead.

To Bath, the same gloomy buildings. Poor Janet — what it
must have been, ill as she was, with not a soul but an
extremely dull old lady whom there was a chance of seeing.
She said she did have the most awful influenza depression . . .
and that it was so difficult to shake it off when you were
thrown so completely on yourself . . . I am so glad she had
been to Tunbridge Wells and to her old school. Her adored —
one of the teachers was there, quite unchanged and 'charmed
to see me, I never knew she cared about me so much, I have
not had such a piece of happiness for years.' She said how
consoling it was to feel how eternal love was, time and place
making no difference.

Flora also often revisited her old (and much older)
friend, Mary Walton:

Here I am at Shelford. It is curious that I always do feel the
stagnation here, and I do feel very much the sadness of
Mary's wasted powers, and I also feel it more than ever about
Etta [Mary's sister]. She really is so clever and original, she is
like Borrow with all her stories of the people she meets
abroad. They are such good stories. She is one of the few
uncommon people we know and it is all so wasted and
thrown away . . . Mary said to me 'Do I seem very cross and
changed — tell me candidly?' So I did say I thought she was
snappy to Etta . . . E. said what she would have loved would
have been studying, classics and philology. Her father wanted
to teach her Latin. Her mother laughed it to scorn. Can't you
imagine that laugh? The box on the ear for learning German
was at 17 . . . I asked why she had never poured out to her
father to help her against her mother. She would not trouble
him. The crushing made her very timid and took away all
initiative. It encouraged natural inertia. She said she often lied
to her mother from sheer terror . . . She was treated exactly as
a child. Her mother paid for her dress and *chose* it. All she was
allowed was *10/- a month*. 'If I had had £5 in my pocket I

would have gone to Austria and never come back.' (Undated letters from Flora to Alice 1907-1911.)

Gradually Flora began to feel that she could understand the descent of so many unmarried women into death-in-life. Her task as a writer, she now knew, was to tell the truth about them, but without sentimentality and without cruelty.

On a first reading, *The Third Miss Symons* seems to be nothing more than a 'degeneration novella'.[6] We watch an intensely loving child become an interesting, clever schoolgirl and then deteriorate, through loneliness and emotional disappointment, into a nagging, jealous, petty-minded caricature of 'the typical spinster', as she bullies the chambermaid or cheats at Patience or turns two hours of her company into a bad-tempered nightmare. Only the wit and beauty of Flora Mayor's prose mitigate the story's 'icy sadness'.[7] Even death does not transfigure Henrietta Symons — 'she looked what she had been in life — insignificant, feeble and unhappy' (ch. 13). One's first impulse on reading such a tale of sorry waste is to apportion blame, first to the Victorians' oppression of women, then to the bourgeois class system, and finally to Henrietta's own character with its Flaubertian *fatalité intérieure*.[8] But that impulse is a mistaken one, for *The Third Miss Symons* does *not* end with Henrietta's untransfigured, lonely deathbed, but with the discovery of her last testament to her sister Evelyn and Evelyn's subsequent vision of Henrietta lifted up into peace and ecstasy at last. And novels, as E.M. Forster said, mean what they say on their last page.[9] Indeed, Alice Mayor wrote to her brother Robin after Flora's death, that: 'The mystical experience at the end was the root of the book round which the whole thing was written.'

That 'mystical' ending has created problems for the agnostic reader ever since.[10] But even without faith in a life after death it is still possible to respect the vision and the yearning behind such a hope. Henrietta Symons, far from being in her essence a damned soul, really deserved to be in bliss and have all 'the bitterness, aimlessness and emptiness of her life ... made up to her,' is what Flora Mayor's last chapter is saying, whether in fact Heaven should prove to exist or not. To reduce *The Third Miss Symons* to nothing more than a pitiful 'degeneration novella' is a misinterpretation, grounded in the reader's own emotional snobbery. For it is an occupational disease of every novel-reader to be reluctant to identify himself or herself with a character who is poor in spirit. An unlikeable, petty, fractious, self-pitying Henrietta Symons is held away from oneself at imaginative arm's length like some unpleasant entomological specimen, whereas the real unpleasantness lies much more in one's own assumption of moral and psychological superiority towards a Henrietta. Time and again the world's moral teachers have declared that it is our very judging of our fellows which is criminal, our righteousness which is 'as filthy rags'.[11] Here, in the last three pages of *The Third Miss Symons*, Flora Mayor overturns this judgemental, 'trial' apparatus altogether, and removes both Henrietta from the dock and the reader from the bench. The posthumous discovery of Henrietta's three poor treasures — her photographs of her sister's babies, the letter announcing their deaths, and a piece of paper on which she had written down her sister's one sentence of gratitude to her many years before — these are enough to humble the reader and to redeem Henrietta. The concluding promise of salvation, after Henrietta's damnation in the hell of this world, redeems God, not her.

Henrietta was a blessed, rather than a damned soul, because of that very longing for love which had caused her so much misery. She had been right to persist in her need for love even 'when existence or when hope is gone.'[12] From first to last she had understood that humans exist for one another, their only meaning being in answering, or in trying to answer, each other's needs. Henrietta Symons had ached to be needed even while she heard the toads of crossness leaping from her lips — her unhappiness at not being needed causing her nastiness, her nastiness making her more and more unhappy. Unthanked, taken for granted, disliked and despised, nevertheless Henrietta Symons had not only continued to pay for a nephew's school fees or a niece's recuperation by the sea, she had continued to *want* to pay for them.

Henrietta's other redeeming quality was her terrible, humble honesty about herself. Perhaps Flora Mayor agreed with Rousseau that we can be cured of anything except vanity. At any rate no one could have accused Henrietta Symons more harshly or more accurately than she accused herself. Whenever she failed in her relationships she was the first to know that she had failed — 'Now I look back, I see the mistakes I have made, and I have done harm instead of good' (ch. 7). Finally Henrietta even perceived an answer to why she had been unloved. It had been her own anger towards all the world which had exacerbated her awful loneliness — her resentment at being rejected had led to her rejecting everyone in her turn, and therefore she had been more rejected still. 'She knew ... she could not trust herself to be pleasant and good-tempered' (ch. 11). Thereafter Henrietta did struggle to master 'the great rage' within her, and although she did not succeed, her maid Annie did finally grant: 'She's funny, I've always said that, but,' she added, 'I've known some I should say was funnier' (ch. 12).

Just as truth and love survived even in a wretched Henrietta Symons, so faith in a merciful, loving God also just managed to survive in Henrietta's creator, Flora Mayor. The book is Christian, but it is questioningly rather than cosily Christian:

If there is any justice and mercy in the world [Henrietta's sister asks] how can they allow a poor, weak, human creature to have so few opportunities, such hard temptations, and when it yields to temptation to suffer so cruelly? (ch. 13.)

Flora Mayor's answer seems to be that there can only be said to be justice and mercy in this life *if* there is a just and merciful afterlife. Her faith was conditional upon that hope. In this she was like Dr Johnson:

Real alleviation . . . of the loss of friends, and rational tranquillity in the prospect of our own dissolution, can be received only . . . from the assurance of another and better state, in which all tears will be wiped from the eyes, and the whole soul shall be filled with joy.[13]

Perhaps Flora Mayor's original impulse in writing the book had been a transference of anger and pity as felt by one spinster on behalf of all the others who were clearly so much worse off ('I have you, my own girl, and Ernest, and numbers of people have no-one' — (Flora to Alice, 1906)). Perhaps her next impulse was to move beyond mere anger by digging deeper into the underlying causes of 'unwantedness'. So Flora Mayor gives Henrietta some of what she knew to be her (and Alice's) worst qualities of 'horridness' — their judgemental, 'morbid' criticalness of others, and their envy at others' happiness and success in life. 'Sympathy in joy is *so* hard. . . it is facing the successes, and rejoicing in them of people who are more successful than me which is the real difficulty' — (Flora to Alice, 1907 and 1912). But what was more remarkable still was that Flora Mayor also gives Henrietta what she felt to be some of her own better qualities, including her reverence for love and her capacity for grief and self-criticism. In all these ways Flora refuses to hold her Third Miss Symons out at arm's length and so she finally prevents the reflective reader from being able to do so either. To me, it is this below-the-surface element of self-identification with Henrietta by Flora Mayor that makes her book so much greater than any clinical case-study of a stereotypical 'sex-starved spinster'. Flora Mayor was interested in something much deeper — and much more common — than sexual frustration; she was concerned with the psychological destructiveness of emotional failure. We all know what it is to fail at loving as much as we want to love and to fail at being loved as much as we need to be loved. *The Third Miss Symons* is not a feminist tract but a human tragedy.[14] Both Mary Sheepshanks and Flora Mayor were feminists *because* they were humanists; their feminism was humanism applied to women, and it never turned into a solipsistic world-view of, by, and for women alone.

The critical reception of *The Third Miss Symons* in 1913 was respectful and even admiring, but almost every reviewer committed the sin of pharisaical condescension to Henrietta, having failed to notice that she was finally not damned but saved. Therefore the anti-feminist male critics rejoiced in the book as a warning to women — and only to women:

One's first impression is that it is intended to present to those whom it may concern an 'awful example' . . . the futile, unwanted life of a peevish, idle, self-centred woman . . . This it does effectively; and there is nothing else in the book. (*The Times.*)

Henrietta Symons is a woman with absolutely nothing to recommend her . . . a superfluous woman . . . (*Morning Post.*)

There are many like her. What is to be done with them? . . . Perhaps there is no remedy. (*Daily News.*)

Every woman should read this book as a shameful, if pitiable example of a life wasted. (*Irish Times.*)

Feminist reviewers, on the other hand, were uneasy about a book that seemed to confirm the anti-feminist case against women as inferior, irrational, benighted creatures. The pro-suffragist *Englishwoman* 'could hardly bear to read it' and wanted to believe it was 'not as common as Miss F.M. Mayor thinks.' The *Free Church Suffrage Times* (June 1913), reviewed the novel from an explicitly feminist point of view:

The fault lies we are told in a 'want of illumination in the

woman herself and in the life around her'. We agree. And it is
partly to give illumination in such lives that our women's
cause exists. Every one recognises the torments of the sweated
woman or of her fallen sister. But few know of the deadly
suffering of the rich and respectable. Yet the lives of the
sweated and the fallen have in them a spur or a sting. They
are not self-consuming void. 'The Third Miss Symons' is said
to belong to a past generation. We wish we could believe this
were so. But it is our work to make her for ever more
impossible.

Resounding words, but the vote would not have helped
Henrietta, and one cannot legislate for the just distribution
of love. The *Common Cause* was more modest in its com-
passionate hope — 'our movement would, *if it could* [my
emphasis] drive out the spirit that created the misery of
Henrietta.' (1 August 1913.)

The best reviews were those in the *Daily Telegraph* (11
April 1913) and the *New Statesman* (12 April 1913).

In many ways this slim volume represents an extremely
interesting experiment. It ranks as fiction, and yet it is entirely
unlike the average provender of the circulating libraries. It is
very short ... being something between a half and a third the
length of an ordinary novel. It is also completely unpopular in
style, making no concession to the common taste for gush and
sentiment, eschewing decoration of every kind, and keeping
close to the bare, austere presentation of a single character ...
It deserves success more than 90% of the novels which
commend themselves so glibly to the public taste. For the
author, Miss F.M. Mayor, is a true artist, restrained but
confident in touch ... her elaborate study of a spinster's life
... is brilliantly clever, actual, and sincere. Without the
slightest attempt to play upon the feelings, it reaches to the
very heart of things, and leaves the reader with an aching
sense of the intolerable waste of human nature. (*Daily
Telegraph.*)

She is in the tradition, though her performance is not yet on
the level of Jane Austen and Mrs Gaskell. But she uses

English with a wise economy employed by few writers today; she moves the reader strongly again and again without ever resorting to hysterical methods; and she manages, above all, to interest one profoundly in the destinies of a wasted, unloved woman, whom in life nine-tenths of us would have passed by as boring or positively irritating. She enables us (unusual thing) to look at Henrietta from the outside and the inside at one and the same time. (*New Statesman.*)

Flora herself commented on this: 'I have just seen the review in the *Statesman* ... It is much the best I have had, and following the steps of Mrs Gaskell is what I should most like to do.' (Letter to Robin Mayor, 1913.)

Some of Flora's friends were wiser than the reviewers in seeing the relevance of Henrietta to themselves:

One of the rays of light that shine out of the book is the contrast between your study of Henrietta and any previous author's treatment of such a subject. Up till now sarcasm has been felt to be the only possible attitude where a Henrietta is in question. Oh how stupid — and I have been guilty of it. *Blâmer tout c'est ne comprendre rien.* (Georgiana Wilson to Flora, 1913.)

I have just read 'The Third Miss Symons' with great delight and some understanding. There seems a great deal of her in many of us ... Have you no suggestions of a solvent nature for the 'Henriettas' who do not die at sixty? (Blanche Smith to Flora, 1914.)

Your book seems to hit us all in one spot and makes us feel that perhaps we are not making the best of everything. (Melian Stawell to Flora, 1913.)

Sixteen years later, young Daphne Sanger very openly and disarmingly confessed how much she felt 'hit' also:

I have just been reading *The Third Miss Symons* and felt that I must write to you because I think it is so extremely good. The only thing is that it is rather depressing as she is exactly like me at that age. I only hope that I shan't be so bad when I am older. Her being shy and silent and talking too loudly and positively is exactly what I do, but not the kind of thing that most people observe I think. And I felt it almost too cruel to put forward as one of her drawbacks that she was good at looking up trains and arranging sightseeing in Italy as that is exactly what I am good at . . . (5 November 1929.)

Flora replied:

It was very nice of you to write to me about 'The Third Miss Symons', and I am glad you like it and think it good. I am not at all surprised that you think yourself like the Third Miss Symons, — a middle-aged *mère de famille* with three children told me last week that she felt herself the Third Miss Symons, and I cannot tell you how many people, men and women, young and old, have told me the same thing. So I think that . . . all of us have a good deal of her in us.

And nearly seventy years later, Susan Hill's new Introduction to *The Third Miss Symons* substantiates all those first readers' testimonies to the book's depth and significance:

How very little material she is handling after all — and yet she is holding up the whole of human life in her hand and subjecting it to scrutiny . . . we gasp at the simple enormity of what she is saying.

The particular through which Flora Mayor gets us to glimpse the universal is the misery of just one insignificant, un-ideal human being. And in doing this she is anticipating, already in 1913, Karl Jaspers' grim conclusion of 1945:

Without exception, universal shipwreck is the fundamental characteristic of every existence . . . Breakdown and failure reveal the true nature of things.[17]

But 'breakdown and failure' can occur in the collective life of society as well as within the individual heart. It is no mere coincidence that one symptom of Henrietta Symons' sickness of spirit should have been xenophobia, all foreigners being 'those wretches' to her. And while Flora Mayor had been absorbed in the breakdown of one

middle-aged middle-class English woman, Mary Sheepshanks was growing more and more anxiously alerted to
the mounting hysteria and paranoia within country after
country in Europe, so soon to culminate in 'the breaking of
nations' in August 1914.

9

MARY SHEEPSHANKS AND
THE FIRST WORLD WAR
1914–1918

The moment that war broke out the Suffragettes changed their policy from militancy to militarism and addressed recruitment rallies up and down the country. The Suffragists, however, reacted rather differently. It is still not generally realised that a significant portion of the nation's women in 1914 — including over half the leadership of the National Union of Women's Suffrage Societies in Britain — were either pacifists or at the very least 'pacificists'. The pacifists totally renounced participation in any war; the 'pacificists' concentrated on the means of preventing war and of bringing wars to an end.[1]

Whereas the English war poets, among countless articulate men, had to endure the gas, the trenches, the barbed wire and the putrescent corpses in the mud before coming to the conclusion that the whole débâcle was murderous futility,[2] women like Mary Sheepshanks and her friends recognised that the 'Great War' was tragic wickedness from the very second that it began:

The war brought me as near despair as I have ever been. ...
That many of the best men in every country should forswear their culture, their humanity, their intellectual efforts ... to wallow in the joys of regimentation, brainlessness, [and] ... the primitive delights of destruction! For they did ... everywhere, in every belligerent country, [men] were doing the same things; patriotically rushing to the defence of their

homes and loved ones, taunting and imprisoning, (if they did
not shoot) the small number of young men who refused to
join them; [and] disseminating and believing the same
atrocity stories against each other. It was lonely in those days.
I felt that men had dropped their end of the burden of living,
and left women to carry on.[3]

The world-wide women's movement, right up to August
1914, had been not merely international, it had been positively *internationalist*. Whenever feminists had gathered,
they had set themselves to work for international understanding and justice, as well as for the emancipation of
women. Maude Royden had written in *Ius Suffragii*, the
year before:

Internationalism should emphasise the solidarity of human
interests as a fact more fundamental than the bitterest
national or racial dissensions. Certainly the Budapest meeting
of the International Women's Suffrage Alliance brought out
the solidarity of women. The wonder is that delegates from
countries divided by feelings so bitter — in some cases, by
wrongs so deep — should consent to come together on any
subject in the world.[4]

But 'come together' they did, and therefore 'Germany' to
woman suffragists meant not the Prussian-helmeted
Ludendorff, von Bülow or the Kaiser, but Frida Perlen,
Gertrud Baümer, Clara Zetkin, the indomitable Lida
Gustava Heymann and Anita Augspurg, Helene Stöcker,
Minna Cauer and Marie Stritt — anti-Prussians every
one.[5] And to Mary Sheepshanks in particular, 'Germany'
meant the devoted women schoolteachers, doctors and
idealistic German Jews who had given her such hospitality
and friendship during her challenging lecture tour there
the year before.

And so, when, at the end of July 1914, to their incredu-
lous horror, these women saw that war was imminent, the
leading British, German, French, and Austrian Suffragists
then meeting in London, helped by their international

president, the American, Mrs Carrie Chapman Catt, drew up a manifesto addressed to all the governments of Europe. It was drafted at Mary Sheepshanks' International Women's Suffrage Office, 7 Adelphi Street, and presented to Lord Grey and to every European ambassador in London on 31 July 1914. Its words were a true prophecy and the tragedy that developed when its appeal went unheard is not over yet:

International Manifesto of Women
We, the women of the world, view with apprehension and dismay the present situation in Europe, which threatens to involve one continent, if not the whole world, in the disasters and horrors of war ... Powerless though we are politically, we call upon the governments and powers of our several countries to avert the threatened unparalleled disaster ... Whatever its result the conflict will leave mankind the poorer, will set back civilization, and will be a powerful check to the gradual amelioration in the condition of the masses of the people, on which so much of the real welfare of nations depends. We women of twenty-six countries ... appeal to you to leave untried no method of conciliation or arbitration for arranging international differences which may help to avert deluging half the civilized world in blood.

On 2 August 1914, these women made one last attempt to stop the outbreak of war. They called a protest meeting, and on 4 August 1914, the very day that war was declared, two thousand women gathered at the Kingsway Hall. Olive Schreiner was on the platform, together with Mrs Fawcett, Mrs Despard, Mrs Pethick Lawrence, Mrs Barton, Mary Macarthur, Madame Malmberg of Finland, and Madame Roszika Schwimmer.[6] The woman reporter for *Votes for Women* came away from the meeting feeling more inspired that such a gathering should have taken place at all than shocked by what had occasioned it.

It was a protest, passionate, sane, and practical, of the civilized against the barbaric ... Never before had such disaster threatened the world; never before had the conscious,

organised, articulate women of all classes and parties and of
several nations met to make, on behalf of womanhood and
childhood and the home, a protest against the time-honoured
methods of brutal force by which men — regardless of half
the race — have seen fit to settle their national disputes ...[7]

The women dispersed, all foreigners having to leave for
their own countries forthwith, and within Britain itself the
women Suffragists soon found that even they could no
longer speak with one voice about what Mrs Fawcett had
called 'the insensate devilry' of war. Righteous nationalism
was to prove stronger than Christianity, stronger than
Judaism, stronger than socialism — and stronger than
internationalist feminism. The pressure exerted upon the
internationalist few by the patriotic many was immense.
The very next morning after that meeting Lord Robert
Cecil wrote a letter of reproach and biting censure to Mrs
Fawcett:

Dear Mrs Fawcett,
    Permit me to express my great regret that you should have
thought it right not only to take part in the 'peace' meeting
last night but also to have allowed the organization of the
National Union to be used for its promotion. Action of that
kind will undoubtedly make it very difficult for friends of
Women's Suffrage in both the Unionist and Ministerial
parties.
    Even to me the action seems so unreasonable under the
circumstances as to shake my belief in the fitness of Women
to deal with great Imperial questions and I can only console
myself by the belief that in this matter the National Union do
not represent the opinions of their fellow country women.
                                    Yours truly,
                                    Cecil.

Mrs Fawcett did, in fact, subordinate her genuine internationalist sympathies to her even deeper, heartfelt patriotism in war time — 'Women, your country needs you' —
but the first few month of the war were so confusing and so
frenetic that the pacifist feminists did not immediately

perceive that they now held a different position from their greatly esteemed, much-loved leader. Thousands of women were being called on to help the nation as nurses, canteen staff, tool-setters, factory charge-hands and transport workers, and even pacifists felt pride in the humanitarian achievements in wartime Serbia of Dr Kathleen Macphail and Dr Elsie Inglis.[8] Nevertheless, despite this emancipatory side-effect of war, there were still many pacifist British women, Mary Sheepshanks among them, who felt sick at heart over what had now overtaken the world. In October 1914, Mary wrote a signed editorial for *Ius Suffragii* called *Patriotism or Internationalism*. It was as incisive and as politically prescient as anything she ever wrote, and, given the context of irrational war fever then dominating Britain, it was a bravely independent act on her part. Mary began by stressing the tragic and absurd irony of the whole war:

Each nation is convinced that it is fighting in self-defence, and each in self-defence hastens to self-destruction. The military authorities declare that the defender must be the aggressor, so armies rush to invade neighbouring countries in pure defence of their own hearth and home, and, as each Government assures the world, with no ambition to aggrandise itself. Thousands of men are slaughtered or crippled ... art, industry, social reform, are thrown back and destroyed; and what gain will anyone have in the end?

In all this orgy of blood, what is left of the internationalism which met in congresses, socialist, feminist, pacifist, and boasted of the coming era of peace and amity? The men are fighting; what are the women doing? They are, as is the lot of women, binding up the wounds that men have made.

With her characteristic fierceness and trenchancy, Mary saw that with the First World War,

the world is relapsing into a worse, because a more scientific, barbarism than that from which it sprang. [In this situation] Women must use not only their hands to bind up, they must use their brains to understand the causes of the European frenzy ...

She recognised that the roots of war lie deep in the human psyche, in the need to feel dominant, and in the fear of being dominated:

What is the boasted patriotism which started and supports the European war? First of all, pride. Each Great Power has encouraged national pride at the expense of humanity; each big nation feeds it children on pride in its fancied superiority in intelligence, culture, freedom or tradition. To assert and spread this superiority by force becomes a national ideal ... Pan-Slavism struggles with Pan-Teutonism for dominance in the Balkans. British Imperialism becomes involved, and in the struggle civilization receives a wound. The other element which has precipitated the catastrophe is panic. Each Power, armed to the teeth, its legions ready to swoop down on its neighbours, is terrorised into striking, lest it should itself be struck. Hence no time, or insufficient time, is allowed for negotiations which might have succeeded had passion been allowed to cool. False patriotism relies upon armaments to uphold the national pride: the nations which have been impoverished for half a century in the name of 'defence' hurl their manhood against that of their neighbours, and all are involved in massacre and ruin.[9]

Mary Sheepshanks' conclusion, published in November 1914, makes grim reading:

Armaments must be drastically reduced and abolished, and their place taken by an international police force. Instead of two great Alliances pitted against each other, we must have a true Concert of Europe. Peace must be on generous, unvindictive lines, satisfying legitimate national needs, and leaving no cause for resentment such as to lead to another war. Only so can it be permanent.

Mary was using her brains, but she was also using her practical gifts, for with the first world war, the twentieth century's 'refugee problem' had come into being.

A lot of women arrive here with their little ones from the different countries at war, without anything else than what they wear ... I cannot tell you how immense the misery is now already in my country. (Dr. Aletta Jacobs, first Dutch woman doctor and President of Dutch Women's Suffrage Society to Mary Sheepshanks, September 1914.)

After the fall of Antwerp, another friend, the American Adelaide Stickney, (later Dame Adelaide Livingstone) told Mary that thousands of Belgian refugees had now poured into Holland and that the Dutch could barely feed them. Mary took action. Together with Crystal Macmillan, an Edinburgh barrister and leading Pacifist and Suffragist, she obtained a guarantee of £200 from the Belgian ambassador with which to buy food. The two women went on to the headquarters of Lyons' Catering Empire and bought £200 worth of provisions — hundreds of loaves of bread, cases of condensed milk, chocolate and tinned food. They saw the cases loaded on to lorries and dispatched to the docks. Then she and Miss Macmillan

collected the things necessary for a couple of nights and joined the ship for Flushing. We were the only passengers and the North Sea was as empty of shipping as our boat was of people. We had one qualm when we saw a periscope, but it turned out to be a British submarine.

Flushing was a tragic sight, swarming with refugees. The walls were covered with notices of missing persons, and hundreds of families were sheltering in huge railway sheds, with the arc-lights full on and Dutch soldiers keeping guard. The weather was damp and bitterly cold, and in the big square large tarpaulins were set up to give some shelter.

Standing at the end of a bridge guarded by Dutch soldiers, we could see the German soldiers holding the Belgian end. Hundreds of women and children were on barges, many without warm clothing and often clutching some useless thing such as a bird-cage. That was the first wave of the tragic flood of refugees that has swept across large tracts of the world ever since, involving broken homes [and] broken lives ...

We returned on a ship packed with refugees and the next

day I reported to the Foreign Office. (Mary Sheepshanks, *Autobiography*, ch. 8.)

Mary had crossed the U-boat patrolled North Sea with what was the first food convoy to Flushing. Her fluency in French and German was an asset in interviewing the stricken people there, and on her return Mary did her utmost to agitate for the admission of vast numbers of Belgian refugees into Britain. Together with Dr Elsie Inglis and the Quaker Isabella Ford, she addressed several overflow meetings in the Kingsway Hall:

Miss Sheepshanks, in an admirable speech, gave an appalling account of the burden which Holland is shouldering. In one province, with 300,000 inhabitants, there are 400,000 refugees. In a village with 800 inhabitants, 2,000 refugees. The situation is impossible, and it is clear that the Belgians must either come here or return to Belgium where their sons would be liable to German military service, and their daughters be unsafe. Public opinion in Great Britain should demand their coming here, and should back the demand by large offers of hospitality from municipal authority ...

[Next week] Miss Sheepshanks, whose speech made so deep an impression on her audience, is to speak again, we hope at greater length.[10]

There was also international relief work to be done nearer home. Hundreds of German women now found themselves stranded in Britain. As many as 800 of them had to be escorted by women from neutral countries back across what were now enemy frontiers to Germany, and it was Mary's International Women's Suffrage Office which undertook all the arrangements for the changing railway, steamer, customs and passport regulations each week. Many of the stranded 'enemy aliens' were destitute and totally dependent on what Mary's office could raise for them; others wanted to emigrate to America — and that had to be organised, also by Mary. Her International Women's Relief Committee was simultaneously sending food, clothes, and money to Belgian refugees in Holland, trying to cater for the needs of German civilians now interned in Britain, organising correspondence between Germans in England and their families in Germany, as well as helping German-born wives of British internees and English-born wives of Germans who had either been deported or interned. Repeatedly, Mary appealed for funds — 'especially such as may be used for the relief of distressed Austrian and German women'. (*Ius Suffragii*, 1 January 1915.) It must have brought back memories of her early days as a social worker in the 1890s in Lambeth for once again she found herself helping to take down family case-notes and organising adequate relief. Helping Germans, however, was not a popular cause:

Our relief work has roused the evil spirit of the [popular] Daily Press and I have had to open a special file for 'anonymous abuse'. I am rather pleased, I always wanted to be associated with an unpopular cause. It is all very strenuous and ten hours a day in a crowded office in this heat is uphill work, and one hears the German girls waiting for the money we are giving them, gloating over what will happen when they bring up their big guns! There really are some advantages in being pessimistic, these things are no shock. (Mary Sheepshanks to Bertrand Russell, September 1914.)

That all this stress was putting a great strain on Mary Sheepshanks' abrasive temper and sharp tongue can be seen from a confidential letter sent by the National English Suffrage President, Mrs Fawcett, to Mrs Chapman Catt, National President of the American Women's Suffrage Movement and International President of the International Women's Suffrage Association:

My dear Mrs Catt,
   I think affairs at 7 Adelphi Street are settling down satis-factorily. We are aware of Miss Sheepshanks' strong points and also of her defects as regards office organization ...
   The relations between Mrs Coit [treasurer] and Miss

Sheepshanks have been a good deal strained but have already
improved and I hope will improve still more. A great deal was
due in my opinion to the overcrowded condition of the office
during the great press of relief work. People were running up
against one another; a dozen different pieces of business were
being transacted in the same room at the same time, the
telephone bell was constantly ringing: you can imagine the
result in nervous tension and exasperation. These very trying
conditions are no longer acute owing to the pressure of relief
work having been very largely diminished. I had a long talk
yesterday with Mrs Coit; she fully appreciated Miss
Sheepshanks' strong points and will I am sure loyally
cooperate with her and help her all she can.[11]

In addition to all her international relief work, Mary still
had to edit *Ius Suffragii*. 'I have to do my paper in bed, so to
speak.' To edit a neutral, international (and internationalist) paper in the capital of one of the belligerent nations
during wartime is not a straightforward task, but it was
done. On 1 October, Mary inserted the following notice
concerning what was to be her editorial policy and practice
throughout the war:

Ius Suffragii, like other international organs, finds its present
position difficult. The editorial office being in a belligerent
country, all news from other countries is subject to
censorship, and it has not been possible up to the present to
obtain news except of a very meagre nature. It appears almost
inevitable under the circumstances that news from England,
America, and neutral countries should predominate, and
though, of course, the policy and sympathy of the paper is
and must be entirely international and untainted by national
or partisan bias, it will be difficult to maintain its all-round
character. We appeal earnestly to readers in neutral countries
to furnish news and articles, especially news of women's doing
in Germany and Austria, and if the paper reaches our
German and Austrian subscribers, we appeal to them not to
attribute the dearth of news from their countries to anything
but its true cause, the impossibility of obtaining news.

Four years later as the war was coming to an end amid cries
for vengeance by the victors and feelings of bitter resentment among the defeated, Mary Sheepshanks repeated her
pledge of absolute neutrality:

Notice on the Policy of Ius Suffragii
In the present critical position of affairs, when any reference to
political conditions may hurt national susceptibilities, it must
be clearly stated that the International Woman Suffrage
Alliance maintains a strictly neutral attitude.

Throughout the war Mary consistently published as much
news as possible from the two opposed sides as would
present the human face of the 'enemy' to all women readers
whatever their nationality. She reported the befriending of
French and Russian prisoners of war by German women,
and the German Women's Suffrage Society's thanks to
British women for their help to stranded Germans. In
December 1914, she published a report from Berlin
revealing how a patriotic voluntary social service was now
being organised all over Germany, exactly paralleling that
then being undertaken in Britain by Mrs Fawcett and
Eleanor Rathbone, among others. Family allowances
were being allocated for the German working-class
dependents whose German breadwinner was at the war;
German soup-kitchens, crêches and second-hand clothes
depots were being set up in all poor city districts, and
German Boy Scouts and Girl Guides were making themselves useful as couriers. In effect, Mary was saying to her
British women readers: 'Look at your German selves.' The
resemblances in tireless self-sacrifice would have been
comic had they not been so terribly sad. In that same
number, December 1914, Mary also published a trans-
lation of the German socialist leader, Clara Zetkin's attack
on militaristic German chauvinism — as evidence that not
all Germans worshipped 'Prussianism'. She also
published, both in English and in German, a declaration
from leading German woman suffragists containing 'warm

and hearty greetings in these wretched bloody times — for true humanity knows no nationalist hatred.'

In January 1915, Mary published an open Christmas letter to the women of Germany and Austria, signed by 100 British women pacifists. The signatories included Emily Hobhouse, Margaret Bondfield, Maude Royden, Margaret Llewelyn Davies, Sylvia Pankhurst, Eva Gore Booth, Dr Marion Philips, Clara Moser and several Quakers. The letter ran:

Sisters,
    Some of us wish to send you a word at this sad Christmastide, though we can but speak through the Press ... those of us who wished and still wish for peace may surely offer a solemn greeting to such of you as feel as we do. Do not let us forget our very anguish unites us, that we are passing together through the same experiences of pain and grief ...
    We pray you to believe that come what may we hold to our faith in Peace and Goodwill between nations; while technically at enmity in obedience to our rulers, we owe allegiance to that higher law which bids us live at peace with all men ...
    Do you not feel with us that the vast slaughter in our opposing armies is a stain on civilisation and Christianity? ...
    As we saw in South Africa and the Balkan States, the brunt of modern war falls upon non-combatants, and the conscience of the world cannot bear the sight ...
    Relief, however colossal, can reach but few. Can we sit still and let the helpless die in their thousands, as die they *must* — unless we rouse ourselves in the name of Humanity to save them? There is but one way to do this. We must all urge that peace be made ...
    We are yours in this sisterhood of sorrow.

In all these ways Mary Sheepshanks' editorship of *Ius Suffragii* was neutral as regards apportioning praise or blame to the combatants, but it was quite the opposite of neutral as regards the wicked lunacy of the Great War itself. To illustrate this, she also printed articles such as Romain

Rolland's 'Our Friend the Enemy' and 'The Immortal Antigone', or C.K. Ogden's 'Militarism versus Feminism' and several contributors' detailed proposals for a Permanent Peace Settlement. Some of her readers, at least, were grateful:

We in Denmark are very much satisfied with the good work you are doing in London. We feel proud of you.

It is always a joy now to receive *Ius Suffragii* . . . Special thanks are due to the Editor, who . . . has avoided [everything] that could in any way hurt the feelings of women in the belligerent countries. (Else Luders, Berlin.)

Ius Suffragii was never so useful as now to the Suffragists of all countries as a medium of intercommunication. (*Irish Citizen.*)

It could not have been done better in a neutral country. (Signe Berman, Sweden.)

But there were others who thought rather differently of Mary Sheepshanks' reports to and from Germany via neutral intermediaries throughout the war — even though all these reports had been subjected to the censors of both sides. In 1916, a dinner was held at the Lyceum Club to celebrate the promise made by the British government to give the vote to women. Mary read out to the guests a telegram of congratulations she had received on the occasion from German women suffragists. A few days later she was banned from the Lyceum Club and a letter appeared in the press from the Club Committee declaring that henceforth she was to be a prohibited visitor there. After the war, the chairman of the Lyceum Club offered to reinstate Mary on receiving her apology. Mary replied that she had nothing to apologise for. Much worse than that public obloquy was a deep personal hurt. Mary's brother, John, the next one down from her in age, heard while he was away at the Front of the Lyceum Club's action against Mary for 'treason' — 'and he never saw or spoke to me again'. (Mary Sheepshanks, *Autobiography*, ch. 8.) Another great grief was the death in action of her second-to-youngest brother, William, a gentle, gifted boy of whom Mary had been very fond.[12]

Meanwhile, for all the rhetoric about the shared internationalist idealism to be found among feminists, there was now growing dissension among British women suffragists on the issue of the war. Before August 1914, most of these women had thought of themselves as feminists *and* pacifists, as pacifist *because* feminist, for was not feminism rooted in the rejection of the rule of force by physically more powerful males? But now, just a few months after the war was under way, they were forced to realise that they would have to choose between their feminism and their pacifism. The whole of Britain was aflame with militant patriotism. If leading feminists were now to identify themselves publicly as *un*-patriotic, Peace-At-Any-Pricers, they would, so it was argued by Mrs Fawcett and the rank and file, sink the cause of women's suffrage in Britain for generations.[13] Mrs Fawcett believed that the pacifists among the feminists were both mistaken in themselves — though genuine idealists — and that their beliefs and actions would prove fatally counter-productive to the cause of British feminism.[14] A break had to come, as the pacifists for their part became more and more convinced that the absolute priority was to end the war as soon as possible and in such a way as to prevent there being any pretext for fighting a second World War. The 'Peace issue' had to take precedence for them over both the feminist and the patriotic issues. 'Mary Sheepshanks was a pacifist first and a feminist second.'[15] It was another instance of her subordination of her feminism to her humanism.

This polarisation of views finally came to a head over the issue of an International Women's Conference. The next International Women's Suffrage Association Conference had been scheduled to take place in 1915, in Berlin. Clearly that was now out of the question. But should there still be an IWSA Conference in some neutral country, its emphasis being on what women could do to end the war in a just, negotiated peace? That proposal was put forward by Crystal Macmillan[16] and circulated to all the officers and national presidents of the IWSA, urging them to press their International President, Mrs Carrie Catt, to call such a Congress next April. Mrs Fawcett was appalled. She wrote to Mrs Catt:

Private

15th December 1914

I am strongly opposed to the above proposal, mainly for the reason that women are as subject as men are to national pre-possessions and susceptibilities and it would hardly be possible to bring together the women of the belligerent countries without violent outbursts of anger and mutual recriminations. We should then run the risk of the scandal of a *Peace* Congress disturbed and perhaps broken up by violent quarrels and fierce denunciations. It is true this often takes place at Socialist and other international meetings: but it is of less importance there: no one expects the general run of men to be anything but fighters. But a *Peace Congress of Women* dissolved by violent quarrels would be the laughing stock of the world ...

When Miss Sheepshanks was in Holland Aletta Jacobs told her she had heard recently from Elsa Luders who had complacently remarked how much for the welfare of the world the victory of Germany would prove because it would enable Germany to impose her culture upon all the other nations of the world. Aletta Jacobs was furious: here you have an example of the sort of thing that might happen during every day and hour of the proposed international congress ...

I feel so strongly against the proposed convention that I would decline to attend it, and if necessary would resign my office in the I.W.S.A. [she was Vice-President] if it were judged incumbent on me in that capacity to take part in the convention.

This is not at all a nice Christmas letter but you know dear

Mrs Catt how cordially and affectionately I think of you and
rely upon your leadership.

Always yours affectionately,
M.G. Fawcett

No official IWSA Conference was called, but leading
British pacifist/feminists went ahead instead to support the
Hungarian Roszika Schwimmer's efforts to get together an
American delegation to attend an International Women's
Peace congress now being mooted by neutral Dutch
women, who had offered to host it at The Hague. Mrs
Fawcett was still adamantly opposed. At the first Council
meeting of the National Union of Women's Suffrage
Societies early in February 1915, the first to be held since
the war, Mrs Fawcett declared that until the German
armies had been driven out of France and Belgium 'I
believe it is akin to treason to talk of peace.' She sat down to
thunderous applause. It was the turn of the pacifists among
the leadership of the women's movement to be appalled.
After a stormy executive meeting in Buxton all the officers
of the National Union (except the Treasurer) and ten
members of the National Executive resigned. Late in
February, some of these women — Crystal Macmillan,
Kathleen Courtney, Emily Leaf and Catherine Marshall,[17]
called a meeting at the Caxton Hall to urge British support
for the Women's Peace Congress at The Hague.[18]

By mid-April a list had been drawn up of 180 British
women anxious to attend this Congress. It included Mary
Sheepshanks. But the government promptly objected to
'the holding of so large a meeting of a political character so
close to the seat of war.'[19] After much negotiation with Mr
Mckenna, the Home Secretary, and the Cabinet, the
Cabinet decided that only twenty-four out of the 180
women would be issued with passports and permits. Again
Mary Sheepshanks was one of the twenty-four nominees.
But Winston Churchill at the Admiralty thought differ-
ently from the Cabinet. He 'closed' the North Sea to British

shipping for the whole period of the Congress to prevent, as he thought, any British women from attending. Mary Sheepshanks, Maude Royden, Margaret Bondfield, Catherine Marshall and Mrs Philip Snowden were among those prevented from going. They 'waited at an hotel facing the Thames at Tilbury, watching the steamer on which their passages were booked lying at anchor. They waited in vain.' (Mary Sheepshanks, *Autobiography*, ch. 8.) However, Crystal Macmillan and Kathleen Courtney were already at The Hague, and Mrs Pethick Lawrence came over with Jane Addams and the American contingent.

Jane Addams had had no illusions about the possible futility, absurdity and even harmfulness of an international women's Peace Conference:

The undertaking, of course, offers many possibilities of failure; indeed it may even do harm ... but it seems to me to be genuine. I think, too, that women who are willing to fail may be able to break through that curious hypnotic spell which makes it impossible for any of the nations to consider peace ...[20]

The press, predictably, had a field day about what fools all these women were to tackle problems which even men could not solve: 'Blundering Englishwomen', 'Folly in Petticoats', 'These feminine busybodies', 'Pro-Hun Peacettes', 'This amiable chatter of a bevy of well-meaning ladies', so ran the headlines before the Congress. But in the event it was not just 'amiable chatter'. The women's speeches at The Hague, advocating continuous mediation by neutral powers, national self-determination, open diplomacy and disarmament, were rather the voice of latter-day Cassandras, doomed to prophesy truths no men would believe, let alone act upon. And their hard-headed, well-thought-out resolutions that covered the non-annexation of territory by force, the institution of inter-national bodies for arbitration and conciliation, (modelled on the International Court of Justice at The Hague), their proposals for disarmament involving the abolition of all private arms manufacture, and their advocacy of new (and more just) rules for international trade and economic co-operation — were to supply Woodrow Wilson with the basis of his Fourteen Points, just three years later.[21]

Finally, the Women's Peace Congress voted to send Jane Addams and Dr Aletta Jacobs as their official deputation to all the war capitals of the world.[22] Their brief was to request each government to declare its war aims in May 1915, with a view to ending the war by negotiation rather than by continuing with the competition in massacre. All the foreign ministers listened politely to Jane Addams' reasoned plea and then ignored it, insisting instead that they had no alternative but to continue on their way — that way which was to take so many men to the Somme, Verdun and Passchendaele.

When Jane Addams reached the London stage of her unsuccessful mission, Mary Sheepshanks invited her to dinner at No 1, Barton Street, to meet Bertrand Russell and Goldsworthy Lowes Dickinson. Mary later heard from Jane Addams how she had been received in Germany, Austria, Hungary, Italy and France — worst in France, where she was followed everywhere by the police. 'Delcassé frankly Jingo. No negotiation, even the best. Destroy Germany so that she will not come up for 100 years.'[23]

After The Hague Congress, the rupture between the 'pacifists' and the 'patriots' within the British Women's Suffrage Movement became irreparable. At the June 1915 elections not one of the resigning pacifist members of the National Executive was re-elected, whereas every one of Mrs Fawcett's supporters was elected in their stead. And in 1916, Mr Asquith at last committed himself to promising British women the vote. In the immediate term, Mrs Fawcett's political judgement, her realism as opposed to her opponents' idealism, would seem to have been completely vindicated. But in the long term, that new age of 'a worse because a more scientific barbarism' which had been prophesied by Mary Sheepshanks in 1914, did indeed come to pass and it was much much worse than even she had foreseen: the gas ovens of Belsen; the systematic starvation of Leningrad; the fire-storm bombing of Dresden; the devastation of Shanghai; the reducing of Hiroshima to a radioactive inferno; the chemical poisoning of tracts of Vietnam; the plastic fragmentation pellets, the napalm, the Neutron bomb, and the promised end of all the world through computer-controlled nuclear incineration from pilotless rockets in outer space — all this followed on from August 1914.

But in 1915 it was still possible to hope that humans would learn from the horror of a 'total' war. And so Mary Sheepshanks concentrated increasingly on the problems of post-war reconstruction. She worked (as did Bertrand Russell) for the Union for Democratic Control [of Foreign Policy], which concentrated on how to end World War One in such a way that it should not breed a subsequent war.[24] In this connection Mary whole-heartedly endorsed Vernon Lee's masterly and prophetic pamphlet *Peace With Honour* [25] published by the UDC in 1915:

We must ask ourselves whether [Germany] would be more likely to be cowed into submission or exasperated into revenge by ... measures of repression? This is a question of psychology. And psychology is merely the study of human nature by means of observation of our own thoughts and feelings ... How should we feel and behave if a victor ... tried to crush us? Would we not use all the resources of a stimulated birth-rate, of improved intellectual and industrial training, in defying or circumventing the restrictions placed upon us? ... Should we spare any sacrifice, any intrigue, to attain freedom and revenge? ... A humiliated, insecure, or hemmed-in Germany would probably mean a Germany arming once more for a Leipzig after a Jena.

In June 1916 Mary wrote an editorial for *Ius Suffragii* defining what she meant by positive internationalism, called 'Is Internationalism Dead?':

Internationalism is the feeling and belief that humanity is a stronger bond than mere racial and political boundaries ... and that co-operation should be [our] object and motive, not destruction. What is the alternative to this gospel of peaceful development, mutual help and fruitful intercourse? The alternative is race hatred and national jealousy, leading to tariffs, militarism, armaments, crushing taxation, mutual butchery and the ruin of all progress ... Internationalism is not dead; it remains an ideal worthy of our devotion as ever, and waiting for the fumes to clear from men's brains for them to recognize it as the only escape from barbarism ... Just as surely as 'no man liveth to himself', no country can now live to itself; co-operation is the law of life.

Mary's life was not totally consumed by public affairs, however, even during the First World War, for it was at this time that she met her closest woman friend, Margaret Bryant,[26] possibly the only friend with whom she was able to sustain a close, unbroken relationship until death. Mary's tribute to her is characteristically high-minded and reticent:

Margaret had a very good brain and a warm and tender heart. I also heard her described as having a noble face, and I think the word noble fitted her character. She was incapable of an unworthy thought; and ever since I knew her I have mentally used her as a standard below which I do not wish to fall, though in practice I do. She became my greatest friend, and I owe her more than I can say. (Mary Sheepshanks, *Autobiography*, ch. 8.)

We must believe Mary's declaration that Margaret Bryant became her greatest friend; we know nothing more.

In March 1917, came the news of the first Russian Revolution. Mary, like so many others, hailed it as a second, greater, Fall of the Bastille:

Women Suffragists all over the world will welcome the liberation of the hundreds of millions of inhabitants of that vast empire ... Freedom of speech, of religion, of the Press, of public meeting; freedom to work or abstain from working; freedom for nationality.[27]

As a pacifist, Mary rejoiced in the apparent bloodlessness of the first Russian Revolution and its prompt decision to abolish capital punishment. But she was too canny, politically, to be totally sanguine: 'At present everything is in the melting-pot, and who knows what may emerge from the mighty cauldron?' In answer to her urgent enquiries, the Russian women's leader Dr Schishkin-Javein, sent her a telegram: 'Women excluded from liberties proclaimed; we demand, we protest, we demonstrate.' The 1 November 1917 number of *Ius Suffragii* carried a stirring four-page special report on how the All-Russian League of Women's Enfranchisement had organised a 40,000-strong women's demonstration in Petrograd on 19 March, standing in the cold and wet, immovable, until they had obtained from the new government a 'Yes' or 'No' to their demands:

Women also have filled the prisons, and boldly marched to the gallows ... We have come to tell you that the Russian woman demands for herself the human rights to which she is entitled as a human being.

They were given the answer 'Yes'.

In the period of euphoria, several meetings were held at Mary's house 'to plan a social club for Labour. Eventually it took shape and was established in Gerrard St. Soho.' (Mary Sheepshanks, *Autobiography*, ch. 8.) It was a lively place, the 1917 Club, hosting every possible shade of left-wing opinion, as well as arty Bohemians and eccentrics, and inspiring the memorable, if inaccurate, verse:

In nineteen seventeen they founded a club,
Partly as brothel and partly as pub.
The members were all of them horrible bores,
Except for the girl in Giotto-pink drawers.[28]

But the 1917 Club survived longer than did the libertarian revolution that had inspired it. Already by March 1918 there was an ominous clamp down on all Russian reports to *Ius Suffragii*. And when the brief German Revolution of January 1919 took place, bringing with it the suffrage for all German women over twenty, Mary Sheepshanks wrote:

Our joy ... is only moderated by uncertainty ... until a really stable government is established. We cannot but remember that the Russian Revolution in its early days also promised universal suffrage, but subsequent events have at least deferred its exercise.

Soon after the end of the First World War, and now that the vote had been won in North America, Scandinavia, Britain, Germany and much of Eastern Europe, Mary decided to resign from the editorship of *Ius Suffragii*, in order to do something more urgent and practical in response to the post-war hunger and desolation. But even before her resignation was announced, tributes were paid to Mary's stalwart internationalism during the war. Jessie McKay wrote to *Ius Suffragii* from New Zealand:

What has been the abiding bow of promise on four years of cloud and storm? Not creed, not art, not science, not Socialism — all these have failed. But the thin gold link of our International Suffrage Press has held us all together in one high sisterhood — British, Germans, French, Hungarians, Latins, Slavs, and Teutons.[29]

And, as Harriet Newcomb, Secretary of the British Dominions' Women Citizens' Union testified, Mary's was 'a unique achievement, and only possible to one to whom was given spiritual vision.' Miss Newcomb added:

During the terrible years of war Miss Sheepshanks ... held the women of the whole world *au-dessus de la mêlée*, united on matters which are above material warfare. It [was] a magnificent contribution towards constructive peace.

Even though most of the women of the world had been no more *au dessus de la mêlée* than the men, it was still impressive that tributes should come to Mary's fair-mindedness in

1919 from the United States, Sweden, Italy, Germany, South Africa, Denmark and Austria as well as from the British Women's Freedom League. The editor of the French edition of *Ius Suffragii* spoke for them all:

It was certainly under most difficult circumstances that Miss Sheepshanks so ably directed *Ius Suffragii* during the war. When communications were more or less cut, when suffragists of various countries were necessarily employed in activities other than woman suffrage, and when the international reports were 'burning' on several points, Miss Sheepshanks, with marvellous generosity and tact, to which everyone pays homage, knew how to maintain the only possible link between the countries affiliated to our Alliance; how to give the news of each country to the other feminists who were working with the same object in view, and in this way to throw a ray of light into the darkness of even the darkest days.

10

FLORA MAYOR DURING
THE FIRST WORLD WAR,
1914–1918

Flora's war could not have been more different from Mary's. Never were the two women further apart in spirit, although, surprisingly, they continued to write and to visit. From one point of view it was clearly Mary who was more at the centre of affairs — reporting back to the Foreign Office about the plight of Belgian refugees and editing her internationalist women's paper in London. But from another point of view it was Flora Mayor, stuck away in a boys' public school boarding house for most of the war, who was more closely in touch with the mainstream of English opinion at this period. For the school in question was Clifton College, cradle of officers in the Royal Artillery and Engineers, and of Field-Marshal Haig himself. The ethos of Clifton was as unquestioningly patriotic and military-minded — even jingoistic — as that of Mary Sheepshanks' circle was internationalist and pacifist.[1] Although Flora did feel somewhat alone and apart at Clifton, the pressure on her to acquiesce in Clifton's patriotic war spirit was too overwhelming to be withstood:

The bad news makes me feel very low, and I am still *very* unhappy about the bad recruiting. I think the English *really* are deteriorating and then wretched sports going on, and the papers clamouring about the Censorship ... We all felt very dismal the general retreat day, but of course middle-aged people have great control and we all made jokes ... I went to see some good reproductions of Raemeckers yesterday in Bristol. There was such a beautiful one of Christ being mocked at by the German soldiers, the face had just the Old Master dignity. (Flora to Alice, 1915 and 1916)

Other letters of hers refer scornfully to 'the Bertrand Russell gang' and wish that 'the Lytton Strachey set' were being sent to the trenches rather than better men. More than by anything else in the war, Flora declared herself upset by the fall of the Tsar. And while most of her views coincided with those of the vast majority of Britons during the First World War, where she did differ, both from pacifists like Mary Sheepshanks and from the rest of England, was in the relative unimportance of the war to her. Insofar as she did think about it at all, she endorsed the conventional patriotic attitude, but she did not think about it very much — in spite of living in a school community of men and boys who were suffering a 66 per cent casualty rate.[2]

What Flora *was* deeply concerned about, between 1915 and 1919, was a quite different, smaller war that was raging within Watson's House, Clifton College, where in January 1916, Henry Mayor had been appointed Housemaster, and where Flora and Alice had to take turns as surrogate Housemaster's wife. It would be as tedious as it would be impossible to chart an accurate historical account of all the shifting *casi belli*, the alliances, the reciprocal accusations of dereliction of duty, the skirmishes, the casualties, the strategic retreats and major victories over disputed territory within Watson's between 1916 and 1919. The deeply upset, involuntary disputants included Henry, Flora, Alice, the chaplain, the house-tutor, the matron, the cook, six maids, one butler and forty-five public schoolboys, aged thirteen to seventeen. In addition, of course, the boys' parents and the rest of Clifton College were all-too-interested bystanders. Everyone wanted to do their best for the House at this grim time, but everybody's lights dictated different signals, and the result was pitiful. The long-established homely Matron of Watson's was dismissed by Flora immediately on Henry's appointment, causing many of the boys to feel bereft and indignant; the new staff brought in by the Mayors were regarded by the older boys as 'intruders'. The new Matron was inclined to have tête-à-têtes with senior boys in her room until midnight, so she also had to be dismissed although, after a tearful pleading, she was temporarily reinstated by Flora. The new cook's efforts, never good, became increasingly awful as war-rationing grew worse. The house-tutor showed that he was quite unfitted to be a boys' schoolmaster, and he too had to be asked to leave. And there was even something of a cabal against Henry Mayor himself, led by his resentful — and much more charismatic — predecessor as Housemaster at Watson's. And all the time the casualty lists from that other war across the Channel were growing longer:

July 1916 — 250 Old Cliftonians killed ...
July 1917 — 365 dead — one in eight of those serving.
December 1918 — 530 dead. (*The Cliftonian*.)

Under the stress of this multiple bereavement and the strain of the continuous conflicts within Watson's, Henry Mayor finally suffered a nervous breakdown.

Meanwhile, Flora and Alice, in trying to help their brother, contributed to his distress — and he to theirs. Flora, in particular, was hopelessly miscast. There was she, at the age of forty-four, the author of *The Third Miss Symons*, hailed as following in the steps of Jane Austen and Mrs Gaskell, now having to allocate beds in a schoolboys' dormitory and make unpopular decisions about their jam ration. Henry's reserve had, if possible, deepened over the years and Flora could never feel that she was in his confidence. Flora and Alice alternated at Clifton, month by month, so continuity as well as inter-communication was lacking. Only one master confided in Flora — and he was the very one whom she was the first to realise had to be asked to leave. From Flora's perspective, she and Alice were pearls cast before Clifton's youthful swine — 'I think eternal boy at dinner a strain.' (July 1916.) But from the boys' point for view, Flora, and to a lesser extent, Alice, were a menace — haughty, interfering and needing to be 'pulled down a peg' by the fee-paying young gentlemen. They were nicknamed 'Flora and Fauna' by the boys, who waxed merry at their difficulty in telling the middle-aged twin sisters apart. The senior boys would tell Flora tall stories at mealtimes and they would stonewall any scheme she might have for introducing drama or glee-singing — 'the thought of Flora in control is rather terrible and she had arranged the details without consulting the Sixth.'[3] The boys even practised crude practical jokes on Alice, of whom they were less afraid, sending her to Coventry, and putting mustard on her chair.

Not surprisingly, both Flora and Alice came to loathe their tours of duty at Clifton — it was 'the kind of thankless worry which makes one earn one's keep.' And the rows themselves were quite horrid. After her attempted dismissal of the second Matron, Flora wrote to Alice: 'I feel pretty cold and shaky you may be sure.' There was no question of 'popularity' or of 'comps' now; instead there was criticism, resentment, snubs and unfriendliness on every side. 'I have asked four men to supper and have got *four* refusals. This is depressing me.' (Flora to Alice, c. 1919.)

I am rather *intriguée* at the thought that we are not liked in Clifton. I should have thought we should have been *worshipped*. I think I was very popular in the old days. Has one got more angular and laying down the law? (Flora to Alice, 1918.)

Whenever one of the sisters was having her time away from Clifton she would be suffering in spirit with her twin. At one bad time Flora wrote to Clifton-bound Alice:

Oh that I was with you. At any rate it would be *two* criminals. I shall never forgive Clifton for this, whatever forgiveness I may extend to individuals. I still feel very weary. I hope you keep no horridness from me ... All the obstinacy in my nature revolts at giving up the House as a failure either on our part or Henry's ... but of course Henry is to blame together with the Matron and the House Tutor for bad discipline in the House.

Our failure is *so* hard and so undeserved.

Oh you have had a time and still have. What I want someone to proclaim *loudly* is that we have all behaved like Christian stars and that if you lost your temper you had *ample provocation* ... What persecution we're enduring. What I want is some *eloquence* — I want hot warm sympathy. My darling I do feel for you. I quite dread getting your letters ... When I had my *affaires* [period] on I had a wave of fury against the whole damned lot of them. (1919.)

At another bad time Alice wrote to Clifton-bound Flora:

Stuff about the games and the food — they're getting more not less. I do feel it very much for you. I thank God, oh how I do, I'm out of it, but I'm truly in it with you. What hateful places Public Schools are. I don't see where we need blame ourselves, if anyone more me — but if that good wasn't good enow I don't know what's wanted ... Only three weeks more of those boys. (1919.)

Once again, as in that other failure of her stage days, which she had also been obstinately reluctant to acknowledge as failure, Flora had to soothe her pride by telling herself and Alice that those who would succeed where they had failed would have to be thoroughly inferior sorts of people:

I agree with you that the House-master had better be rather commonplace, and not too high a standard intellectually or morally. This also applies to the House-master's ladies ... Most of the Newnhamy people I know would have felt it rather a degrading position. (Flora to Alice, 1919.)

More sympathetically, her novelist's ear and eye did take in much of the psychological interest within the boarding-school world:

It was rather pathetic — I asked the fags what time they liked

best in the week — they said *bed*. ... It strikes me that the
masters, even people like Henry, are very afraid of the boys.
... If ever a friend wanted someone speaking clear and loud in
his defence, it is Henry, ill and strained. But it requires moral
courage — and apparently none of these men have got that.
... I said I felt the power of strong love was the greatest thing
in the world and he must not wish he had not got it. I do
think it is a pity friendship is not encouraged when the other
thing [homosexuality] is rightly discouraged in the school.
(Flora to Alice, 1916 and 1918.)

But despite all these insights, Flora Mayor never wrote
about life in a boys' school. Nor did she write much while at
the school — 'I don't like writing here ... it's most dis-
integrating intellectually — I should have no powers of
concentration left if I led this life long.' After four years of
'this life' Flora left Clifton for good. Henry had been
relieved of his Housemastership temporarily on account of
his breakdown and the two sisters thankfully left Watson's
at the same time. But thankfulness was tempered by the
pain of her realisation that she would not be missed. Un-
cannily, Flora was acting out precisely what she herself had
written about her own Henrietta Symons ten years earlier:

When she went away, there were kind wishes for her
prosperity, interest in her plans, many hopes that she would
visit them, but no regret; with a clearness and honesty of sight
she unfortunately possessed she realized that — no regret.

    What was the use of [four] years in which she had sincerely
tried to do her best, if she had not built up some little
memorial of affection? ... there is not much consolation when
one fails where it seems quite easy for others to succeed.[4]

Perhaps Flora would have succeeded better at Clifton
had she felt more affection for the boys, but that was not
possible. All the unfavourable circumstances surrounding
Henry's wartime period of Housemastership ensured that
the boys themselves had started out by being set against
Flora out of loyalty to their old order — and Flora could

never like those who did not make the first overtures by appreciating her.

There were two other events in Flora's life at this period, both connected with the Mayor family, which contributed to Flora's dangerously lowered sense of self-esteem. First, her elder brother, Robin, had quite suddenly fallen very deeply in love with a woman seventeen years younger than he, Beatrice Meinertzhagen, one of the nieces of Beatrice Webb. In 1913 they married and by 1919 they had three children. Flora tried loyally to affirm Robin's marriage but, in fact, it came to her as a severe blow. Just two years before, in 1911, Robin and Flora had set up house together in Campden Hill Square in London — Alice having happily agreed to take Flora's place with Henry. And Flora had much preferred her London life with Robin to sharing the school-dominated life of Henry at Clifton — even before the latter's Housemastership. When Robin married and Beatrice moved in to Campden Hill Square, Flora moved back to her parents at Queensgate House and thus lost what she felt was the first truly independent, congenial home she had ever had. The situation was further aggravated for Flora by Beatrice's beauty and talent. Not only was she much younger and more attractive than Flora but her family background was more dashing and artistic as well as a good deal wealthier. Beatrice proceeded to have several children, and to write poetry and plays, and to suffer from serious health problems causing much anxiety within the family. Flora could not help feeling outshone in every way — she was not even the interestingly ill one. There was no hint of open friction, of course — they were all far too civilised and much too anxious to preserve family harmony for that. But there was a constant undercurrent of defensive, jealous judging of Beatrice by Flora and Alice, which Flora at least, would occasionally have to check in shame.

The other family event was the last illness of Flora's father. By 1916, the Rev. Dr Joseph Mayor was eighty-eight and had outlived all his eleven brothers and sisters but one.

Flora and Alice agreed that Flora's health simply could not cope with the demands of nursing two very old parents, the one dying, the other dreading her husband's death. Nevertheless, Flora felt ever afterwards that she had let Alice down at this time of crisis in permitting her to shoulder it all ('I feel I have funked it too much ... I shall *always* feel that I am not brave or to be relied on in an emergency.')

There are no details extant revealing Flora Mayor's writing routine at this or any other period of her life. Her daily bulletins to Alice mention everything except her writing — conversations with friends, visits paid and received, servants, illness, books read and family concerns. One can only deduce that her writing was fitted in whenever all these other daily preoccupations at Clifton, or Campden Hill Square or Queensgate House allowed. As we have seen, she could not concentrate enough to write in the jangled atmosphere of Watson's at all.[5] The Mayor family did take Flora's writing seriously; Robin, Henry and Alice all read and discussed her work in manuscript and used whatever contacts or influence they had to help her win recognition, though she commented once to Alice: 'No one has been as snubbed by publishers as I have been'. Much of what Flora wrote did not satisfy her; she would cross it out or leave it unfinished. But there was one story she wrote at this time which she did finish and which has some lasting interest. *Miss Browne's Friend — A Story of Two Women*, published in the *Free Church Suffrage Times* in serial form in June, July and August 1914, and (the delay caused by the outbreak of the war) finally, in March 1915.

Miss Browne's friend was a prostitute and prostitution was the one subject on which all feminists were united: they wanted to see it abolished. Male writers were not so sure In male fiction prostitutes were treated with fascinated horror or else with sentimental wish-fulfilment. But Flora Mayor's treatment of her prostitute, Mabel Roberts, is as original as her treatment of that other outcast, the emotionally starved, respectable spinster, Henrietta Symons. For once again Flora Mayor treads between cruelty and sentimentality, refusing either to dehumanise or to idealise her subject.

Miss Browne, a gentle, cultivated suburban lady, adopts Mabel Roberts from a Rescue Home in order to befriend her on her re-emergence into the respectable world outside:

'They are so solitary, poor lassies,' said the article, with ... bright pathos ... 'not a soul to care for them. Who will take them by the hand?'

The story then explores all that is involved in 'caring for' Mabel. But in doing that it probes further. Just what do we mean when we talk about 'caring' for someone? In what sense does Miss Browne 'care'? Does Mabel ever 'care' for her — or is the title wholly ironic? Is it the gruff, unglamorous Florrie, Mabel's mate in the Rescue Home, who really cares most deeply and effectively both for Mabel and for Miss Browne?

Part of the strength of the story comes from Flora Mayor's explicit acknowledgement that one ingredient in Miss Browne's heroic perseverance in caring for Mabel — and it is heroic — is her romantic attraction to the girl. Miss Browne falls in love with Mabel at first sight, instantly idealising her in a somewhat novelettish fashion and soon growing to feel more and more committed to her. It is a convincing inversion of the stereotype situation that it should prove to be the lady who is awed by and even deferential to the much greater beauty (and sexual experience) of the young prostitute, rather than the prostitute who is awed by her first encounter with the lady. Miss Browne grows ever more involved with Mabel, the girl's letters giving her 'more pleasure than she realized.' But Miss Browne's response has to be tested time and again over the next eighteen months as Mabel either leaves or is asked to leave 'place' after 'place'. Finally, in the climactic scene in an ABC tea-room, Miss Browne has to force herself, loudly and publicly, to plead with Mabel, despite the intimidating presence of Lena, who has got Mabel back on the game:

'I want you to give up this life, Mabel. Do, do, *do* give it up, dear. Lena, don't persuade her to stay!'

But Mabel is not to be rescued. And when Miss Browne learns from the Madam herself how Mabel and Lena had 'had a hearty laugh' about her, in anguish she gives up Mabel's place in her heart. 'She had not even been able to make Mabel care for her.' Once Miss Browne is convinced that Mabel does not care a button for her, has never, in fact, cared a button, although she still visits Mabel, ill in the workhouse infirmary, 'in her heart she felt repulsion to Mabel ... she was glad when the kiss was done.'

We never see inside Mabel. Flora Mayor wants us to be almost as much in the dark about her as Miss Browne had been. Ingratiating, manipulative, disloyal, a compulsive liar and a 'stirrer' wherever she goes, whether at the Rescue Home or in service or, finally, in the infirmary, Mabel would seem to have no redeeming quality at all — unlike her working-class friend Florrie. Prostitution has so corrupted Mabel that she now automatically sets out to seduce whomsoever comes her way. She is even prostituting herself to Miss Browne, selling her what she thinks will be a 'nice' Mabel and thereby extracting another five shillings. Behind this psychological sordidness and all the physical squalor of the 'poor, tattered openwork stockings, lacy petticoat, transparent blouse, and underclothes all over dirty bows', the crucial question remains both for Miss Browne and for Flora Mayor: does any trace of authentic feeling remain in Mabel at all? For what Flora Mayor means by the redemption of the soul — as in her *The Third Miss Symons* — is the survival of the heart. In all Mabel's chameleon changes there is one thread of consistent response. Whenever Miss Browne caresses her Mabel is, for a moment or two, genuinely moved. It is only when Miss Browne 'suddenly put her hand imploringly on her shoulder' in the ABC cafe that Mabel turns round, 'her eyes swimming in tears.' Flora Mayor never sentimental-ises Mabel, but neither does she put her beyond the pale of feeling altogether, making out, as Miss Browne's art student sister airily does, that 'those girls like that sort of life.'

Flora sent the story to John Masefield for his comments, he having been so deeply impressed by *The Third Miss Symons*. On 25 January he wrote to her, praising the story but wanting it to be expanded by incidents showing 'those sides in Mabel which wanted and attracted men. You are a shade too discreet about that. It was the vital point for Mabel.' Then in December 1915, Masefield wrote to Flora Mayor again, returning a new, much-expanded version of *Miss Browne's Friend* (which has since disappeared without trace). He was still not satisfied about

what it was that Mabel found in men, whether she really liked them and could not resist them, or whether she simply did not care what she did when sufficiently lonely ... and the matter is important, for it concerned Mabel's heart.

Nevertheless, Masefield thought the story 'brilliant'. It is revealing that Masefield should have been so curious about Mabel's feelings for men, or lack of them, whereas what Flora Mayor is clearly concerned with is Mabel's feelings, or lack of them, for Miss Browne. Flora's own subtitle for the story, after all, was *A Tale of Two Women*.

How can one possibly 'connect' Flora Mayor's pre-occupation with that most inward of all dramas, the survival or extinction of an individual's capacity to feel, between 1914 and 1916, with the mass-murdering shambles of the Great War? War would seem to be the obverse of the human capacity to care. And yet it too is a perverted offshoot of caring since it is in 'the defence of our loved ones' that every war is declared. However much as a citizen Flora acquiesced in the conventional patriotic acceptance of the Great War, in her private life, and as an imaginative writer, Flora Mayor was in her own way quite as much concerned with how to keep alive the human bond between people as was the pacifist Mary Sheepshanks in her relief work for refugees or her editing of *Ius Suffragii.* And the personal conflicts within Watson's House taught Flora Mayor all that she needed to know about the horror ensuing when relationships break down.

Personal relationships were all in all to Flora Mayor both in her life and in her writing. When those relationships became bedevilled as they did during the conflict-ridden years in Watson's House, 1916-1919, she could hardly write at all. Towards the end of the war, however, something occurred in her personal circle that was to be very fruitful in her writing. In 1917 Mary Walton died. It was Mary Walton who had once said that if ever she had had children she would have wished them to have been like Alice and Flora, and who had written after Ernest Shepherd's death how gladly she herself would have died instead of him, for Flora's sake. And it was of Mary Walton that Flora had written c. 1910, 'I always do feel the stagnation here, and I do feel very much the sadness of Mary's wasted powers.' Flora brooded for months on Mary Walton's life of apparent unfulfilment in the obscurity of Little Shelford, Cambridgeshire. The many years of her caring for elderly, infirm and querulous relatives, her unconsummated love for the local rector, and his for her, that had to be channelled into decorous, neighbourly affection, the passing seasons of dedicated, creative gardening — and Mary Watson's occasional flash of near-rebellion:

I do long to see you both, and hear everything about your foreign visit and have a good talk, but I don't think I shall ever be free to do anything until I am too old to care. (Mary Walton to Flora, undated.)

Slowly, in 1919, Flora Mayor began to sketch the beginning of a novel she called *Dedmayne*, which was in time to become her masterpiece, *The Rector's Daughter*.

11

MARY AND FLORA
IN THE AFTERMATH OF WAR —
1919–23

At the end of the war came famine. In Vienna, 'in the summer and autumn of 1918, from seven to eleven per cent of the total mortality was certified as due to starvation.'[1] In Finland people were eating the bark off trees, in Rumania they were dying of cold, in Budapest's hospitals abandoned babies had to be wrapped in newspaper, while in Germany and Austria bread was being made from sawdust and tree-bark and in the cities there was almost no milk at all.[2] 'Collect acorns!' 'Collect fruit kernels to make oil!' 'Collect apple peelings!' So ran the official posters of a Germany now on its knees. Nothing like it had been experienced in Central Europe since the Thirty Years' War. And soon there was to be famine also in Russia. The famine was caused in part by a totally exhausted and defeated war-economy. But even after the war was over the two-way blockade imposed by the vengeful victors meant that the defeated were still prevented either from exporting industrial goods or from importing food and raw materials for industrial production — and so the hunger went on.

There was a litter of ruin, not only the ruins which covered the old battlefields, but in the hearts of men and women, where smouldering fires were waiting to light the torch of war again ... It was a ghastly time.[3]

The Treaty of Versailles — that 'Peace to end Peace', as

Helena Swanwick called it — was the political expression of that 'ghastly time'.

News of the famine first reached Britain through the pacifist journal, *The Cambridge Magazine*, which had translated and summarised news reports from all enemy and neutral countries throughout the war. When Dorothy Buxton and her sister, Eglantyne Jebb, first learned about the children starving in Central Europe, they organised a meeting in the London house of Kate, Lady Courtney of Penwith,[4] and in response, the British Fight the Famine Council was formed.

In an amazingly short time the Council gained the support of a number of the most enlightened people in England: university professors like Gilbert Murray, Gooch and Tawney, writers like Masefield, Olive Schreiner, Leonard Woolf, Jerome K. Jerome and J. L. Hammond, economists like Maynard Keynes, Beveridge and Cole.[5]

And in August 1919 the Fight the Famine Council appointed as their new Secretary Mary Sheepshanks. The Council had two immediate aims — first to relieve the hunger in Europe and secondly to educate public opinion about the need for a new, just and rational international economic system which would abolish hunger altogether. The relief aspect of the Council's work was soon taken over by its off-shoot — Eglantyne Jebb's Save the Children Fund which is still in operation today.[6] The other, economic and eduational aspect of the Fight the Famine Council has now perhaps been taken over by the FAO at the UN and by the Commission of the Brandt Report.

Mary Sheepshanks participated both in the immediate relief measures and in the longer-term attempt to educate the British public. The most poignant instance of relief work which Mary helped organise was the German Babies' Teats Fund. By the end of 1918, Germany had no rubber; German babies were too weak to suck from the substitute bone-made teats and their mothers were too undernourished to have any breast-milk for them. And so between January and March 1919 over a million rubber teats were distributed to baby clinics throughout Germany, paid for and dispatched by British women members of the Women's International League, including Mary, who was then on its British Executive Committee.[7]

In July 1920 Mary Sheepshanks was active in procuring and distributing aid for Europe from America. She wrote to Jane Addams:

I am so glad to hear you are speaking in America on famine conditions here. Many of us feel that only America can save Europe from disaster, and all our friends who have been in America tell us that they are not in the least aware of the terrible conditions. I am very glad, however, to see that the American Dairy Cattle Farmers are proposing to send over 100,000 milch cows. I am informed, however, that there is neither transport for them nor fodder when they arrive, and as soon as we get full details of this, I hope that my Council will take up the matter and do all it can to urge the provision of transport. I am in communication with Miss Ray Beveridge, an American worker in Berlin, who puts forward excellent plans for the provision of fertilizer and fodder to restore agriculture in Germany and enable peasants to take the town children and feed them ... The economic situation in Europe is getting rapidly worse ... Our economic and financial experts consider that there will be a terrible crisis in the autumn ... We have had a good deal of talk about sending Miss Royden[8] or someone of that sort to America in the autumn to try and arouse sympathy for starving Europe, but we are told that America does not want to listen to English people on this subject, and that they would do more harm than good ...[9] (12 July 1920.)

When her head was not full of fodder and fertiliser and transport for milch cows, Mary Sheepshanks was trying to organise one conference after another in order to promote the international control of the distribution of food and raw materials and the provision of credit through internationally guaranteed loans via the League of Nations. At the

same time her Fight the Famine Council was waging a
campaign in the British press to try and dispel the demand
for enormous reparations payments from Germany.
'Public opinion in this country is improving, although
much too slowly,' as Mary Sheepshanks wrote to Jane
Addams in July 1920.

It was to the League of Nations that most internationalists first looked for hope after 1919.[10] But the League was
too morally timid, too locked in the old mental habits of
suspicious, nationalistic diplomacy as Mary Sheepshanks
herself was to discover, when, at the age of forty-eight she
went as the representative of the Fight the Famine Council
to lobby the League in Geneva in November 1920. Everywhere she went in Geneva she found national animus, over-
caution and buck-passing. Lord Robert Cecil warned
Mary against pressing for the admission of Germany to the
League and against raising any questions concerning
revision of the Treaty of Versailles; another British delegate
told her in confidence that both the British Government
and the Treasury were totally opposed to any kind of
international economic body and were instructed to block
any move towards instituting such — that it was, in fact, the
British who had killed the Supreme Economic Council.
The French were equally adamant against trade with
Bolshevik Russia. The delegates from the small nations
told her that they were powerless and that she must
concentrate on influencing the British government.
Rumania and Italy spoke bitterly of the aggressive
economic policy of Britain and the Dominions, saying that
British coal prices strangled the trade of other nations.
Portugal was more stirred by fear of the Bolsheviks than by
anything else and Argentina thought that Germany and
Austria must be made to revert to being merely agricultural
producers for ever more.[11]

Mary's growing impatience at all this callous self-interest
which paralysed any humanitarian response may be
detected in a cryptic allusion in one of Flora's letters to Alice

at this time: 'M.S. too pugnacious for F. the F.C. [Fight the Famine Council].' Occasionally, Mary would even vent her frustration and anger upon a colleague, releasing the old Sheepshanks devil of bad temper:

All went well for two years. Mary was pleasant to work with, and generous in giving the other women their chances. Then she suddenly [would become] crazily unreasonable to some woman she took a dislike to ... She is alone in Hampstead always changing servants and suffering a good deal from arthritis. Emily thinks she likes the pacifist set she has round her but that she is very lonely. (Flora to Alice, reporting a conversation with Emily Leaf, c. 1921. Mary had given up the lease of No 1 Barton Street at this point and moved to Hampstead.)

It was a relief for Mary to turn from the constant negativism of men in power to the life-nurturing resolutions of the Women's International League — quite powerless though these women were. The League had held its first post-war International Congress at Zürich in May 1919:

On my way there I stayed a night or two in Paris where I heard the first news of the terms of the Treaty of Versailles, and I still remember sitting in the Tuileries gardens and realising their meaning ... The Zürich Congress was a deeply moving experience. After four years of the suffering, losses and anxieties of the first world war in history, women from the warring as well as the neutral nations joined hands in grief and horror at the misery and devastation, the loss of millions of lives, the mutilation and ruined health of millions more, and the wretched plight of the refugees ... deprived of everything that makes life worth living ... We picked up the broken threads of international friendship and worked again for the settlement of all disputes by conciliation. (Mary Sheepshanks, *Autobiography*, ch. 8.)

One of the Austrian members of the Women's International League had actually died of starvation; another, so emaciated and shrunk with hunger as to be hardly recognisable, died a few weeks after attending the Zürich

Congress. The shocked delegates from the victor nations immediately concentrated on food for Europe as the first priority. Mrs Pethick Lawrence of Britain proposed the first resolution immediately after the Congress's formal opening. It was carried unanimously and then cabled to President Wilson at the Victors' Conference in Paris:

This International Congress of Women regards the famine, pestilence and unemployment extending throughout great tracts of Central and Eastern Europe and into Asia as a disgrace to civilization.

It therefore urges the Governments of all the Powers assembled at the Peace Conference immediately to develop the inter-allied organizations formed for purposes of war into an international organization for purposes of peace, so that the resources of the world — food, raw materials, finance, transport — shall be made available for the relief of the peoples of all countries from famine and pestilence.

To this end it urges that immediate action be taken:
1. To raise the blockade; and
2. If there is insufficiency of food or transport;
    a) To prohibit the use of transport from one country to another for the conveyance of luxuries until the necessaries of life are supplied to all peoples;
    b) To ration the people of every country so that the starving may be fed.[12]

President Wilson cabled back saying that the resolution appealed 'both to his head and his heart . . . but there were infinite practical difficulties.' In the event, neither his head nor his heart could withstand 'Tiger' Clemenceau, so the 'practical difficulties' remained insuperable.

Next the Women's International League tackled the punitive terms of the Peace Treaty. Again they cabled Wilson and the other leaders at Versailles:

By guaranteeing the fruits of the secret treaties to the conquerors, the terms of peace tacitly sanction secret diplomacy, deny the principles of self-determination, recognize the right of the victors to the spoils of war, and create all over Europe discords and animosities, which can only lead to future wars ... By the demand for the disarmament of one set of belligerents only, the principle of justice is violated, and the rule of force is continued ... By the financial and economic proposals a hundred million people of this generation in the heart of Europe are condemned to poverty, disease, and despair, which must result in the spread of hatred and anarchy within each nation.[13]

As Mary Sheepshanks sadly commented forty years later, if only the Allies had strengthened the liberal elements in Germany, 1919-20, after the fall of the Kaiser, instead of pursuing a policy of vindictive oppression 'the rise of the Nazi party might have been forestalled.'[14] (Mary Sheepshanks, *Autobiography*, ch. 8.)

The Zürich Women's Congress welcomed the League of Nations but they were quick to diagnose its potentially fatal flaws — including the non-membership of the defeated and the failure of the Covenant to accord with all of Wilson's fourteen Points. The women urged that membership of the League should be freely open to any state desiring to join and that there should be an immediate reduction of armaments on the same terms for all member states. In addition, the women recommended that the League should 'abolish the protection of the investments of the capitalists of one country in the resources of another' and that it should 'guarantee the civil and political rights of all minorities within each nation, including those of language, religion and eduation.' Total freedom of communication and travel, the abolition of government censorship, a League of Nations Charter for women, and proposals for world-wide education in internationalism were among the other ideals it was still possible to believe in then. Once again the women internationalists were hooted at in the press for being mere 'Alices in Blunderland'. Nevertheless they had felt compelled to speak out against the misconceived, punitive Treaty of Versailles — and they were the very first people in the world to denounce it —

even though they knew perfectly well that their protest would go unheeded.

In 1921, at the age of nearly fifty, after twenty-six years of working for one aspect of the public good after another, without any extended break or conspicuous success, Mary Sheepshanks felt sufficiently tired — and perhaps dispirited — to grant herself a rest. But it was a characteristically strenuous and unconventional rest. She travelled for four weeks in a cargo boat to the Argentine, spending her days on deck learning Spanish from a Trappist. Her destination was Uruguay, where her younger brother, Robin Sheepshanks, was managing a ranch.

That section of Mary Sheepshanks' autobiography which describes her months in Uruguay reveals the softer, more vulnerable, affection-seeking side of her personality. Always one to latch on to a lame duck, Mary had, in effect, adopted Robin, who was regarded askance by the other Sheepshankses on account of his consistent lack of worldly success. Mary remained loyally protective towards Robin and his family for the rest of her life.

After a hair-raising car journey along appalling Uruguayan roads (worse, she said, than those in pre-war Poland), during which the usually intrepid and atheistic Mary found herself clinging to the side of the car and praying, she had her first sight of Robin's two children. They were then aged two and four 'walking hand in hand in the garden, dressed in white suits and looking unnaturally angelic, all ready to impress the newly-arrived aunt.' Six months later, Mary decided 'with great regret' that she must leave them and travel through more of South America. 'It was the end of a memorable and happy visit and I wept as I waved to Robert, who stood on the quay holding John and Pita by the hand.' (Mary Sheepshanks, *Autobiography*, ch. 9.) Those were the only tears Mary's memoirs recorded.

While in Uruguay, Mary had taken the opportunity to visit Montevideo where she had discussed political, social and moral problems with the great feminist leader, Dr Paulina Luisi — 'a woman of outstanding ability and genius ... whose vitality and dominating personality would make her a leader in any country in the world.' (Mary Sheepshanks, *Autobiography*, ch. 11.) Mary left Uruguay for Buenos Aires and then travelled across Argentina in the direction of Chile because she wanted to see the statue of Christ of the Andes. In order to do this, Mary had to struggle up to the summit by mule. Once in Chile, Mary visited child-clinics, hostels for women university students and the department of education in Santiago. It was in Chile that she found greater promise of a just society than in all the rest of South America's 'peonage' system, poverty and oppression of women.

After Chile, Mary ventured by boat, by narrow-gauge railway and by hand-trolley, into Bolivia and Peru. Perhaps she remembered her father's travels through Siberia by horse-drawn, brakeless *tarrantass* in the 1860s, as she now entrusted herself, at 12,000 ft. to a hand-trolley which was nothing more than

a small platform on wheels, worked by two Indian boys by hand-pump. There was no brake, the boys enjoyed getting up speed, and when an occasional animal strayed on the track a collision seemed imminent. (Mary Sheepshanks, *Auto-biography*, ch. 13.)

Stiff with cold, discomfort and fear, Mary sat the journey out. Her goal was the ruined city of Tihuanacu, twenty miles from Lake Titicaca. Next, Mary journeyed to Cuzco, the ancient Inca capital of Peru. What struck her there was the immense poverty of the Indians and the immense wealth of the Catholic church:

In Cuzco, the living descendants of the conquered race are, in their downtrodden misery, a perpetual reproach to the regime that has replaced the prosperous Inca rule ... A rough track leads out of the city ... into the hills. A constant stream of bare-footed Indians laden with heavy burdens passes along it.

Two or three miles up this track ... every Indian, man or woman, steps aside and, looking down at the ancient City of the Sun, bares his or her head and stands a moment in silent prayer ... For a moment the poor Indian, downtrodden and oppressed during three centuries of Spanish domination, assumes the dignity of ancient tradition, and is one with the ghosts of the heroic past. (Mary Sheepshanks, *Autobiography*, ch. 14.)

Both Bolivians and Peruvians spoke to Mary with apprehension of their 'Indian enemies'. Mary recognised that the Indians wanted the restoration of their traditional communal land tenure system, and she did meet a few white liberals who also recognised that confiscated land was at the heart of the oppression.

Mary Sheepshanks was one of those born travellers who are not merely intelligent social observers but who are also alive to the beauty of strange places and filled with a zest for adventure. Climbing the hills above Cuzco, for instance, at over 15,000 ft, Mary found to be slow, breathtaking work:

But as I mounted the winding path in the delicious freshness of the early morning looking for the fortress of prehistoric Sacahuaman I felt a keen joy and exhilaration ... The little town sparkled below in the sunshine, the beautiful Vilacota river wound its way through the wide fertile valley, and the snowy peaks of the Sierra rose beyond the nearest hills. All around were fresh spring flowers, vetches, calceolarias, blue lupins and sweet thyme. The waving fields of barley and oats were ripening and the hay was being cut. A herd of llamas came over the hillside, shepherded by an Indian and his little girl. (Mary Sheepshanks, *Autobiography*, ch. 16.)

By now it was summer, 1922, and Mary was soon to return to the cold and darkness of hungry Europe. But first she went north to Chicago to stay with her revered Jane Addams, whose temperament, as Mary attested, was always 'calm and equable, and whose manner and whole bearing was of the utmost simplicity.' Mary Sheepshanks recounts one anecdote about Jane Addams in her autobiography which is notable partly because it shows that Mary could tell a story that reflected not altogether favourably on herself, but which is even more significant because it reveals the exceptional humanity and wisdom of Jane Addams:

I said to her once that I did not envy Americans their colour problem. To this remark her somewhat startling reply was, 'There is no such problem properly regarded. Every man, woman and child has a right to be treated fairly and justly and on a footing of equality.'

'Would you allow mixed marriages?' I asked.

'If they are desired,' she replied, 'I hate all pretensions of superiority. For anyone to despise any other human being is to me the unpardonable sin.'

This was the only occasion on which I heard her speak vehemently. (Mary Sheepshanks, *Autobiography*, ch. 16.)

After having made her first acquaintance with that startling 1920s phenomenon, the American 'flapper' and crying 'More strength to her elbow!' (Mary Sheepshanks, *Autobiography*, ch. 16) Mary said a reluctant goodbye to America and sailed with Jane Addams to a special Economic Conference at The Hague.

Back in Europe, Mary found herself immersed yet again in the familiar, interrelated problems of economic injustice and political instability. In 1923 she was invited to Germany to lecture in Munich, Berlin and Dresden on 'International Conciliation'. She had chosen a bad moment for such a theme. The French had recently occupied the Ruhr and in response the German government had issued vast quantities of paper money. It took a rucksack now to hold the equivalent of just £1. Mary's Munich friends had to cycle out into the country each day in search of food, while German police tried to control the mothers outside the American Red Cross centres, jostling and fighting to get tinned milk for their children. The political scene was correspondingly ominous:

At the time of my meeting in Munich, Hitler was holding his beer-cellar rallies. So I was escorted home by two immense Bavarian railwaymen as protectors from the Nazis ... Berlin had arranged a meeting, but my hotel either could not or would not give me any messages of information and the telephone to the organiser was cut off. (Mary Sheepshanks, *Autobiography*, ch. 17.)

However, that peace meeting did eventually take place, and it was a most memorable one for Mary since her fellow speakers were Albert Einstein and his friend, the French physicist, Langevin. After Mary had delivered her speech in German, Einstein turned to her and said: *'Das war meisterhaft'* [masterly]. He inscribed his place-card for her *'Mit aufrichtiger Bewunderung'* [with genuine admiration] and the little card became one of Mary's greatest treasures. On her return to England Mary sent food parcels to all who had given her hospitality, and was then left to her own forebodings as to what would be seen next on German soil.

But war has many repercussions besides that most material and pressing one of hunger. People's spirits had also taken the strain and a sensitive non-combatant like Henry Mayor had, in his own way, also been a casualty of the war. His burden of grief for all the dead boys, so many of whom had been in his own Classical Sixth at Clifton, was a burden that was all the more insupportable because it was part of Henry Mayor's rock-like character to force himself to carry it in silence and alone. In 1919, Henry, then aged fifty, suffered an acute depressive breakdown. He had to take many months off work and rumours circulated within Clifton College either that he would be asked to retire or else that the Headmaster had recommended to Henry that he think of marrying as a possible solution to his problems.

Both Flora and Alice Mayor had been urging Henry to marry for many years — 'Oh I *do* hope he'll marry' (Flora to Alice, c. 1910). They were far from being possessively jealous in relation to him, realising how much at risk he was in his desperate need for someone else besides them — and besides Clifton:

I feel as if I never shall be free of worrying about him, and I'm no help to him at all ... If only one could get near to him. I do reverence him so, sometimes I feel he is already like a person in heaven, and I should think he does cling very little to life. He would be perfect if he had more human affection, but that is a big 'if' ... Henry's devotion to Clifton is absolutely unique ... If he has to retire it will nearly break his heart. (Flora to Alice, 1917-1919.)

The woman whom Flora and Alice had long thought of as an ideal possible wife for Henry was thirty-seven-year-old Kitty Howard, daughter of Canon Howard of Weekley, near Kidderminster, Northamptonshire, and younger cousin of Ernest Shepherd. The Mayors had known her all her life. Kitty Howard was in many ways a younger Mary Walton and she was to be almost equally important as inspiration for Flora Mayor's creative work during these years, 1920-1922, when Flora was writing *The Rector's Daughter.* Brought up in almost total seclusion by her elderly parents, and much given to the solitary pleasures of reading, music, sewing, gardening and brooding in a brown study, Kitty was a rare creature. She was a 'natural' writer and a fine pianist but her only recognised social role was to be a lady and look after her widowed mother. Kitty had a very beautiful speaking voice and eyes that glinted with her sense of humour but she was much too shy and awkward to be a success with people. 'Kitty says it takes her five years to make a friend so people get tired of trying' (Flora to Alice, 1906). Only those who knew Kitty intimately recognised her exceptional sensibility — and even they sometimes needed her letters in order to discover and interpret her aright.

In April 1920, Alice took her courage in both hands — 'As to my darling Henry ... I shall write and tell him how Uncle Henry [Kitty's father, Canon Howard] wanted him to marry Kit. I *do* think it's not too late.' Henry answered with his customary reticence and sad lack of belief in himself:

Your letter needed some thought, and it is not easy to answer. I may say that I have thought before now of Kitty Howard; but though it is easy enough to say, 'She would suit me,' the other is the more serious question 'Should I suit her?' And when I ask myself, I can only say, that I fear I should make a very poor husband for anyone; and if one could not make a woman happy, it is not fair even to ask ... I feel I have so little to offer.

Undaunted, Flora and Alice invited Kitty down to Clifton for a long visit in July. Henry and Kitty took several walks by themselves during which Henry talked earnestly about the school and politics and such assorted impersonal topics, while Kitty listened. Kitty feared that she was falling in love with Henry, but was only too certain that he felt nothing of the kind for her. As she confessed with brave openness:

I was for the most part very unhappy at Clifton. After a few days I thought I was falling in love with Mr Mayor. I am easily swayed by passing attraction (I don't mean I have ever felt as then — I haven't; but slightly so) and therefore merely thought myself a fool. The feeling persisted and I became very sad because I was entirely convinced that he — not disliked me — but was trying most politely to be pleasant to your friend, and finding it rather a bore ... Our conversations were stiff and formal enough heaven knows but I somehow learnt a little about his extraordinary sincerity, and fineness of character. In fact the 15th psalm[16] tho' I didn't think of it then! Well there it was — a dream.

Then came Sunday and that awful walk in which I tried in a nightmare to talk and got no support!

Now this is the difficult part to tell you. When he spoke to me — when I could take in the words (very few of them to take in) it was as if my remote dream had suddenly become a fact. This ought to have been happiness, instead of which my only feeling was terror — (Kitty to Alice, July 1920.)

Kitty gave Henry no direct answer at once but suggested that they write to one another — he being just about to go off to a cure for rheumatism at a French spa. But when Henry's cool, reticent letters began to arrive, Kitty felt more bewildered than ever:

... even tho' I know in the depths of my heart that to be his wife would be a happiness and honour almost too great, I simply feel I *can't* write to him and say 'I love you and I will be your wife.' He has never said or written that he loves me, and though you may say 'idiot — you ought to know', I can't help it — it does make a difference.

I think you know me well enough to know that I am the last person to stand on my dignity and expect to be ardently sought but I feel as if there were a sort of barrier that I can't get through. (Kitty to Alice, July 1920.)

Kitty was suffering from that same barrier of reserve on Henry's part which had so often hurt Flora and Alice in the past. But for that very reason, Flora and Alice were able to help Kitty by interpreting the 'real', hidden Henry to her. Kitty asked Flora and Alice bluntly:

I want you to tell me plainly ... whether it is your opinion, that I should now write to him and tell him that I am ready to be his wife — that indeed I love him with all my heart — surely, surely I can't be deceived in that?

Both Flora and Alice answered yes — indeed Flora felt they might have gone too far — 'I think we won't urge her any *more* about telling; we have urged her a good deal.' Kitty tried to screw her courage to the sticking-point, and she did finally write her letter to Henry — 'I see my way now and that it is cowardice to hold back' — but before she could send it she received from him a serious rebuff:

The chronicle shall continue — indeed it is most necessary that it should! If ever people wanted help in the world it is Mr Mayor and myself.

After profound thought I wrote but did not send a letter to him last evening in which I quite plainly told him the truth. It was not purple patchy or Mrs Asquith like as you may well believe, but it did show him exactly what was in my heart, though in sedater language naturally than in a letter to you. This morning I received a long letter from him, and after the first shock I simply laughed till I cried! for the contrast was so ludicrous.

It was a very well written neat account of his journey, of Brides-les-Bains and of the European situation. He began with thanking me for my welcome letter and then without a word of comment went straight on as I have described. Of course it was like *buckets* of cold water and the further I got into the intricacies of the relationship between Germany and France, the more I felt it to be absolutely impossible to send my letter. Yet I have made a tremendous venture of faith and have done so. Why? Most of all from your letters — yes it is your responsibility — Also, towards the end of his letter though it still seemed stiff and formal to a degree as a whole, it became more personal and there was this sentence which gave me a momentary feeling of seeing as through a glass darkly. It was — 'In music I should be the small child trotting along, holding by its mother's skirts.' And then I began to cry, and to think that perhaps it was a little like that in everything, and that I *must* leap first and forget everything but the idea of fighting for his happiness in spite of himself. You understand don't you? And what a difficult road it is to tread and how terrified I am of making mistakes? ...

Alice dear if you think you can do any interpreting by writing to him I really think you had better do so for it seems to me we are getting stuck in a perfect morass of reticence. If the next letter — in answer to mine — is a lecture on the European Situation, I *shall* feel that everything's at an end — and Europe can smash up if she likes, I shan't be in a position to care![17] (Kitty to Alice, August 1920.)

Henry Mayor did not answer Kitty's declaration of love with another lecture on the European situation.

Alice dear, [Kitty wrote] I have just been sitting in the garden, crying for joy so I couldn't stop ... I have just received a letter in answer to my second one. I suppose I could never tell any human being quite what that letter meant to me. It had a 10 centime stamp! and I would cheerfully have sold all that I had to possess it.

In my letter I had made a leap forward and had been sick with fear that I'd done wrong. I had described all my own feelings of loneliness and reserve, and had said — which was the exact truth — that I felt as if it was like at last meeting somebody one had thought of and wanted for years without knowing it, and that if it came to the best of all it would be like coming home.

Well dearest Alice that sentence unlocked the doors. He said that I had described all his own feelings. That *was* my leap in the dark you know ... He said he felt the prison doors were really opening at last ... (August 1920.)

In her own way Kitty Howard was as wise and as generous in her emotional responsiveness to Henry Mayor's feelings, as her cousin Ernest Shepherd had been in relation to Flora twenty years before.

And, darling Flora, you do know now, don't you that I will never give up — not if fresh clouds come or some inexplicable draw-back — never, I do promise you as long as he wants me. Even if he didn't I should go on wanting him and simply waiting and hoping. ... Do you know that what I feel for him almost terrifies me ... I feel frightened — as if I was giving more than he could possibly desire to receive ... I just want to give him exactly what he wishes to receive, whatever it may be; after all, I needn't be so very complicated and strenuous about it all — for I suppose its simply understanding and sympathy as far as may be, and love and companionship ... My ... love for him has grown so — that I feel sometimes it is almost an anguish ... (Kitty to Flora, September-November 1920.)

Kitty Howard and Henry Mayor were married in December 1920.[18]

Flora felt humbled and stirred by these revelations of Kitty's innermost heart:

I think Kit's letters, particularly hers to you, are so beautiful *et font du bien.* We have seen so little of love affairs, so one cannot compare, but I feel *how* unworthy I was compared to her, tho' glad to think that I felt *some* of what she felt. Henry is being repaid seven fold the unhappiness he has suffered by getting such love from Kit. (Flora to Alice, August 1920.)

Kitty Howard became fused in Flora Mayor's creative imagination both with her own inner life and with her memories of Mary Walton going back many years — 'I felt a strange rush of extreme sadness the other day about dear Mary Walton, and in the summer often have whiffs of Shelford' (Flora to Alice, 1920) — and so 'Mary Jocelyn' was born. For it was just in these months in 1920 while Flora was so involved with Kitty's daily bulletins about her desperate love for Henry Mayor that she was also writing the first draft of 'the kiss chapter' and its passionate aftermath in *The Rector's Daughter.*

12

FLORA MAYOR'S
THE RECTOR'S DAUGHTER, 1924[1]

The Rector's Daughter is the story of an unconsummated, lifelong passion between a man and a woman. This central relationship is juxtaposed with three other kinds of love — between husband and wife, between woman and woman, and between parent and child. All these loves are shown to be fragmentary and imperfect; nevertheless it is they, taken together, which, in Flora Mayor's view, constitute 'our bonds of primal sympathy', revealing 'the universal heart'[2] by which we live.

Despite her deep devotion to the realm of George Eliot and Mrs Gaskell, Flora Mayor harks back in this novel to the more desperate passion of the Romantics, expressed once and for all in Blake's aphorism: 'Those who restrain desire do so because theirs is weak enough to be re-strained'.[3] Unusual as it may seem to place middle-aged, clerical Mr Herbert and dowdy, bespectacled Mary Jocelyn in the tradition of Tristan and Isolde or *La Nouvelle Héloise*, that, nevertheless, is where the central characters of *The Rector's Daughter* belong. Most of the novel's action takes place in one dull East Anglian household consisting of an octogenarian rector, his thirty-five-year-old spinster daughter and their two servants. A visitor or two comes — or does not come — but by the end of the book that dark, quiet rectory has witnessed ecstasy and despair.

Few opening pages are as defiantly unromantic and

unpromising as is the sequence of pejorative terms that introduce *The Rector's Daughter*. 'Insignificant', 'ugly', 'dusty', 'grimy' — that is Dedmayne; the village's very name suggests it is moribund. Yet Flora Mayor adds a caveat: 'What has been known from childhood must be lovable, whether it is ugly or beautiful' (ch. 1) — wonderfully confirming Cowper's lines:

Scenes must be beautiful, which daily view'd
Please daily, and whose novelty survives
Long knowledge and the scrutiny of years.[4]

The interior of the rectory, together with its dank, decaying garden, is evoked bleakly at first too: 'Not a new piece of furniture had been bought ... not a room had been papered ... not a chintz renewed'. But then comes the counterpointing affirmation: 'Books streamed everywhere, all over the house, even up the attic stairs' (Ch. 1). The riches of this household are three thousand years of human culture. The Old Testament, Socrates, Virgil, the Gospels, Early Church Fathers, Shakespeare, Pascal, Dr Johnson — these are the guiding light of that rectory.[5] Mary Jocelyn's bedroom is also book-filled, but it is not merely book-filled: and the books themselves, which include all her old children's books and favourite nineteenth-century novels, as well as Elizabethan poetic drama and mediaeval mysticism, have a range that is at once more homely and more unfettered than those cherished by her father's great intellect.

Romantic lovers exemplify the heroism of the heart. But the history of Mary Jocelyn's heart during its first thirty-five years would seem to have been empty, even starved. Motherless from a child, isolated physically from her brothers, mentally from her subnormal sister, emotionally from her withdrawn and chilly father, and considered 'odd' by all the contemporaries of her own social class, Mary Jocelyn would seem to have had no opportunity to love anyone. But her ardent, responsive nature found nourishment even in that stony ground. In addition to her one-sided devotion to her father, Mary had 'longed for friends' and 'had had some passions for older ladies' as well as for 'two or three bright girls with pigtails' (ch. 2). When these were rebuffed, she had abandoned herself to fantasies featuring Mr Rochester, or Hamlet or Dr Johnson. The only reciprocal loving relationship in her life was with Cook — 'Mary poured out freely to her' (ch. 2). Mary's solitariness ends at last when she meets the Vicar of nearby Lanchester, Mr Herbert, and each falls in love with the other's intense capacity to feel.

Canon Jocelyn was talking about Mr Herbert's father, and his voice was faltering, almost breaking, when he said, 'There was no one like your father — no one.' ... Her eyes met Mr Herbert's; he had turned his head a little to give her father time to recover. He had been moved also, and she liked his expression ... he remembered Miss Jocelyn's face, when she looked at her father. She had a sweet smile. (Ch. 6.)

G.E. Moore's assertion that 'the appreciation of a person's attitude towards other persons, or, to take one instance, the love of love, is far the most valuable good we know',[6] is frequently given convincing imaginative life in *The Rector's Daughter*. But, alas for Mary, one of the people whom Mr Herbert loves, and whom she has to love him for loving, is young, beautiful Kathy Hollings. Mary loses Mr Herbert — or thinks that she loses him — to Kathy, and much of the book is concerned with how, in Anne Elliot's words, one can go on living and loving when 'existence or or when hope is gone'.[7] Mary Jocelyn's first solace is to drug herself with fantasies:

Night after night, she thought of him, imagining with the terror of love, every sort of disaster and of death for him. She dreamt of him also, waking up in an uncontrollable torrent of tears because he was dead in some foreign country ...

After a while she built castles. She described them to herself as concerning someone else, but she knew from her excited joy she was thinking of pleasure she was ashamed to own. She would picture Kathy's death ... She recoiled from herself, but she continued her daydreams. (Ch. 16.)

Between tea and dinner were the special hours she had devoted to reverie. It had become like a drug; her ennui at everything else was almost unendurable ...
    There was a moment in the twenty-four hours which carried her through; it was when she mentioned Mr Herbert in her prayers. She found she counted the minutes to half-past ten, and devised excuses for going to bed early. Thereupon Reason and Duty bade her give up praying for him; she did. (Ch. 17.)

It was for Mary's sake, in order not to impose what he believed to be his unforgivable, adulterous passion on her, that Mr Herbert stayed away from Mary. And it was for Mr Herbert's sake, in order to help a married clergyman keep faith with what he believed to be right, that Mary forced herself to stay away from him. Each goes on loving the other without a shred of hope that they are loved in return. In Flora Mayor's view the very deepest love is precisely that which survives without hope of reciprocity, believing, indeed, that it has been set on one side. Pascal agreed:

The deepest attachment may often be conceived when the beloved object is unconscious of the passion; the most inviolate fidelity preserved when even our love is unknown. But such love as this is of the highest and purest order ...[8]

In all these ways *The Rector's Daughter* is a twentieth-century re-telling of the myth of romantic passion.[9] Admittedly it is difficult to apply the term 'romantic passion' to Mr Herbert, given that even after he has met Mary Jocelyn, he then leaves her and marries her polar opposite, Kathy Hollings. Mr Herbert is prey not to one romantic passion but to two, which seems an absurd contradiction, as well as being a torment. I think it very probable that Flora was basing Mr Herbert on her know-ledge of her brothers, but that it was beyond her powers to compress their two very different personalities and love-relationships — Robin Mayor's for Beatrice Meinertz-hagen, and Henry Mayor's for Kitty Howard — into the heart of one and the same man. But for all her difficulty with Mr Herbert, Flora Mayor's treatment of his marriage to Kathy is still convincing. Paradoxically, it is the very crises in the Herbert marriage which enable it to survive. It is only when they are most deeply troubled that the husband and wife transcend their everyday irritability, insensitivity and mutual incomprehension, and reach out to each other in sudden tenderness and desperate need.

That Kathy Herbert really does possess depths of self-critical vulnerability underneath all her 'county' boorish-ness, emerges most memorably in her relationship with her unsuspected rival, Mary. The two women, who have nothing in common but their love for Mr Herbert, at one point in their lives actually come to love one another. In Kathy's case it is love through need; in Mary's it is love offered as a gift.[10] But Kathy is not the only other woman whom Mary Jocelyn loves and is loved by. There is hardly a woman in the book who is not drawn to Mary or for whom Mary feels nothing; her emotional world does not consist merely of her father and of Mr Herbert, even when she thinks that it does. Not only is there Mary's mentally handicapped, utterly dependent sister Ruth, her adored elderly neighbour, Lady Merton, and her stolid best friend Dora, but the whole village of 'her own faithful Dedmayne ... could not have loved [Mary] more' — from the silent girl in her economics class to the old nurse who asks: 'Are you well, my dear? This dear white hand is so thin.' The greatest of all Mary's women friends is Cook. This small, thin working-woman of sixty-three is Mary's *de facto* mother:

Cook had come when Mary was six ... [she] looked on Mary as a child ... in all practical matters. Mary poured out freely to her ... When Mary cried in Cook's arms, Cook did not reject her. (Ch. 2.)

It is Cook who says lovingly: 'Ah, my dear, you'll be going to the Vicarage once too often.' It is Cook's skinny shoulder Mary hugs when Mr Herbert forgets her, and it is Cook's tearless elegy that moves us to tears at the end.

The longest-lasting relationship in the book, as so often in life, is that of parent and child. At first sight, the eighty-two-year-old canon's impact on his daughter seems totally repressive — words like 'crush', 'quail', 'dashed to the ground' are used. But although Mary does withdraw into silence, she still has something to withdraw — 'she had much seething within her waiting for an outlet.' And far from being a downtrodden, mouse-like daughter, in her inmost soul Mary Jocelyn criticises the canon; she has in the past even hated her father for his icy hardness to her brother; she has 'never ceased to blame him for his indifference' to her mentally handicapped sister, and when she once challenges him with her need for some avowal of his affection — 'If he had repelled her she would not have been heart-broken, but she could not have helped despising him.' (Ch. 13.) Flora Mayor renders the parent-child relationship with justice and compassion for both sides.[11] The true grandeur of the canon's mind, mirrored in his marvellous diction, is never in doubt, even though Flora Mayor also makes it clear that precisely in proportion to the canon's great intellectual work a terrible emotional price has been paid by all those close to him — as by the canon himself.[12] Only after his death, is he known more intimately, when Mary discovers his private journal. There, in a passage written on the night of Ruth's death, he actually confesses to himself that Mary's nature was deeper than his own:

I consider [Ruth's] poor afflicted life, the countless sufferings which I have done nothing to mitigate. I was helpless before them. Mary devoted herself actively to the task; she has been both sister and mother. She told me just now with tears of her grief. I feel no grief. How should I? I have not deserved to grieve. (Ch. 26.)

Such a passage, which renders the very timbre and cadence of an old man's soul, is one of the touchstones establishing Flora Mayor's claim to greatness as a novelist.

The world of *The Rector's Daughter* is poised between the nineteenth and the twentieth centuries, critical of both. Canon Jocelyn is hardly a model father and through him Flora Mayor is attacking the patriarchal, emotionally rigid authoritarianism of the late Victorians and the damage that they inflicted. But 'the Brynhilda set' — inspired by the pre-War Friday Club of Clive Bell, the Stephens, Desmond MacCarthy, Rothenstein, Fry and Henry Lamb[13] — is equally criticised. Flora's twin sister Alice had been the much condescended-to Honorary Secretary of the Friday Club in about 1908, and her tart response to the club's intellectual snobbery, its irreligion, and penchant for declaiming Swinburnian erotica aloud, had been reported back to Flora, then ill in Clifton.

Implicitly, *The Rector's Daughter* is written in resistance to two twentieth-century currents — the current of sexual promiscuity in the name of 'experience', and the current of brutal violence in the name of 'justice'. In taking as her heroine a Mary Jocelyn, Flora Mayor is championing all those social and sexual 'failures' whom she saw as despised and discounted by the young and thriving, and who even, as she believed, would be in danger of execution in post-revolutionary societies. Flora Mayor was no friend to the Bolsheviks.[14] As a successor of Jane Austen, George Eliot and Mrs Gaskell, Flora Mayor in her turn is alerting us to 'a keen vision and feeling of all ordinary human life.'[15] She does so by dramatising the immense effort that is required to respond to every dependent, needy soul in the community. Work, for Mary Jocelyn, is not manual drudgery, but it is drudgery of another kind. It is 'to sit half an hour by an elderly lady getting deaf, another half an hour by some awkward spectacled girl, a third half hour by the shyest curate' (ch. 9). It is to listen sympathetically to the complaints of the village school mistress and to keep up some

response to six hours of chat from rheumatic Miss Davey. It
is to laugh at her father's jokes — loudly enough for him to
hear but not too loudly lest she appear 'unrestrained'. And,
most Sisyphus-like of all, it is to get through day after day in
the company of her Aunt Lottie:

the daily winding-up of two clocks, the weekly winding-up of
three more; the morning paper, which she read all through to
Aunt Lottie and later Aunt Lottie read all through to her, and
the evening paper, in which the same news appeared in a still
brighter form; the cat and dog, who wanted to be let in, and
as soon as they were in to be let out, and as soon as they were
out to be let in again; the knitting, which she set ready for
Aunt Lottie, undid when she was gone to bed, and knitted up
again to be ready for Aunt Lottie next afternoon; the
explanations and answers to questions, which must be
repeated several times, for Aunt Lottie, though not deaf, was
inquisitive and inattentive; the listening to little whining digs
of Aunt Lottie against various people, not made in malice, but
just a habit, like sniffing ... Sometimes in the morning [Mary]
shrank at the day's prospect. (Ch. 27.)

But, as Mary Jocelyn knows, 'Aunt Lottie could turn to
no one else.' 'Sympathy,' Virginia Woolf once noted, 'uses
the same force required to lay 700 bricks.'[16] 'Moral energy,'
said Jane Addams 'is [the] vital thing.'[17]

To refuse to do this work of keeping alive in other people
their illusions about themselves, and hence their will to live,
is to force the unwanted failures of the earth to feel the full
depth and extent of their unwantedness. It is to kill their
spirit. Mary Jocelyn has just one moment of rebellion when
she chooses to attend a theatre matinée rather than to arrive
punctually at the house of a genteel, carping widow. But
when she does arrive at last, she finds that widow crying in
her disappointment and anxiety, and Mary condemns
herself for 'having deliberately given Mrs Plumtree three
hours of avoidable torment.' It is Mary Jocelyn's greatness
that she recognises that she has caused nothing less than
'torment', and it is Flora Mayor's greatness that she insists

that Mrs Plumtree's torment matters. Flora Mayor is saying (as she had said in *The Third Miss Symons* and in *Miss Browne's Friend*) that individual caring is as necessary to a humanly bearable life as are Jane Addams' peace and bread. Her vision is 'conservative' insofar as she is attempting to shore up and conserve the *ewig-menschliche* — the eternal human values of personal love and of life-nurturing work. But her vision is also in its way an ideal, even Utopian vision of how we might live together — an 'idyll' like that of which Schiller wrote: 'a state of harmony and peace ... the state to which civilisation aspires.'[18]

The quality of Mary Jocelyn makes *The Rector's Daughter* a saintly book. But it was no saint who wrote it. On a first reading, such is its inner conviction that one assumes Mary Jocelyn must have been based upon Flora Mayor herself, who, after all, was also the unmarried daughter of a scholarly cleric. But now that the thousands of self-absorbed, judgemental letters from Flora to Alice have come to light, complacently retailing all the 'comps' and *Grandes Passions* that she had scored at Newnham, all her envious bitterness during her time on the stage and at Clifton College, it is clear that Flora Mayor was *not* Mary Jocelyn; that she was, for the most part, the very opposite of her unassuming heroine. Instead, it would seem that it was two other women, Flora's much older friend Mary Walton and her sister-in-law Kitty Howard, who gave her much of the inspiration for her rector's daughter. But this is not to say that there was nothing of Flora in Mary Jocelyn. It was, in fact, central to Flora's nature to love both the Mary Jocelyn figures in her own life, and to testify, twenty years after Ernest Shepherd's death, to the truth that she had first poignantly noted in her *Grief Journal* of 1904: 'Love *is* better than anything else. Goodness and love are the eternal things.' Finally, to complete her portrait of Mary, Flora Mayor does give her some of her own faults: a few spasms of jealousy, of wild self-pity and even of intellectual arrogance — all that Flora meant by her own hateful 'criticalness' and ungenerosity. Given that added dimension, Mary Jocelyn becomes more than a combination of Mary Walton and Kitty Howard; she becomes, in my view, one of the most convincing, lovable characters in twentieth-century English fiction.

After *The Rector's Daughter* was published, Virginia Woolf wrote to Flora:

29th May 1924

Dear Miss Mayor,
   I thought I would send a line to tell you how many people have spoken to me with admiration of the Rector's Daughter. Lytton Strachey, my sister and Duncan Grant have all been reading it with deep interest, and I hear that Mr Raymond Mortimer is also a great admirer, and is, I hope, reviewing it in 'Vogue'. Of course this does not necessarily mean a large public, but it is the kind of success which I feel is worth having, and the kind I felt certain the Rector's Daugher would have.
                    Yours sincerely,
                    Virginia Woolf
We hope to send the announcement forms tomorrow. We have been in a great rush this week.

   Even more gratifying was the letter from E.M. Forster:

Hung [Hurry?] — Hill — Brightstone
— Isle of Wight
16.6.24

Dear Miss Mayor
   This is Dedmayne, plus better scenery and charabancs, and to read and live the same thing results in an extraordinary experience: as if, taking up first a telescope and then a microscope, one saw precisely the same appearance of reality down the tube of each. The book interested and moved me much, and I found in all the end part — after Kathy's operation — a great pulling together and heightening, so that the whole work was lifted from the plains of satire and observation — which are amusing and easy but in the long

run unprofitable — and placed on the level of creation. Mary begins as ridiculous and ends as dignified: this seemed to me a very great achievement; and all the realistic detail delighted me, of course.

Thank you very much for your letter, also. I read what you say about *A Passage to India* with great pleasure. The book is more pessimistic than my own experiences warrant, for I have made at least one permanent Indian friend. But the books one writes usually are either sadder or happier than one's life, there is no subduing them to exactly the same tone. I do blame the English more than the Indians for the present impasse. Faults on both sides but the greater on this, and the O'Dwyer case does seem to be the turning-point for evil in our relationship. I know the dissenting juryman in it: his account is appalling. O'Dwyer certainly was libelled, but I don't believe that in the future, in a case of black v. white, the black can hope for justice in a British court. What the extremists longed to prove, of course. My own friends, all moderates when they are anything, are now discredited, and I have no doubt that this was O'Dwyer's and McArchie's aim.

I should very much like to see you when I return to Weybridge, which I hope to do in July. Thank you again for your book. I am very glad that you consented to the exchange.

> Yours sincerely,
> E.M. Forster

Flora's 'respectful old ally,' John Masefield, also praised *The Rector's Daughter*:

It is a remarkable book and confirms you in your remarkable rank ... It is a great advance in every way on your other two stories, though you know that I thought and still think both of them most unusually good in their own ways ...

I will always back you against all these ladies. You have twice their sense of character, and make all your effects so thriftily: so never heed the reviews; the book has already outlived them ...

In the event, most early reviews of *The Rector's Daughter* were highly favourable. Forrest Reid wrote that *The Rector's*

Daughter was 'a book that should not be passed over.'[19]
Ralph Wright singled it out as being 'far out of the ordinary.'[20] Rebecca West proclaimed Flora Mayor's immense
superiority to Galsworthy.[21] There were also interesting
long articles on the novel by Ellis Roberts and A.C. Benson
in two Anglican periodicals,[22] and Raymond Mortimer
praised the novel in *Vogue*.[23] The two most perceptive
reviews were by Gerald Gould and Sylvia Lynd. Gould
wrote:

Miss Mayor has taken the subject-matter of all the serials in
all the journals suitable for home reading of the last century,
and made it live. The scholarly, selfish old rector, blind to the
needs and hungers of his plain, unselfish daughter: the
neighbouring parson, who loves the plain daughter for her
goodness but marries somebody else who is beautiful and
then finds that beauty in a wife isn't everything: the wife who
is going to run away with a dashing young soldier, but loses
her looks through an unfortunate operation at the crucial
moment and discovers that it was those looks, and not her
spirit's self, that the young soldier wanted to run away with:
the apposite recovery of her looks after she has been
reconciled to her husband — here they are, and yet how
different they seem! Can it be that things really did, and do,
happen thus — that the journals suitable for home reading
learnt them in the first place from life? For in Miss Mayor's
hands they are far more real, far nearer to experience, than all
the sly quests and exquisite analyses which pass for realism
now. She has the true novelist's divine incommunicable gift:
no shadows flit across her pages: she has but to mention
someone, give him a phrase to say or even to write, and he
puts on solidity and permanence.[24]

And Sylvia Lynd declared:

The Rector's Daughter belongs to the finest English tradition of
novel writing. It is like a bitter *Cranford*. Mrs. [sic] Mayor
explores depths of feeling that Mrs Gaskell's generation
perhaps did not know and certainly did not admit to
knowing. Mrs Mayor's genius struggles with exasperation

where Mrs. Gaskell's struggled with the much milder demon
of sentimentality ...

The Rector's daughter, Mary Jocelyn, is one of those sad
figures of whom it is said that nothing has ever happened to
them. Mrs Mayor reveals the meaninglessness of that phrase.
Mary Jocelyn's 'nothing' is a full and rich state of being.[25]

Among all the praise from *cognoscenti* and all the loving
thanks for the book expressed by her own circle of friends
were two letters that Flora Mayor received from Mary
Sheepshanks. No matter how differently each of them saw
their world, something remained in common: a certain
humane idealism and a bond of reciprocal respect and
affection, rooted by now in thirty years of intermittent
meetings and correspondence. If Flora was tempted at
times to think of Mary as the archetypal public-spirited-
but-insensitive social worker of the world — an Ella
Redland write large — then the following letters must have
reminded Flora of that other, gentler Mary who could be so
generously responsive, and so touchingly anxious to be
friends:

                                        30 The Close, Norwich.
My dear Flora —
    May I add mine to the chorus of congratulation and praise
and thanks for your book?
    It is *beautiful*, true, delicate, full of lovely things and so
exquisitely expressed, — a worthy successor to Miss
Symons. It must be a real and deep satisfaction to you to
have produced such an admirable piece of work, and to have
succeeded in giving expression to a considered view of life.
Mary is a noble and lovely creation, and I admire too your
just and fair and discriminating picture of Kathy — who
naturally appealed less to your individual taste.
    It is all first-rate.
    Have you ever thought of writing anything about your
Father? He was so fine. I remember with such pleasure the
times I had the honour of meeting him. I have heard nothing
of you since my visit to the Americas, and don't even know

whether you are still at Kingston. How are Mrs Mayor and Alice?

I live at Golders Green, and shall be back in September — In October I start giving my lecture on Peru in lots of places. I should so much like to meet you; if it is too far for you to come to Golders Green we could meet in town. I am very arthritic, and my feet are bad, so getting about is a great difficulty.

I am here for a week, then a week in Yorkshire, then a week at Maidenhead then home — Golders Green.

I admire your work so much, and it will give great enjoyment to many. I hope it will bring you other advantages besides your own satisfaction and the praise of appreciators —

> Yours affectionately,
> Mary Sheepshanks.

A week later she wrote again:

Dear Flora,

Many thanks for your letter, I must just correct what I seem to have put badly. I didn't for an instant think Canon Jocelyn was your father. I guessed exactly what you say, that the atmosphere of scholarship and refinement was what you had known at home and at your uncles', but I realised that he was an imaginative creation, and I knew something of what your Father was too well to mistake.

I added as quite a separate notion that I wondered if you ever considered a little monograph about him. I shall never forget him, I remember perfectly the charm and human sympathy with which he interested himself in other people's doings, always remembering and inquiring, as you say, about Drywood. I am so very glad you are all still at Queensgate House. I recognised amongst other things a house that had no servant difficulties. But one of the superiorities of the book is that it is no mere transcript, with recognisable photographs. I brought it home for my Mother to read, and she admired and enjoyed it very much. I am afraid my rheumatism has made me very inert and cut me off from people very much. Getting about London suburbs is so much more trying than travelling in the Andes! I went to Germany last summer and to Sicily in the winter, but when I am home in September I hope to see you. I am so glad you are still in the old home.

Yours affectionately
Mary Sheepshanks.

Mary does not make much of her own recent exploits, her exploration of South America or her speechmaking with Einstein in Berlin. And Flora would simply have smiled at the same old Mary, complaining as usual about her bad feet. It was always so easy to caricature Mary Sheepshanks, in the intervals of seeing her, as someone exclusively public-spirited and outward-looking as she stumped (or hobbled) along in her dogged, frowning, reformist way, armed with facts about the latest deplorable world situation, about which something must and could be done. One might have expected her to have as little time as did Beatrice Webb for the intricacies of the emotional life and the sufferings of just one individual. In fact, Mary never believed that she or anyone else had to choose between public causes and private concerns. Therefore she wrote so whole-heartedly to Flora: '*I admire your work so much* ... Mary is a noble and lovely creation.'

13

THE DARKENING WORLD
OF MARY SHEEPSHANKS,
1926–1933

Dedmayne Rectory had symbolised civilisation. The thousands of volumes in Canon Jocelyn's library and the music of Haydn standing on the piano were merely the outer signs of that civilisation; its soul was Mary Jocelyn's daily life as she responded to the deepest needs of everyone around her, obeying Rousseau's imperative: 'Never hurt anybody.'[1] But Dedmayne Rectory was, in Flora Mayor's own words, 'a frail, frail survival, lasting on out of its time',[2] whereas hurting people was soon to become the order of the day.

The late 1920s and early 1930s witnessed a great effort to prevent another World War. But before 1939 came 1933 and the three-fold tragedy of the years 1919-1945 was the tragedy of the failure to prevent the triumph of Fascism, the consequent necessity to fight a Second World War against Fascism, and the subversion of the humanism of the anti-Fascists during that war, until they felt they had to 'become Fascist to win.'[3] And, as E.M. Forster said, 'the nightmare [was] that everything almost went right.'[4] It was during the period from the Locarno Treaty of 1925 until Stresemann's death and the Wall Street Crash at the end of 1929 that 'everything almost went right.' And it was during much the same period — 'the most successful and hopeful in the history of the League of Nations' (Mary Sheepshanks, *Autobiography*, ch. 18) — that Mary Sheepshanks was working in Geneva as International Secretary of the Women's International League for Peace and Freedom.[5]

During the 1920s when many newly enfranchised women were lobbying within their own countries for social reforms,[6] it was also possible to believe that women might successfully join across national frontiers to constitute a powerful reformist lobby in international affairs. The Women's International League for Peace and Freedom (WIL) endeavoured to become that lobby. Its letterhead listed National Sections in Australia, Austria, Belgium, Bulgaria, Canada, Czechoslovakia, Denmark, France, Germany, Great Britain, Greece, Haiti, Holland, Hungary, Ireland, Italy, Japan, New Zealand, Norway, Poland, Sweden, Switzerland, the Ukraine and the United States. The League also had official corresponding links with women in China, Egypt, India, Russia and Spain. Only most of Africa remained cut off, its women without access to basic education or political influence of any kind. Within each country the League's membership tended to consist of well-educated, radical women — doctors, scientists, artists, writers, lawyers, university teachers, social work administrators, journalists and civil servants. Mary Sheepshanks was by no means the only member of whom it was said 'She always knew her stuff.'[7] Between 1927 and 1932, the WIL sent fact-finding missions to Haiti, China, Austria, Palestine and the Ukraine, and published substantial papers on Economic Imperialism, Disarmament, and the protection of the Civil Rights of Minorities. Deputations of women in the WIL also lobbied the League of Nations. These women saw the interconnections between the political, economic, social, military and scientific developments in their world, but the consequence was that they felt compelled to shoulder all the problems of the world simultaneously. Mary Sheepshanks was as competent an International Secretary as any the WIL ever had, but even she found the task beyond her — for she was serving the sentences of Atlas and of Sisyphus concurrently.

Just how idealistic the WIL was can be seen from its Manifesto of 1926:

The League aims at uniting women in all countries who are opposed to every kind of war, exploitation and oppression, and who work for the solution of conflicts not by force of domination but by the recognition of human solidarity, by world co-operation, and by the establishment of social, political and economic justice for all, without distinction of sex, race, class or creed.

But these women had not resolved the problems of how oppression can be ended and justice established without recourse either to violence or to the threat of violence. Moreover, their very rationality and humane (often agnostic) internationalism blinded them to the force of the irrational national, racial and religious fanaticisms then gaining strength all around them. Just as important was their own disunity. The International Executive of the WIL was split down the middle between 'the extremists', the very Left-wing, even revolutionary members from France and Germany, and the more 'moderate' Scandinavian and British women who were willing to envisage partial and gradual reform through arbitration rather than confrontation. Temperamentally, the 'extremists', despite all their theoretical antipathy to every form of domination, were very domineering. They believed that their absolutism proved the greater depth of their commitment and that their commitment entitled them to have their own way. They, and they alone, were the trustees of the spirit of 1915 — the others were compromisers, revisionists, even 'traitors'. It is a familiar scenario. Mary Sheepshanks' predecessor as International Secretary, the American lawyer, Madeleine Doty,[9] reported almost in despair to Jane Addams at the time of handing over the office to Mary:

I do not think our French and German members of the Executive — Perlen, Heymann,[10] Augspurg,[11] Baer, Duchêne,

Jouve, realize that they are dictators and autocrats. I am sure they feel they are voting for the welfare of the WIL, but this suppression on their part of representatives of other sections, (especially Britain) is bound to bring disaster unless it is changed ... I am sure that if Mary Sheepshanks had no Englishwoman [on the International Executive] to understand her, to appreciate what she was doing, it would be intolerable ... I do not think that the French and Germans realize at all that they, a minority, are dictating to the majority. They are so convinced that they are right and that the others are wrong that they can see no other point of view. (August 1927.)

She added a heartfelt postscript:

You can't think what a relief it is to cease to be Secretary. I have learned a lot and it was a great experience, but I doubt if any Secretary can stand it for long under present conditions.

Mary Sheepshanks was very much of her opinion. She had seriously considered resigning her appointment even before she took office. Nevertheless, at the age of fifty-six, and despite her chronic arthritis, Mary did decide to enter the shafts:

My dear Miss Addams,
 ... Well, about Geneva — I am going to risk it and try my hand ... You know I had appendicitis before Xmas and was as nearly as possible dead — it just wanted two hours the surgeons said. And I made a really astonishing recovery, so I feel encouraged to try a real job ...

 I am fully aware of my inadequacy in other ways [than health], but apparently none of our first rate people can or will leave what they are doing each in her own country — I am afraid I shall be a disappointment to all who put confidence in me. I shall make all sorts of mistakes and lose what friends I have, but still I will try if they want me.

 And of course dear Miss Addams I shall be terribly sorry if I let you down.

 I only hope the [national] sections will really take more interest in Geneva ... They can't expect it to go well if they give nothing but criticism. Poor Madeleine Doty hasn't had a bed of roses. (21 February 1927.)

And to Madeleine Doty, Mary wrote: 'I feel that it is the work that lies nearest to my heart.'

One nettle that Mary had to grasp immediately was 'the indifference and hostility' manifested towards the League of Nations by the French and German Left-wingers on the WIL Executive, despite the fact that two of the WIL's agreed functions were to bring its influence to bear on delegates at the League of Nations and to inform its National Sections of significant developments at Geneva. Mary Sheepshanks wrote several articles for the WIL monthly *Pax International*, emphasising the positive humanitarian work that was being achieved by the League. In October 1927, Mary praised its stand against the international traffic in drugs and in child prostitution, and in November 1927, she wrote about the attention that the International Labour Organisation was now paying to the universal need of working women to statutory leave before and after childbirth. She urged WIL members to read the devastating work of reportage by the British Women's Co-operative Guild called *Maternity*[12] which revealed the full extent of women's 'preventable suffering' in one of the richest nations of the world.

In December 1927, Mary wrote a powerful, carefully reasoned article against all capital punishment — 'punishment must be restorative', which also expressed her even more heartfelt revulsion against the use of torture. During the 1920s a White Terror was in progress in Hungary, Bulgaria and Romania where suspected political radicals were being imprisoned and brutally tortured. In December 1927, Mary Sheepshanks wrote on behalf of the WIL an appeal, in French and German, to all these governments to release their political prisoners as a Christmas act of clemency. She also put forward the idea (fifty years before Amnesty International) that an international movement was now needed to work for an amnesty for *all* political prisoners who were not terrorists.[13]

Mary Sheepshanks' other work during her first two months in office included: monitoring the case of Indonesian political prisoners in Holland; backing the investigation of allegations of torture of Macedonian students in Yugoslavia while simultaneously protesting against the Macedonian comitasjlis' policy of political assassination; bidding farewell to the WIL delegates to war-torn China; planning and writing lectures on the connections between colonial imperialism and war for her tour of peace groups in Scandinavia and Germany in the New Year; attending as many sessions of the League of Nations Council and its Commissions as possible; and, finally, alerting the WIL to the initiative for world disarmament first proposed by the Soviet Foreign Minister Litvinoff — 'It is hoped that all National Sections will support the Russian proposal for immediate, universal, total disarmament, and undertake propaganda for the proposal.' (Mary Sheepshanks' letter to the WIL International Executive, 27 December 1927.)

The list is not exhaustive but it indicates Mary Sheepshanks' sense of her new, global brief.

The major world issue on which the WIL had to take a stand during 1928 concerned the rival peace initiatives of the Soviet Union and the United States. Mary Sheepshanks welcomed them both but she was acutely aware of the dangers in backing one without the other: the Soviet proposals for Total Disarmament would be unconvincing so long as the Soviet Union continued to support violent revolution abroad, while the Kellogg proposals for the Outlawry of War would be mere verbiage without either any radical progress in disarmament or the participation of the Soviet Union. Mary wrote to Jane Addams:

The American proposal coming at the same time as the Russian disarmament proposal makes a critical situation. . . . It is difficult to know where to stand on this question. On the one hand we feel bound to support all proposals for disarmament; on the other hand we are accused of being

Bolsheviks in supporting the Russian proposal and it is said that the Russians' only object is to get the other countries to disarm and at the same time to leave revolvers in the hands of their citizens so that revolution may be promoted. (28 March 1928.)

After months of internal consultation, the WIL sent a telegram to Kellogg which they also released to the press:

IN INTERESTS UNIVERSAL PEACE THIS LEAGUE URGES UNITED STATES GOVERNMENT TO INVITE BEFORE PARIS CONFERENCE SOVIET GOVERNMENT TO JOIN IN DELIBERATIONS ON KELLOGG PACT.

Mary followed this up with the following letter sent to all the fourteen governments that signed the Kellogg Pact in Paris:

The omission of a country as powerful as the USSR from the list of original signatories to the Kellogg Pact appears to those who really desire peace a very grave matter.

If it should happen that all of Russia's neighbours were included in the treaty while she was outside, a very serious menace to the peace of the world would, it seems to us, be created. It is obvious that Russia herself is very uneasy about such a situation, which may be and is already interpreted in some quarters as showing that the Pact is directed against her.

We therefore urgently beg the representatives of the Powers gathered at Paris for the signing of the Treaty for the Renunciation of War to make it clear to the USSR that their immediate adhesion to the treaty is cordially desired. (25 August 1928.)

On 11 September 1928, Mary Sheepshanks headed a deputation of the WIL to the Secretariat of the League of Nations in Geneva to present an urgent memorandum on Disarmament to the President of the Ninth Assembly of the League of Nations — Herr Zahle of Denmark. Having first introduced all the women delegates from ten countries (including Dr Hilda Clark from Britain[14] and the future

Nobel Peace Prize winner Emily Balch from the United States[15]), Mary Sheepshanks went on to deliver a solemn warning from the WIL. She pointed out that unless either the Russian or some alternative proposals for disarmament were approved and acted upon, new wars were bound to ensue. In order to avoid an imminent loss of faith in the League of Nations, she urged, on behalf of the WIL, that a World Disarmament Conference be convened by the League of Nations without delay, and its delegates instructed 'to make every sacrifice necessary for the transition from a state of organisation for war to a state of organisation for peace.'[16]

Herr Zahle listened politely. He congratulated the delegates on their 'generous efforts' and 'greatness of heart' but warned them against trying to go too far too soon. He countered this assault on the part of urgent female 'idealists' with a reminder of the 'slow but steady' approach preferred by male 'realists'. It was, after all, men who were actually in power all over the world and who were therefore more likely to be in touch with the real world of international politics:

I fear ladies that in advocating solutions of a too positive character, too brusque, too imperfectly adapted to the present-day world you may add to the difficulties which the men who are responsible for their countries' destinies are trying to smooth away by slow and loyal means.[17]

Perhaps Mary Sheepshanks had sounded 'brusque' — she often did — but the 'slow and loyal means' favoured by Herr Zahle were to block the calling of a World Disarmament Conference for the next three and a half years, until May 1932, by which time it was too late.

At the end of 1928 Mary Sheepshanks published an article, *Did the War End War, 1918-1928?* which began sardonically: 'The tenth anniversary of the end of the war has been celebrated, generally by military displays.'[18] She was disquieted by the evidence that each nation's politicians and Chiefs of Staff were once again relying on military power in order to maintain or expand their respective countries' security and influence:

Armaments, in spite of all the disarmament discussions, are everywhere gigantic. Britain is spending well over 100 million pounds a year on them, while the population groans under taxation and unemployment ...

In Europe ... more men are under arms than in 1913, besides the terrific developments in air forces and the apparatus for chemical warfare. The United States ... seems to have caught the war fever from its participation in 'the war to end war'. Mr. Coolidge in his speech on Armistice Day expressed his belief that European armaments had prevented war coming sooner than it actually did [i.e. in 1914]; this is in our view a profoundly mistaken judgment. It will indeed be disastrous if America thus follows the worst precedents of European politics.[19]

In this situation, Mary Sheepshanks put all her hope in public opinion and its capacity to influence government. In order to strengthen anti-militarist European public opinion at this crucial time, Mary organised an important scientific conference at Frankfurt-on-Main in January 1929. The subject of the conference was: Modern Methods of Warfare and The Protection of the Civilian Population. Two women scientists, the Swedish chemist, Dr Naima Sahlbohm and the Swiss biochemist, Dr Gertrud Woker (who were also members of the WIL), had witnessed a demonstration of 'Gas manoeuvres in War time' at the Edgewood Arsenal in America in 1924 (including phosphorus and other incendiary bombardment), and ever since they had been determined to alert the world to this new menace of warfare on civilians from the air.

Airplanes without pilots, steered by radio and carrying poison gas bombs and incendiary bombs can in a few minutes destroy simultaneously great cities like London, Paris, Berlin ... A new war would thus be a war of the *simultaneous extermination of peoples*, and would imperil the whole of civilisation.

Thus ran the WIL's Disarmament appeal put out in conjunction with the Frankfurt Conference, eleven years before the Blitz.

Three hundred people attended the conference, including many scientists and technologists and representatives from sixty-eight newspapers from all over the world. Einstein sent a message of support:

To me the killing of any human being is murder; it is also murder when it takes place on a large scale as an instrument of state policy.[20]

The speakers included the German toxicologist Professor Lewin who, having devoted his whole life to the study of poisons, expressed his horror at the idea that mass poisoning was to be a method of warfare. Poisoners, said the professor, had always been regarded as the worst criminals, and to flood a country with clouds of poison against which there was no defence, would turn civilisation into a desert. Dr Hoejer of Sweden said: 'Modern war will be a war of men against children, mothers and invalids who cannot defend themselves.' A woman doctor from Poland, Dr Budzinska-Tylicka, gave a first-hand account of what it had been like trying to treat the casualties of the first gas-attacks in a Polish field hospital during World War One, and Dr Gertrud Woker demolished the notion that a gasbomb would be 'more humane and cleaner' than previous competitions in massacre. She prophesied that in future wars would not be fought so much against the enemy's armies as against the unarmed enemy populations whose cities and industrial centres would be in the front line.[21] The conclusions reached at the end of a very sombre conference were that no effective protection could be afforded from these horrors, and that the only way to rescue civilisation and humanity itself from destruction was to achieve total disarmament and to organise the peaceful settlement of all disputes. In addition, the great French physicist Langevin drew up a declaration that was published with the conference proceedings, and signed by Einstein, among many other distinguished scientists. It declared:

As there can be no idea of limiting the development of science, the only alternative is to put a stop to war itself ... to denounce the futility of seeking security in armaments, [and] to proclaim with the utmost energy our conviction that the speedy establishment of international justice is a question of life and death for the human race ...[22]

Mary Sheepshanks felt that the Frankfurt Conference was in many ways one of the greatest successes that the WIL had ever had — it had certainly received more notice in the European press than anything they had ever undertaken. But the conference had been nearly wrecked, she felt, by the domineering ways and the tactlessly obvious Communist leanings of one of the German women organisers who had allowed a Communist deputy to the Reichstag to dominate the open discussion time with a long set speech denouncing 'Imperialist' war. Mary fully believed in the liberty of Communists and of Communist sympathisers within the WIL to express their views as publicly as they wished, but she could not be happy about the Communists' wish to dictate a 'correct' line, because it in no way reflected the views of the majority of members within the WIL and because it clearly weakened the League's claim to objectivity in international affairs, and hence any slight moral influence that it might have. She wrote to Jane Addams:

The Communists may be right, but there is not the slightest chance that all the different Sections of our League will agree on this point. Some groups think the racial question, minorities, etc., is the burning one; others think we should concentrate on co-operation with and development of the League of Nations, and so on, and it is only by a very great spirit of tolerance that we can get all our various kinds of people to co-operate. Strong opinions, and still more violent forms of expression, lead to a certain amount of trouble. (4 February 1929.)

Just a month earlier, in December 1928, Mary had had to engage a Geneva lawyer on behalf of the WIL to counter public allegations by a mysterious 'Entente Internationale' that the WIL was a Bolshevik-infiltrated 'cell', operating in the interests of the Komintern.[23] The last thing the WIL needed at this point was well-publicised domination by its Left-wing. In January 1929, Mary wrote gloomily to Dr Alice Hamilton in the United States: 'there are such unfortunate elements of friction that I fear very much there will be a rupture ... Prague weighs very heavy on my mind.' (19 January 1929.)

Prague was the locale fixed on for the WIL's triennial International Conference later that year. But in Prague there was a Czech section of the WIL, a German section of the WIL and a Jewish section of the WIL — and none of them could get on with the others. Clearly there could be no hope for an effective international women's peace organisation if it were unable 'to manifest a spirit of conciliation in its own ranks.' Mary put all her hope for the survival of the WIL in Jane Addams — if only the latter were not now so old and ill:

If Miss Addams were in the best of health, the mere fact of her influence would have a wonderful effect, but as she is at present she ought not to be subjected to the strain that this sort of thing means. Personally I feel completely exhausted after three days at Frankfort simply with the worry of it. (March 1929.)

In the event, despite still suffering from the after-effects of a serious heart attack, Jane Addams did rally sufficiently to go to Prague for the Congress in September 1929. The Congress hall was tense with suppressed friction and the anticipation of open conflict. But when seventy-year-old

Jane Addams walked slowly on to the platform to take her place as presiding officer, an extraordinary calming influence went out from her to everyone present.[24] She did not pretend that there was nothing wrong; instead she faced the divisions within the WIL, both the split between the 'compromisers' and the 'non-compromisers', and the split between those members who belonged to what were felt to be oppressive majority groups and those who belonged to ethnic minorities within the various countries represented. Jane Addams urged all the women present to work to achieve a new synthesis — 'Not compromise, but a new solution born of good-will and pooled intelligence.' For the sake of this 'pooled intelligence' Polish, Ukrainian and German women thereupon held joint meetings to plan a concerted programme of internationalist action for the following year; the German group, the Jewish group and the Czech group within the Czech branch agreed at last to form one joint national Section; and individual delegates relinquished 'cherished pet projects' for the sake of strengthening consensus decisions by the WIL as a whole.

Mary Sheepshanks' other preoccupation at the end of 1929 was the eruption of alarming situations in Palestine and in Austria. Mary had many Jewish friends and while in London in 1929 she had attended several Zionist meetings called to protest against the slackness of the British authorities in protecting Jewish settlers from Arab attacks. Regarding Palestine, Mary reported to Jane Addams:

There is no doubt that the disorders were due to the negligence of the British officials, that is to say, they could and should have prevented and guarded against them. The Zionists are of opinion that the Arabs have been carrying out a policy of rioting and agitation and that as this had on two previous occasions been followed by concessions from the Administration, they have been encouraged to continue, hoping that if they make themselves unpleasant enough the British will relinquish the Mandate. Their view is, and it seems justified, that the British officials have not given the whole-hearted support to the Balfour declaration that they should have done, and that the Arabs have felt that the British were fundamentally indifferent to the Jews. It is even possible that, as my Jewish informant said 'Arabs are more popular with the British because they are more distinguished and romantic than our unattractive Jewish population'. In any case the view put forward to me was that the British Administration should in future state emphatically that they intend to carry out the Mandate and protect the Jews, or if the British Government is really weakening about the Mandate and intends to give it up, it should say so and give the Jews proper warning so that they may take what steps they can to protect themselves. (2 November 1929.)

The suggestion was made that a WIL delegation should visit Palestine to mediate between Arab and Jewish women community leaders but Mary did not hold out any hope for its effectiveness. She wrote on 19 December 1929 to Jane Addams:

There has recently been a congress of Arab women which went in deputation to the Governor and strongly supported the Arab nationalist claims and demanded the withdrawal of the Balfour Declaration and the checking of Zionist immigration. There is therefore a nucleus of women to be got hold of though they would certainly not to begin with be easy to deal with.

Mary Sheepshanks was quite prescient enough to realise that any conciliation between the two communities in Palestine would take many years of patient reciprocal interpretation and concessions: it was not a matter to be effected by any outsiders' flying visit — and least of all by a delegation of Engishwomen, however well-meaning.

As for Austria, the situation there was rapidly approaching that of civil war between armed Right-wing nationalists and young socialists. At the request of the WIL in Austria, a fact-finding deputation visited Vienna at the end of 1929. The women reported that they found virulent anti-Semitism, hatred between Catholics and socialists, ominous discontent among many former army officers and a blatantly dangerous build-up of private armies, all aggravated by the deepening economic misery of the masses. All the pre-conditions for the triumph of Fascism, not only in Austria but also in Germany, Hungary, Bulgaria and Romania, were diagnosed in 1929 by these women who were quite powerless to stem it. 'If only,' they said, 'the League of Nations would proclaim that any state that refused to disarm the illegal and extra-legal forces within it borders would be exposed to League sanctions.' But nothing was done.[25]

1930 was to be Mary Sheepshanks' busiest year as International Secretary of the WIL, and it was also to be her last. Two issues prominent on her working agenda were the Five Power Naval Conference[26] and the confrontation between the British Raj and the Indian Independence Movement.[27] But the most urgent appeals of all now beginning to come to the WIL international office in Geneva were those from Central and Eastern Europe. On 14 August 1930, Mary received the following ominous message from Romania:

Les Juifs de Bucarest se sentent en grand danger et supplient de faire à Genève tout ce qu'il est possible pour insister auprès du Gouvernement roumain pour qu'il prenne les mesures efficaces nécessaires pour éviter de nouveaux pogromes ... J'attends vos instructions au sujet de cette démarche. [The Jews of Bucharest consider themselves to be in great danger and entreat Geneva to do everything possible to insist that the Romanian government take effective measures necessary to avoid new pogroms ... I await your instructions concerning this development.]

The Jews of Europe were soon to find themselves belonging to a new category of human beings — the so-called 'stateless persons', or 'Apatrides'. These people were either members of minority groups within the new nation states called into being on the dissolution of the Hapsburg Empire after 1919, or else they were political exiles deprived of citizenship by their own country of origin, or else they were Jews. All too soon it was to become clear that to be thus 'de-nationalised' also entailed being 'denaturalised' — looked upon by their enemies as something other than belonging to human nature.

The denationalized White Russians were followed by the Spanish Republicans, the Armenians and, of course, the Jews ... The stateless were truly men without any political community. No country wanted them or cared about their fate ... Stateless persons were ... among the first Europeans in the twentieth century to experience unrestricted police domination.

They had been deprived of all political status by bureaucratic definition. As such they had become *superfluous men*. These *apatrides* in the detention camps were among the living dead ... They lost all right to life and human dignity.[28]

Because of Mary's many contacts in Romania, Czecho-slovakia, Hungary, Yugoslavia and Poland she was one of the first people in the world to realise something of the peril that the new stateless citizens of Europe were in. It was not surprising, given Mary Sheepshanks' constant determ-ination to get something done, that it should have been she who organised the first Conference on Statelessness to be held in Europe, in Geneva in September 1930.[29]

That Conference, which she chaired and introduced, was attended by representatives from the International Council of Women, the Society of Friends, the Inter-national Suffrage Alliance, the League for the Rights of Man and the League of Nations Union. A message from Romain Rolland as well as a letter of support from Albert Einstein were read out. Frau Aszkanazy of Vienna summed up the total vulnerability of the stateless person:

To be stateless means death by starvation, for the stateless cannot secure work anywhere without permission of the authorities. The authorities rarely grant this permission on the grounds that hundreds of thousands of their own subjects are without work! ... The stateless citizen has no consular protection anywhere, he cannot get a passport or visa, and on the other hand, he may be expelled from a country at any time without any reason.[30]

All that the WIL Conference could do was to alert sympathetic members of the British Delegation to the League of Nations — Charles Roden Buxton, Mary Agnes Hamilton and Ellen Wilkinson, MP — to the plight of these 'undesirables' of Europe. In the following year, a WIL deputation presented detailed proposals for dealing with the stateless problem (including the extension of the precedent of the 'Nansen passport' — a passport issued to fugitives from the Russian Revolution) to the legal section of the League of Nations. No effective action was taken, however, partly because no one was then able to foresee what would soon be the frightful consequences of their inaction.

Mary Sheepshanks had organised that conference on statelessness despite having already, in April 1930, officially resigned as International Secretary of the WIL. She had been driven to resign by the increasing hostility between herself and some of the dominant members of the International Executive. Deep personal antipathies had presented themselves as arguments about tactics and, as a result, these pacifist women were now warring with one another. The leading German members of the WIL, especially Lida Gustava Heymann and her young disciple Gertrud Baer, supported by the French Left-wingers Gabrielle Duchêne and Camille Drevet, always passionate and high-handed, had, understandably, become still more passionate and high-handed under pressure from the menace of Fascism. But Mary Sheepshanks could be equally implacable. She was quite as anti-Fascist as were Heymann or Baer or Duchêne, but she was convinced that their 'Left-extremism' was alienating the very support against Hitler and Mussolini that they so desperately needed; they would be left out in the cold, calling for 'total disarmament and the overthrow of capitalism', with nobody listening. As indeed they were.[31] They, for their part, did not approve of Mary's efforts to increase the influence of the WIL at the League of Nations and they wanted her to act merely as the subordinate officer of the International Executive of the WIL. But, as Mary herself admitted in her old age: 'I never learned to be a good subordinate.' Not even Jane Addams herself, to whom members of the WIL all over the world were whole-heartedly devoted, could succeed in mediating between the different national and political groupings:

Perhaps it takes more moral energy than any of us possess to compose this situation in which we find ourselves [i.e. the polarisation between Left and Right in 1930]; like the bulk of our generation we may be finding international comity too difficult, even upon the very small scale in which we are trying it.[32]

But the conflicts that racked the WIL went deeper than any arguments between Left and Right. For all their altruism and far-sightedness, these women were just as much at the mercy of their own febrile righteous indignation and of the will-to-power within themselves as were the benighted citizens whom they were trying to influence. 'We are all merciless', as Herzen says, 'and most merciless when we are in the right.'[33] And their self-image as intelligent, humane women blinded them to their own irrationality and capacity for hate. Jane Addams put her finger on what was wrong:

After a session in Prague in which Frau Perlen had been quite difficult and I had tried very hard as presiding officer to be fair to her, she came to me and said, 'You don't really like me and a Pacifist can't do any good unless she likes the people she is dealing with; you can't even be just unless you do.' Of course I instantly remembered that statement of Tolstoy's, because she had used almost his very words, 'We think that there are human situations which we can manage without love but there are no such situations.'[34]

The pity was that these women had loved one another once — both in 1915 and in 1919, and yet here they were in 1931 experiencing a total breakdown of relationship. Finally, there was nothing left for Mary Sheepshanks to do but leave. Polite regrets followed her departure but also sighs of relief.[35]

After handing over the Maison Internationale in Geneva to her successor, Mary — now nearly sixty and very arthritic — went on to undertake the most important and the most personally devastating task of her whole political life. At the request of Ukrainian members of the WIL, she went on a fact-finding mission to East Galicia and to Poland in order to investigate reports of recent Polish atrocities in the Ukraine. What she found there was that, in her own words, 'The bullied had become bullies.'[36]

Mary arrived secretly at Lvov one very cold morning in late November 1930. Instead of registering with the police as she was supposed to do, she left her luggage at the station and went straight to the house of her Ukrainian woman contact. The latter then took her to secret interviews with journalists, doctors, the head of the Women's Cultural Organisation, patients in the Ukrainian Clinic and to the Bishop of Lvov who was sheltering some of the stricken peasants in his house. Everywhere she went Mary gathered the same account from eye-witnesses, all of whom were now risking years of imprisonment, and worse, by talking to her.

Two months previously, ostensibly as a reprisal for some rick-burning committed by Ukrainian schoolboys, but really in order to terrorise the whole Ukrainian minority, of some five million, the Polish dictator Pilsudski had ordered savage police and military raids to be made throughout the country by night.

Each village had been surrounded, machine guns set up, and

contributions in live-stock, grain and cash levied from each household. The villages were forced to wreck their reading-room, library and co-operative store; and for this they were not allowed tools but had to use their torn and bleeding hands. They were then made to sign a declaration that they had carried out this demolition of their own free will.

The leading men of the village were then rounded up, the storekeeper, the schoolmaster, the custodian of the reading-room, the priest and others. They were driven into a barn, where they were stripped and beaten unconscious with the thick sticks used for threshing corn. They were then revived with cold water and beaten again.[37]

No medical treatment was allowed — the survivors had to be smuggled out of the villages in farmcarts to find a doctor in the town who would treat them in secret. Mary inter-viewed many such patients who insisted on showing her their now gangrenous wounds. 'In some villages the troops took the roofs from their houses, or forced the peasants to destroy their roofs, stoves were damaged, agricultural machinery broken up and the drinking water supply destroyed.'[38] Mary could not visit any of the terrorised villages because they were now all cordoned off by police and militia. But by correlating the reports of lawyers, deputies, doctors, women's leaders and clergy and peasants, she was able to deduce that at the very least some five hundred villages had been involved. She concluded that:

this so-called pacification has been carried out with a ferocity which can only be compared to the previous atrocities carried out in the early 19th century by the Bashi-bazouks in the old Turkish territories; [they] ... were inflicted without trial and wholesale on an entire population.[39]

When Mary reached Warsaw she was dismayed to discover that the very nationalistic Polish members of the WIL flatly refused to believe what she told them about the happenings in Galicia. Only Madame Semplowska, who had championed the cause of political prisoners for nearly forty years, and the woman senator Kruschianska believed Mary, both of them being only too well aware of the Polish military dictator Pilsudski's reliance on torture and brutality.[40] Mary obtained still more appalling evidence of this in Warsaw itself when she saw the results of what Pilsudski had ordered to be done to his own most eminent political opponents within Poland. Men such as the head of the Socialist Party, the Procurator of the State Tribunal, the former head of the Government, the chief of the Christian Party, the socialist editor, Dubois, and five Ukrainian Deputies had all been imprisoned for the past three months in the fortress of Brest-Litovsk. Mary was taken secretly to see the recently released Libermann, former State Procurator, now lying in a sanatorium:

It was extremely moving, indeed heartrending to see this fine old man, the champion of social democracy suffering and broken ... He told me how in September he had been summoned to the Police Station and taken by police agents in a motor car into the country and told to run into the woods. Realising that that meant shooting for pretended flight, he refused and was then stripped naked, his head muffled in a coat, held down and beaten so frightfully that he was unconscious for four days, and had twenty-one wounds on his body. He was taken in this condition to the fortress of Brest Litovsk and put into a damp, dark, dirty cell without even bedding ... On one occasion he and his companion were each taken to adjoining empty prison cells and told that everything was to be now finished. They were stripped and made to stand facing the wall for several hours while revolvers were fired in adjacent cells so that they believed that prisoners were being executed one by one ...

Now as he lay in the sanatorium he said he trembled at every sound, fearing it was police come to re-arrest him. This final and terrible interview finished my stay.[41]

Mary Sheepshanks prefaced her confidential report to the Executive of the WIL by stressing that no one must know she had seen Libermann — 'He begged me not to let that appear in print because it ... might lead to his re-arrest, which would probably involve his death.'[42]

Mary Sheepshanks did everything possible to rouse world opinion. First she went to Berlin. She wrote up her report and contacted sympathetic socialists in the German Reichstag including the woman deputy, Toni Pfülf. While still in Berlin she saw Lewis Lochner of the Associated Press of America (the US government was very pro-Pilsudski) and she had a long conference with Frederick Voigt of the *Manchester Guardian*, who gave her his whole-hearted support. From Berlin she went on to Amsterdam where she saw the leader of the International Transport Workers' Union, Edo Fimmen, who promised her that he would urge industrial action by his men, including the 'blacking' of Polish iron. From the Netherlands she went on to London. She knew that both the British Consul in Warsaw and the *Times* correspondent there were pro-Pilsudski and that the British public knew almost nothing of what had been perpetrated in the Ukraine. She reported on her experiences to the Trades Union Council and to the Labour Party's international information section and she saw several MPs at the House of Commons. She had interviews with the Editor and the Foreign Editor of the *Times* and finally, after much difficulty, persuaded them to print a letter from her (published 1 January 1931).[43] She also had a long interview with Wickham Steed, the former editor of the *Times*, who promised to see a representative of *Le Figaro*. Philip Noel-Baker, then Parliamentary Secretary for Foreign Affairs, told Mary that the important thing was to 'get at France'. Therefore, Mary urged her successor in Geneva, Camille Drevet, to organise as many protests as she could to be delivered to the Polish Embassy in Paris and to get a French speaker to the WIL's meeting in Geneva which had been timed to anticipate the League of Nations'

Council meeting and which, it was hoped, might influence the issue of a Swiss bank loan to Poland that was being negotiated just then. Mary's letter to Camille Drevet, dated 24 December 1930 ended: 'I am dead tired.' Three days later, however, Mary was preparing to make a secret trip to Dublin in order to lobby the Irish Foreign Minister because she thought there was a good chance of getting Ireland to bring up the matter of Poland and Galicia at the League of Nations Council. 'I think if we really succeed in getting something done [about Galicia] it will help other minorities.'

In the short term, Mary thought, the widespread publicity about the 'pacification' of Galicia did have some effect on Pilsudski. Certainly when she was invited to visit the Ukraine again, three years later, Mary was welcomed openly as a celebrity and, although she was occasionally stopped and questioned, there was no longer any need for her to dodge the police. She attended public meetings, saw Mass celebrated in the open air and received the traditional offering of bread and salt in the houses where she stayed. In another few years, of course, this part of Europe was a battlefield, after which it was absorbed into the Soviet bloc under Stalin and no further contact with Western Europe was possible. Mary's only consolation in her old age was to be told by a Ukrainian emigrant that there were 300,000 Ukrainians in Canada who loved her. 'The very thought keeps me warm.' (Mary Sheepshanks, *Autobiography*, ch. 20).

Elsewhere, between 1931 and 1933, the world became ever darker. The economic system of the West was clearly in a shambles; atavistic nationalism became for many of the demoralised a wonder drug. The World Disarmament Conference at Geneva in 1932 did nothing to answer the petition of millions that the arms race be halted.[44] And in March 1933, Hitler came to power. Mary Sheepshanks foresaw much of what would now follow. Some of her friends in Germany and Austria went immediately into exile, others went 'underground'; Toni Pfülf, the socialist woman deputy to the Reichstag, whom Mary had interviewed about Galicia in December 1930, killed herself. Hers was the first violent death in Mary's circle that was directly attributable to the triumph of the Nazis.

The civilised, humane vision inspiring Mary Sheepshanks' pacifist socialism proved impotent against the irrational human drive to dominate lest one be dominated, kill lest one be killed. Mary brooded time and again on why she and those like her had failed. Had her own inability to make common cause with her fellow anti-Fascists within the women's peace movement been a significant weakness at a vital time? Or had it not mattered one way or another, given all the economic and political power ranged against them? When, in any case, had been the 'vital' time? 1932? 1929? 1919? — or August 1914? E.M. Forster's conclusion at this same period was: 'As a matter of fact, one's activities (and inactivities) must have been doomed for many years.'[45]

14

THE LAST YEARS OF FLORA MAYOR
AND MARY SHEEPSHANKS

The years 1926-1932 were dark ones for Flora also. Flora agreed with Mary that the political and economic world of the late 1920s was becoming increasingly grim — but for quite different reasons. Far from being either a 'Left extremist' or a 'Left moderate', Flora was a Conservative. She and Alice lived on the interest from their inherited capital and during the 1920s they felt both economically vulnerable and politically beleaguered. It would be hard to say whom Flora and Alice Mayor feared and detested more — the iconoclastic, 'arty', avant-garde, or the now militant British working-class with its strikes and marches and Labour Party winning a first general election. One of the last books that Flora Mayor re-read with deep approval was Matthew Arnold's *Culture and Anarchy*. The fifty-five-year-old sisters saw the cultural domination of one half of the world by jazz, cocktails and worship of the motor car, and the imminent political domination of the other half by Bolshevik Russia.

In a letter to Alice, Flora wrote: 'I feel the duty of all is to preach patriotism'; and in September 1926, a long letter from Flora was published in the Church of England weekly newspaper, the *Guardian*, bitterly criticising the British miners for continuing their strike after the General Strike had failed. She accused the miners' leaders of exploiting the 'natural weaknesses of greed, intellectual laziness and moral cowardice', and the miners themselves of refusing to help England at a time of national economic crisis and of ruining Britain's coal industry with their bad habits of ca'canny and absenteeism. She contrasted the miners' refusal to work a longer shift with the clergy, the house-masters at public schools and the civil servants, all of whom (like her own father and brothers) were willing to work much longer than eight hours a day out of their sense of duty.

It was left to the editor of the *Guardian* to point out, in a lengthy reply, 1 October 1926, that miners, unlike public schoolmasters, do not have three-and-a-half months' annual holiday, nor do they earn more money when they are sixty than when they are twenty, nor can they ever afford to retire before they are old. The editor refrained from adding that none of the professional men whom Flora had instanced were squatting half-naked in a tunnel two-and-a-half feet high, hacking at the coalface while inhaling the dust that would later kill them. But even without those facts, it is still rather terrible to read the editor's entreaty to 'Miss Mayor, the distinguished authoress of *The Rector's Daughter*' to be more 'human': 'It is [the] human factor in the situation which I plead with you to take into account.'

What caused Flora's extraordinary outburst against the miners was not merely her belief that the whole strike was ultimately orchestrated by Moscow, but also her passion-ate, outraged sense of loyalty to her own people — to her brother Henry whose work as an unappreciated housemaster at Clifton had so nearly broken him, and to her brother Robin, Principal Assistant Secretary in the Department of Education, created Companion of the Bath in 1919. 1926 was the year in which both her brothers were asked to take early retirement, and Flora was adamant that neither of them had been granted anything like their due in return for all the selfless, unstinting service that each of them had rendered. And she was 'd—d' if she was going to join with the 'sentimentalists' in their exclusive pity for

coal-miners and their righteous contempt for the govern-
ing class: 'At what stage does an employer cease to be
vermin and outside the pale, and become a man?'[1]

Flora could sometimes laugh at her deepening conservatism. In her last novel, *The Squire's Daughter*, she wrote
'They all stood for Church, King, Public Schools and
Primrose League. One can guess their many, many
aversions.'[2] But Alice never could. And Flora, due to her
increasing invalidism, was becoming ever more dependent
upon Alice.

The embittered *The Squire's Daughter* is the product of
these class anxieties. All that Flora believed deserved to
survive in England is seen here to be on the verge of dis-
integration, if not of extinction. By the end of the book the
De Laceys are compelled to sell off their centuries-old
ancestral home, the squire loses his mind through stress
caused by the Great War and anxiety over his children, and
there will be no grandchild to carry on the family tradition.
'The lights are going out for all of us', grieves one of the
characters over the departure of the De Laceys.[3] 'Carne
stood for all that is best in our fair England ... and that
"went under" after 1914-1918' agreed a sympathetic
reviewer in the *Critic*. 'Fall of England's "Caste" system
again provides material for Miss Mayor', wrote a less
sympathetic American reviewer in New York. Another
American reviewer put his finger on the book's central
weakness: 'I felt that Miss Mayor was using her characters
and events as a frame on which to build her analysis.'[4]

Flora Mayor was not on intimate terms with 'county'
families, and her 'squire' of the title, Sir Geoffrey De Lacey,
is a fantasy figure — a winner of the Victoria Cross, devoted
reader of Dante, Shakespeare and Cervantes, indulgent
landlord, beloved neighbour and the very pattern of
fatherly forbearance towards his maddeningly irresponsible youngest daughter. But this idealisation makes him
such a nonpareil that — despite some touching moments
— Sir Geoffrey De Lacey is neither a convincing social type

nor a credible, un-ideal, human being. The problem with the squire's daughter, Ron, however, is not one of over-simplifying authorial idealisation, but the reverse. What was meant to be complex psychological realism becomes muddled self-contradiction. Ron De Lacey is not one girl, but two. She is the girl whom Flora Mayor could imagine and sympathise with — honest and serious and brave despite being blown hither and yon by the febrile sensation-seeking of the 1920s. But she can also be a quite different girl, so rootless as to become blasé and unserious, a mocker not just of herself but of everyone else, and a hurter of others just for the devil of it — the very type of 'modern girl' whom Flora Mayor most despised and feared.

To L.P. Hartley, Ron was:

a nightmare girl, a Victorian parent's bad dream of what his offspring might be like, come true. We want to know whether a heart really animates her casual and indifferent demeanour; sometimes it seems as though the modest ticking of that organ might be discerned amid the louder throbbing of her motor-car.[5]

And the essayist and critic Gerald Gould, in his review headed 'A Girl as the Modern Byron' was even more severe: 'apparently she had some sort of charm and attractiveness which her creator never succeeds in com-municating'.[6] He found Ron's selfishness and emptiness unbearable. Flora Mayor herself was very uneasy about the book, telling Virginia Woolf that she was 'writing a bad novel' and fearing, after it was finished, that she had failed to bring it off.

What Flora had hoped to write was an elegy, but what emerged was more like a disapproving moan. Hitherto she had always extended the range of her reader's emotional and imaginative reach but here she explicitly prohibits any sympathy for Ron's mother, sister, brother, friends, neighbours or the much-despised Americans who become

Ron's in-laws. Thus there is a cumulative, antipathetic fusion of intellectual, spiritual, social and emotional snobberies until, instead of everyone mattering, hardly anyone seems to matter very much.

But Flora rallied from that Slough of sour Despond to write a few last short stories which do awaken sympathy for people whom one had hitherto overlooked or been tempted to condemn. 'In her last stories Flora again recurs with pity to the lonely and unwanted', Alice wrote to Robin Mayor in 1932. These characters are the elderly and infirm residents of guesthouses and nursing homes, living from breakfast to lunch to tea along the south coast of England. Seventy-year-old Mrs Gwynne, for example, in *Christmas Night at the Almira*,[7] once vivacious, pretty and much loved, has now nothing to live for but a grown-up married son, who never visits her. Whenever her true situation of abandonment becomes too real, she goes up to a furtive bottle of brandy in her bedroom. Forbidden to keep a pet by the boarding-house regulations, Mrs Gwynne is only permitted the

birds that flew past her window. She spent long hours willing them into confidence. This was her solid occupation; her relaxations were dozing on the sofa at half-past ten in the morning, at five, at any unchartered hour, and talking to all listeners she could lay hands on.

The catastrophe comes when Mrs Gwynne's son at last pays his duty visit, only to announce that he must immediately be off again — 'on business'. Over-excited and desperate at this imminent desertion, Mrs Gwynne drinks too much at the Christmas dinner table:

Her loud vulgar singing, her laughter, her shouts made Mrs Wallington's decorous Christmas party ready to sink into the floor . . .
    She was trying to get at more champagne, fighting with him, screaming and abusing him . . .
    'She's a mother to be proud of, isn't she?'

Next morning Mrs Gwynne wakes to remember her disgraceful scene, swallows an overdose of sleeping-pills and cries herself to death.

Another late story, *Innocents' Day*, also focuses on 'the last, most cheerless stage'[8] of life, but this time it shows three solitary, ageing women who nevertheless manage, during one winter's afternoon, to sustain and nourish one another. 'Sometimes in the jog-trot of life comes a week, a day, an afternoon, lit up with some special sweetness, which sets it apart, and makes it treasured in the memory.' The three elderly friends' shared memories, which go back more than fifty years, and the loving fellowship that they feel during their reunion, enable them, however briefly, to constitute a family. Unconsciously they mother one another, even calling the youngest of the three, sixty-year-old Miss Perrin, 'child'. (Similarly, and equally significantly, whenever Flora and Alice Mayor were apart they began their daily letter to each other with 'My dear child', all their adult lives.)

Flora Mayor's last and longest story, *Mother and Daughter*,[9] involves 'three harmless chronics' at 'The Nookery': Miss Robins with her pathetically darned underwear and trembly hands; eighty-year-old Rev. Mr Selby, anguished as he senses the approach of senility; and Mrs Fairholme, the sixty-year-old Mother of the title who tries to protect these two 'comrades' from the tyranny of the proprietress. For there are dictators, as Flora knew, in the small world as well as in the great. Mrs Fairholme's daughter, Helen, is a thirty-five-year-old Labour Party activist, who rejects all her mother's weak-minded liberalism in the name of 'progress'. To Helen, old Miss Robins is not quite human — but a 'small species of weasel', too leech-like to be harmless:

She's a blot on the landscape; such people ought not to exist. I'm thankful to say they won't, once this generation's gone. We shall eliminate that type; we shall give women more self-respect.

With an unerring, prescient ear Flora Mayor records that ominous: 'We shall eliminate that type.' Precisely at the time when Mary Sheepshanks was being alerted to the inhumanity of Fascism, Flora was alive to the inhumanity that is also at times detectable behind the righteous rhetoric of the Left. Flora's sympathy and respect are clearly for elderly Mrs Fairholme, but Helen is no mere caricature. The crucial confrontation between the two women comes when Helen tells her mother that she no longer feels any need to believe in a reunion with her dead father and brother. But at the end of the story, it is Helen, by then bereft of her mother also, who cries in desolation. She is still unable to believe in a reunion after death but she is no longer superior to the need to believe.

The need to believe in immortality had been a necessity for Flora herself ever since Ernest Shepherd had died nearly thirty years earlier, and it was this that inspired her sporadic attempts to write ghost stories. Many of these stories centre on the possibility of communication between the living and the beloved dead, and most of them were written during and just after the Great War when there was a revival of interest in spiritualism. Flora Mayor herself went through a short period of participation in spiritualist meetings in 1918. In Flora's opinion her ghost stories contained the best prose she ever wrote but few of her readers would agree, and they were rejected by publisher after publisher. Only one of her supernatural stories, *Letters from Manningfield*,[10] is distinctively by 'F.M. Mayor' as it probes the brief ambivalence in the response of a usually tender, middle-aged daughter towards her very old parents.

As the 1920s advanced, Flora, who was still living with her mother and Alice at Queensgate House, grew increasingly thin and frail. She was racked by frequent attacks of severe bronchial asthma, through which she was always nursed by Alice. The lifelong interdependence, camaraderie and reciprocal 'mothering' between the sisters had deepened with the years. Throughout the 1920s Alice would always champion Flora to all comers as a writer whose great gifts neither the critics nor the reading public had ever adequately acknowledged, while Flora would openly admire Alice's singing and constantly prod her into doing more with her painting. On the very rare occasions when Alice and Flora quarrelled — for instance during their wretched Clifton College period in 1916 when neither of them succeeded in being a good surrogate housemaster's wife at Watson's — Flora would be the first to make it up: 'You have done so much for me, I must just try and think about that.' Whenever they were apart it was Flora who would insist on her absolute need of a long daily letter from Alice, and, whenever she compared herself with Alice, Flora would always assert that if she were the more intellectual one, Alice was the more many-sided and had the stronger character. Time and again Flora would try to tell Alice what she felt for her:

I have been thinking much of you. Oh, may God spare us to live together all our lives. I often pray so. I sometimes think what our loneliness would have been without one another. You would have married Frank I think and I should certainly have married Ernest at once and might have had my baby. But without that, excluded entirely from Father's and Mother's confidence, and treated as the little, wayward young creature, Henry immersed only in Clifton and Robin in his marriage — of course one would have thrown oneself into friendship and friendship can give much, but we are unlike all our friends. If we do lose oneanother [sic] untimely, we shall have had oneanother. (1921.)

In 1927, Flora wrote to Alice: 'I *cannot* be happy if you are not happy.'

It was also in 1927 that their mother, the redoubtable Mrs Mayor, died, at the great age of ninety-eight, having kept all her faculties, except her hearing, to the end. When *The Rector's Daughter* had been published, in 1924, only those of Flora's own generation within the immediate

Mayor family had realised that the portrait of the intimidating and unbending old lady, Mrs Herbert, was, in fact, based on Flora's own mother. With the death of Mrs Mayor the old familiar life in Queensgate House was over at last. The house, together with its eighteenth-century paintings, was sold and Flora and Alice moved to 7 East Heath Road, Hampstead. A few months later Flora had to undergo a serious operation. At first she seemed to make a good recovery, carefully nursed by Alice. But every bout of illness that she suffered after that weakened her more. Eventually Flora went down with pneumonia and had to go into hospital. Hers was the first generation in which an English lady found herself being nursed in a public institution and Flora's reactions to life in Braintree Cottage Hospital at the end of the 1920s are revealing:

My dear child,

Well it is an experience to be in a Hospital and not really an unpleasant one. They seem to be good natured souls, and of course I am Thank God a paying case in my own room. I wouldn't be in any ordinary ward an ordinary patient for all you could give me. The central mistake ... is to treat all patients alike — to standardize. You would get the patient on much quicker clearly if you would consult their taste a little in the matter of food — and oh this bed-pan fetish. It's much less tiring just to get out, not that anybody makes a fuss over bringing it, but it's such a bother asking for it, and then finding you don't want it, that you rather put off, and then I get a pain. The Sister of course is rather shocked at the towzle of my bed: 'I don't know what they would say if you were in a General Ward.'
Me: 'Yes I'm afraid I would break Sister's heart.'
Sister: 'Or Sister would break your heart.'
I felt inclined to say 'If she tried that, she would regret it.'

I'm perfectly certain all patients in wards are treated like children who are inclined to be troublesome and are in need of admonition. Of course you must have a certain amount of discipline in a Ward, but I am certain discipline is administered with a lavish hand.

In a later letter from the same hospital Flora wrote:

I told my little G.P.[11] nurse she must never get used to
suffering and always sympathize with it and she said she
would: she did hate the way the nurse who calls me 'Miss' is
so callous and says 'Oh they don't feel it'.

In December 1931 Flora suffered another attack of
pneumonia on top of her chronic asthma and, in January
1932, she also contracted 'flu. Alice caught the same 'flu
and the last letters that the twin sisters ever wrote to one
another were on pencilled scraps of paper passed from one
sickroom at 7 East Heath Road to the next. These were
among Flora's last written words:

Oh don't the days seem lank and long ... My dear child,
Hand shaky. Fair night but one bad attack of coughing ...
Well, my darling I am a bit better today, and am so glad. Yes
... now at last I know what constant suffering is, but being
alone with the fact *m'a aidée* ... I do pray and *try* to be brave,
you know ... I know my darling you must feel very miserable
about my health ... but let us feel more *thankful than words can
say* that it is only physical.

Finally she managed to write: 'Lying here with my Lord I
look forward to my long rest.' The night before Flora died,
Alice was brought in to see her. Together with Robin, their
elder brother, Alice marvelled at 'That look of radiant
happiness on Flora's face' (Robin to Alice, February 1932).
Next morning Flora's long struggle to breathe was over.
Alice was too ill to be at Flora's side when she died, but
Henry and Kitty were with her. Kitty later spoke of Flora's
look of transfiguration — 'Flora's was the only beautiful
passing I have seen.' She was fifty-nine. The funeral service
included Richard Baxter's seventeenth-century hymn,
'Lord, it belongs not to my care' set by Purcell:

Lord, it belongs not to my care
    Whether I die or live ...

Christ leads me through no darker rooms
  Than He went through before;
And he that to God's Kingdom comes
  Must enter by this door ...

Flora Mayor is buried among the crab-apple trees, roses, cypresses and long feathery grass of West Hampstead Cemetery, next to her seven Mayor aunts — Anna, Lizzie, Kate, Charlotte, Emily, Fanny and Georgina. On her gravestone are her favourite words from Bach's B Minor Mass: *Exspecto Resurrectionem.*

John Masefield, the Poet Laureate, wrote an obituary note on 'F.M. Mayor, Novelist' for *The Times*, but *The Times* refused to print it. In contrast to this official disdain, the personal tributes to Flora poured in to try and comfort Alice. There was one letter from a farmer's daughter which said: 'I did not know Miss Flora wrote novels' as well as the very literary tribute from Rex Littleboy: 'I like to think of her now talking with Cowper and Jane Austen, and Trollope.' Ernest Shepherd's sister, Gertrude, wrote:

How I hope she and Ernest are together, two of the best. I suppose *the* two best of all our generation. There never, again, was anyone like him I think: he was in a class alone just as she is.

And Ernest's brother wrote to Alice:

at least you have the satisfaction of knowing that you had always done everything you possibly could have done for Flora, and not even Ernest could have found even the smallest thing to complain of.

Many other friends stressed the extraordinary achievement that the lifelong loving friendship between the twin sisters had been:

I should think hardly any two sisters were as much to each other as you two have been.

Your life has had Flora for its pivot.

Flora herself told us that it was *you* who made it possible for her to take up her life again as she did after Ernest's death, and to enjoy it.

That capacity of Flora's for enjoyment, her vitality, and her humour, were what many of her friends cherished most:

Flora was so gay and so very gallant herself — she would have approved of the thing the organist played at the end of the [funeral] service — there was such a note of triumph about it.

... even when Flora was so ill ... she seemed to forget all that and see fun in things when most of us would have done our best to be patient and resigned but would certainly not have risen to brightness and fun.

When she was here gay times were gayer ... there was such joy in her friendship, and no one made me laugh so much; she had the knack of making other people feel almost clever.

She had more humour than anyone I have ever known.

Flora could never be a Sunday memory. She is a Sunday, a Monday, and every other day memory.

Flora's great courage in fighting against constant illness was also underlined:

When I saw you and her together last summer I was struck then as I had been before by the way she could rise out of these serious discomforts and the moment the asthma or the coughing gave her respite she would be bright and gay and almost as of old. What courage she had.

She was a brave unselfish woman — if ever there was one.

What Flora's friends emphasised most of all, however, was her extraordinary gift for making them feel loved. Among the papers in the Mayor archive there is a large bundle of letters signed 'Yours respectfully, L. Hotton.' Lily Hotton had been housemaid at Queensgate House until she had had to leave for reasons of health, but she and Flora and Alice wrote to each other and visited to the end of their lives. When Flora died, Alice wrote to Lily Hotton that same day to tell her, and Lily replied:

And so dear Miss Alice you have lost her for a while ... I have indeed lost my best friend — for Miss Flora in so many ways has been more than a friend, she has been a sister, more feeling and understanding than my own ... I should so have loved to see her just once more ... The little shawl I should like [to keep] for she has worn it and that is enough.

Another friend, the historical novelist Margaret Irwin, wrote: 'So many have been more themselves because of [Flora's] love and understanding.' And this was repeated in tribute after tribute:

dear Flora understood me as probably *no* one else did — or ever has.

Her friendship was, and I feel *is*, something perfectly *wonderful*.

that wonderful sympathy of hers that began for me all those years ago at Clifton when she became my first friend.

I wonder how many people have told you she was their 'best friend'? She was without equal in my experience for understanding and good counsel.

I shall never, never forget how she came to meet me after my Helen's death, and came back with me to my empty house. That was true friendship.

She loved life, as she loved her fellow-beings. And she was one of the most lovable of God's creatures herself — with her it was always the same plunge into lively, witty, *kind* talk.

Flora absolutely poured sympathy.

Lots of people like one, Alice dear, but I know of no-one with the real *love* that Flora gave so unsparingly. I used to wonder why she gave me so much, but it was like the air one breathed when one was with her — she just radiated it from her whole heart.

And Alice herself wrote:

That warm love is what I think of and is what helps me so very much. (Alice to Robin, 1932).

No one knew of Flora Mayor's gift for transmitting love except those who had received it, and they, being English and upper middle-class, could never bring themselves to speak of it until after Flora was dead. And it was impossible to deduce Flora's great lovingness towards her friends from her letters to Alice, since Flora, perhaps unconsciously, always protected Alice by concealing it from her.

Flora Mayor's standing as a writer of serious fiction has taken half a century to establish itself. Although her original reviewers had dared to predict that her first two novels would outlive her, after her death Flora Mayor's work was forgotten for decades. There was only one obituary notice, Melian Stawell's in the *Newnham Letter*, 1932.[12] G.B. Stern told Flora's friend, Margaret Irwin, that she wanted to write an article about Flora Mayor's work for *Time and Tide* — 'it made her furious that there should be so much fuss about Edgar Wallace in the press and nothing about Flora.' But if such an article were written, it did not get printed, and there was no further allusion to Flora Mayor's fiction for nearly ten years. Then, on 28 February 1941, *John O'London's Weekly* published an eloquent tribute by Rosamond Lehmann, entitled *These Novels Should Live*:

In its quiet and personal way *The Rector's Daughter* is a piece of history. We dwell within a way of English life that was once, in the far-off 'twenties, and is now no more. Yet the book is timeless because within its social framework, its subject is permanent: the problems and pains of love in human relationships ...

[It] is the daughter, Mary Jocelyn, who makes the book particularly memorable. She is my favourite character in contemporary fiction: favourite in that she is completely real to me, deeply moving, evoking as vivid and valid a sense of sympathy, pity, and admiration as do the Brontë sisters each time I live with them and through them again in the pages of

Mrs. Gaskell's biography. The poignancy of the sisters lies in their moral grandeur. The same is true of Mary Jocelyn.

Plain, not young, dowdy, shy, and from shyness awkward, proud, passionate, reserved, she is herself, an individual, to an extraordinary degree — At the same time she becomes, to me at least, a kind of symbol or touchstone for feminine dignity, intelligence and truthfulness ...

Flora Mayor would have been pleased that her Mary Jocelyn, together with Mrs Gaskell and the Brontës, propped the mind of Rosamond Lehmann during the Blitz.

No further mention of Flora Mayor as a novelist was made for over a quarter of a century. Then, in 1967, Leonard Woolf published volume IV of his autobiography *Downhill All The Way*, and in his reminiscences of publishing during the 1920s, he included one sentence about *The Rector's Daughter*.[13]

Encouraged by Leonard Woolf's opinion of the novel, and at the suggestion of his sister Teresa, Flora's nephew, Andreas Mayor, then approached Penguin Books in 1969, asking them to consider republication of *The Rector's Daughter*. They issued it in 1973 under the distinctive imprint of a Penguin Modern Classic.[14] In 1979 *The Third Miss Symons* was republished as a Virago Modern Classic with an introduction by Susan Hill. Now, slowly, Flora Mayor is beginning to take her rightful place in English fiction as one of the most perceptive writers on the inner life of women — a significant link between Mrs Gaskell and Virginia Woolf.

It was when I was looking for further clues relating to the life of Flora Mayor that I came upon the following entry in the Electoral Roll Returns for Hampstead Ward, 1933:

7 East Heath Rd.,
Householders: Alice Mayor, Mary Sheepshanks.

That among all the Mayor sisters' many friends it should

have been Mary who moved in with Alice upon the death of Flora was almost perverse. If the two women had 'differed exceedingly' in the 1890s, now, in 1933, they were poles apart on every conceivable issue — from contraception to education, capital punishment, the Church of England, disarmament and the Labour Party. Not surprisingly, they very soon decided to part — Alice Mayor left Hampstead permanently to settle in Cambridge, where she died in 1961, and Mary, who was sixty in 1932, moved to Highgate in North London.

Mary Sheepshanks outlived Flora Mayor by twenty-six years. They were years of cumulative horror for this fiercely humane woman, recently so active in politics, now constrained to watch impotently on the sidelines as one nightmare after another was perpetrated in the world.[15] Mary, being Mary, still tried to prevent or at least alleviate the triumph of brutality under Hitler, Stalin and Hirohito. One member of the Sheepshanks family reports that it was Mary who passed on to the *Manchester Guardian* correspondent, Voigt — perhaps by word of mouth as well as letter — the first conclusive evidence of the existence of Nazi concentration camps in the 1930s, only to be deeply disappointed when he did not make — or was not allowed to make — what she considered to be adequate public use of her information.

In 1934 Mary Sheepshanks put together a report on The Admission of Women to the Diplomatic and Consular Services, still believing that if only women could have access to decision-forming positions in international affairs their counsel would be humane. And in June 1935 Mary mourned the death of the one woman above all others who had inspired that faith in her — Jane Addams.[16] Throughout the Spanish Civil War, Mary Sheepshanks was active in helping Dr Hilda Clark and Edith Pye in organising relief for its child victims and, in 1938, for Basque child refugees. Mary also gave asylum to a stream of refugees in her own home in Highgate. First she housed Trotskyist refugees from Stalin, then refugees from the Sudetenland, then more and more German and Austrian Jews. One refugee tried to keep goldfish in her bath and he had to go, but his place was soon taken by such a constant flow of obvious 'foreigners' that Mary had hostile slogans painted over her house wall. Many of the refugees, especially those from the Sudetenland, were accepted as immigrants to America, and Mary would organise English lessons for them at her home before they embarked.[17]

During World War Two, Mary, who was now in her seventies, went on holding these English classes and discussion groups for refugee university women; she also worked for the BBC, translating from and into German, and she knitted for the Merchant Navy. Like most of her colleagues in the WIL, she had had to renounce her lifelong pacifism and support this war against Nazism.

Here we are still in this grim and horrible war, poor London is still being bombed. It is impossible for you to imagine what it means ... in the sixth year of this misery and suffering. It absolutely spoils life for everyone and makes me despair of human beings ever being able to live in peace and happiness. People have been and are most heroic, working so hard, old and young and being so brave, but very tired and worn and living in frightful discomfort in overcrowded and damaged dwellings. (Mary Sheepshanks to her niece Pita in Buenos Aires, 26 November 1944.)

In 1945 Mary Sheepshanks was utterly opposed to the decision to drop the atomic bomb, and in the general election she was anti-Churchill and very pro-Labour:

My dear, how could you ever think that I might be a conservative? I *never* was. In my youth I was a liberal, in fact a Radical, and I have long been a Socialist. I admit that this war has made me deeply pessimistic, the incredible savagery and beastliness of the Germans and the immeasurable suffering they caused make me despair of human nature, and now I expect this ghastly atomic bomb will be used to destroy

the world. There are decent and wise people but they are
bested by the evil ones ... (Mary Sheepshanks to her niece
Pita, November 1945).[18]

Mary had had so many friends among those martyred by
the Nazis: the Hungarians, Eugénie Meller and Melanie
Valbery, deported to extermination camps, the Czech
members of the WIL, Milena Illova, Elsa Kalmus and
Frantiska Plaminkova, all executed in Prague, the Dutch
organiser of the 1915 Women's Peace Congress at The
Hague, Rosa Manus, executed in a German concentration
camp — and the list was undoubtedly much longer — it is
not surprising that she should have come to 'despair of
human nature.'

Mary's private life was also becoming more and more of
a struggle. In addition to her chronic, crippling arthritis,
she was threatened by approaching blindness, and, at the
age of nearly eighty, she had to be operated on for cancer.

I hoped I might have quietly gone out under the anaesthetic,
but no such luck. Modern surgery and anaesthesia are too
well done ...

I must say the family have been awfully nice, perhaps we
are more mellow in our old age ... presents just flow in ... I
think they thought it would be the end of me. (Mary
Sheepshanks to her niece Pita, 10 March 1951).

That new 'mellowness' within the Sheepshanks family
was far from general, however. There were still several
brothers and sisters with whom Mary would have nothing
to do or who would have nothing to do with her; it was
during this last stay in hospital that Mary not only refused
to be seen by one sister but actually flung her propitiatory
bunch of flowers out of the window after her. If she could no
longer stump, she could still throw. One of Mary's
nephews, now Lord Wilberforce, cannot remember that
his aunt Mary ever visited his mother. As for Mary's
youngest brother — 'I haven't seen Tom for years. Of
course we were never a united family; too many of us all

pulling against each other.' (Mary Sheepshanks to Pita, August 1954.) It was the black sheep among her generation of Sheepshankses with whom Mary did keep in touch and it was the younger generation of nephews and nieces with whom she got on well. They did not know another talker to equal her, they said.

Although Mary Sheepshanks outlived many of her contemporaries, younger people (including Kathleen Courtney and Ellen Wilkinson, MP) continued to visit her, fascinated by her reminiscences and by her incisive political judgement.[19] Dame Margery Corbett Ashby remembered Mary Sheepshanks as one of the most many-sided women she had ever worked with: 'She had so many general interests — music, books and art as well as politics. She looked on mankind as a family, and she did not hate men — oh dear no — she was most human.' And when Denis Richards, a former principal of Morley College, went to interview Mary in her eighties, her once large, vigorous frame now confined to a wheelchair, he found that:

Her best feature was undoubtedly her eyes, which even at her late age were brilliantly blue and alive with intelligence and humour. Apart from that, and the general alertness of her face, she looked very much like a German caricature of an English spinster in the early years of this century.

But those who were closest to Mary in her last years felt the warmth of her affection even more than her sharp intelligence. 'Take off your hat and let me look at you', would be her characteristic greeting — every goose being a swan to the once 'difficult' Mary then.

But despite these friendships, and despite her stoicism, Mary Sheepshanks found old age very hard to bear. She who had once travelled across whole continents, making speeches on the great twentieth-century issues of feminism and internationalism, was now confined to one room and even to one chair.

I have the radio by my chair on one side and a table with
'phone, papers and books all within reach ... One just
scratches along ... I read as much as my eyes permit; but
there are sixteen hours in the day and six is the outside limit
of reading for me. (Mary to Pita, 1950s.)

It was then, when Mary was well over eighty and suffering acutely from boredom, that her woman doctor suggested she write her memoirs.[20] When Mary Sheepshanks
looked back she saw her life as having been nothing more
than a sequence of 'pieces of work'. But her memoirs are no
mere *curriculum vitae*; instead they become a roll-call of all
the splendid men and women — especially women — she
had ever known: Jane Harrison and Melian Stawell at
Newnham, Margaret Sewell at the Southwark Settlement,
Emma Cons at Morley College, Virginia Woolf, Dr Hilda
Clark, Dr Aletta Jacobs, Margaret Bryant and the great
Jane Addams herself. And in remembering all of these, and
others, less famous, like them, Mary Sheepshanks finally
came to modify the pessimism of her latter years. Thus, at
the age of eighty-three, she wrote: 'When I have felt
tempted to take a dim view of human nature I think of the
hundreds of decent people I knew at Morley College.' And
her French and German colleagues on the International
Executive of the WIL with whom she had fallen out so
fatally a quarter of a century earlier she now finally saw to
have been disinterested idealists, although tactically mistaken:

They were a body of high-minded women ... fighting for
unpopular causes for which they had made genuine sacrifices;
and that is a quality of supreme value. I often crossed swords
with my colleagues and superiors, but I always respected and
admired them, and I count it as one of the blessings of my life
that in all my various activities I had such fine people to work
with. (Mary Sheepshanks, *Autobiography*, ch. 18.)

It was also at this, the last period of her life, that Mary

Sheepshanks paid her marvellous tribute to Margaret Bryant, her closest personal friend, now ten years dead:

She was incapable of an unworthy thought; and ever since I knew her I have mentally used her as a standard below which I do not wish to fall, though in practice I do. I owe her more than I can say. (Mary Sheepshanks, *Autobiography*, ch. 8.)[21]

To her great disappointment, Mary Sheepshanks' autobiography was rejected for publication. The publishers all wanted her to add many more 'gossipy' comments on the famous, but she, characteristically, 'absolutely refused to alter it or touch it again.' (Dr Drew to the author.)

Mary had wanted to call her memoirs 'The Long Day Ended' from Henley's 'My task accomplished and the long day ended'. Sometimes she would ask a close friend, or one of her nieces who was visiting her, whether they thought it would be all right for her, a lifelong agnostic, to have an Anglican funeral service. She would add apologetically: 'I have always loved the words so.' That 'always' evokes the many times during her childhood and youth that Mary had heard her father intone:

We brought nothing into this world, and it is certain we can carry nothing out ...
    My heart was hot within me, and while I was thus musing the fire kindled: and at last I spake with my tongue;
    Lord, let me know mine end, and the number of my days: that I may be certified how long I have to live ...
    Deliver me from all my offences: and make me not a rebuke unto the foolish ...
    Thou turnest man to destruction: again thou sayest, Come again, ye children of men.
    For a thousand years in thy sight are but as yesterday: seeing that is past as a watch in the night ...
    ... earth to earth, ashes to ashes, dust to dust.

In 1958 Mary Sheepshanks' daily help had a quarrel with the people who lived on the floor above and told Mary, then aged eighty-six, that she wanted to leave her. Mary could see nothing but compulsory institutionalization ahead. Very nearly blind and paralysed, but still competent to the last, Mary Sheepshanks wrote a loving note to her nephew John, and then killed herself.

EPILOGUE

The two baby girls who had been born in October 1872 into their respective clerical families, would seem to have ended their lives at diametrically opposite poles — Flora, the conservative, Anglican, patriotic English lady; Mary, the socialist, atheist, pacifist citizen of the world. The content of their work would appear to be a simple contrast also: Flora Mayor, the tragic novelist focused on the eternal problems of the emotional life which no law can change or cure, while Mary Sheepshanks, the meliorist, constantly attempted to prevent or to alleviate some specific case of economic or political suffering.

And yet were the preoccupations of Flora and Mary really so utterly opposed? Gradually I have come to think that, underlying their very different lives and work and opinions, both women were haunted by the same tragic fact — the gulf that exists between how we want to live with one another and how we do. Writers as well as reformers are confronted by this gulf between the ideal and the actual and by the bitter fact of human inhumanity; oppression and war exist not only in the world outside us but are experienced at one time or another within every household on earth. The 'deliberate [infliction] of avoidable torment' is a phrase taken not from one of Mary Sheepshanks' protests against torture or chemical warfare, but from Flora Mayor's *The Rector's Daughter*. What Flora and Mary both abhorred was cruelty. To both women it was an abomination to categorise any human being as 'superfluous' or 'vermin' and to treat them accordingly — but each woman had very different 'superfluous vermin' in mind. Flora championed the unwanted, derided, middle-class, middle-aged spinsters and widows against those who saw them as 'parasites' needing to be 'swept away'. Mary championed the 'superfluous' unemployed, the stateless persons, and the political refugees. What matters is not the difference between those for whom Flora or Mary felt pity and indignation, but rather the fact that both women loathed 'the deliberate [infliction] of avoidable torment' equally.

At its greatest, the idealism in Flora Mayor's work and in that of Mary Sheepshanks had something about it almost of sanctity — yet neither woman was anything like a saint. Both had known the damaging cruelty of failure and the compensatory demons of censoriousness, righteous anger and bitterness of spirit. Flora's almost exclusive emotional dependence on her small family circle could blind her to the fellow-humanity of those who were not Mayors, while Mary's sense of isolation from her huge family caused a predisposition in her at times of crisis to treat her later alternative families of friends as yet more hostile brothers and sisters against whom she had to wage a private war. But both Flora and Mary were able to transcend their 'damagedness', and give expression to their greatest quality of all — their reverence for the greatness in others. Underneath her considerable self-esteem, Flora had a deep layer of self-critical humility before those whom she felt to be more loving than she herself really was. She recognised her debt to the tremendous love that she had received both from Alice and from Ernest Shepherd and she had the eyes to see within the unpretentious exterior of her two friends Mary Walton and Kitty Howard the marvellous soul of a Mary Jocelyn. Mary Sheepshanks could break out of her defensive, unhappy, unloved shell and respond with immense energy and selfless devotion to all those in her life whom she thought infinitely more 'worthwhile' than she was.

True to her faith that one human being can reach out and save another, the novelist Flora Mayor stressed those life-giving moments when one person truly cares for someone else — Milly Hammond for Bobby, Henrietta Symons for Evelyn, Miss Browne for Mabel and Mary Jocelyn for almost everyone. Similarly Mary Sheepshanks reached out time and again to try and build a network of mutually supportive people, whether at Morley College, or within the women's movement, or in the Fight the Famine Campaign, or through the Women's International League, in order to create a more humane and civilised world. These two women who had first met at Newnham in the 1890s were the contemporaries (and overlooked counterparts) of Cambridge humanists like Roger Fry, Goldsworthy Lowes Dickinson, G.E. Moore, Bertrand Russell, E.M. Forster and Flora's own brother, the moral philosopher Robin Mayor.[1]

Flora Mayor focused on fellowship and reconciliation between individuals; Mary Sheepshanks worked for fellowship and reconciliation between groups. The tragedy is that our quest for one kind of fellowship so often entails the negation of another. Our intensity — or our failures — in caring within our private lives can incapacitate us from effective caring as citizens of the world. And our attempts to be committed political reformists can lead us to override or neglect the needs of individuals. 'You must make your choice between the man and the citizen, you cannot train both.'[2] But we are compelled in every generation to try, and therefore we need both writers and reformers, both Flora and Mary. Flora Mayor forces us to 'see feelingly' that every human being is irreplaceable, vulnerable, and yet also capable of inflicting hurt — saint and sinner both; Mary Sheepshanks inspires us to commit ourselves in the dark world of politics in order to try to prevent the infliction of mass-pain. The two women are not alternative heroines between whom we have to choose, but rather, complementary figures pointing along different roads to the same goal.

> We read their life, we read their death,
> Their life and death are our bread,
> Their death the bread of the living.
>
> Gottfried von Strasburg, *Tristan*, c. 1180.

NOTES

PROLOGUE

1 See Howard Channon, *Portrait of Liverpool*, Robert Hale, 1970, ch. 3; and Ramsay Muir, *A History of Liverpool*, published for the University of Liverpool by Williams and Norgate, 1907, ch. 16.
2 Mary Sheepshanks' unpublished *Autobiography* written in her eighties, c. 1953, ch. 1.
3 *ibid.*
4 *ibid.* However surprisingly, St Mary's Vicarage, Anfield evidently lacked all the sanitary amenities that were absent in the parish as a whole. There is no reason to suppose that Mary Sheepshanks invented or exaggerated such details; on the contrary, she was conscious of 'softening it a good deal'.

1. TWO CHILDHOODS, 1872–1882

1 Dorothy Muir, *Lift the Curtain*, Jonathan Cape, 1955, ch. 1.
2 Mary Sheepshanks' unpublished *Autobiography*, ch. 1
3 Dorothy Muir, *Lift the Curtain*, ch. 6
4 Adrienne Rich, *Of Woman Born*, Virago, 1977, ch. 9.
5 Mary Sheepshanks, *Autobiography*, ch. 1.
6 Dorothy Muir, *Lift the Curtain*, ch. 5; see also *A Bishop in the Rough*. [Extracts from the journal of John Sheepshanks, Bishop of Norwich.] Ed. by Rev. D. Wallace Duthie, Smith, Elder, 1909.
7 Mary Sheepshanks, *Autobiography*, ch. 1.
8 *ibid.*
9 Dorothy Muir, *Lift the Curtain*, ch. 7.
10 Mary Sheepshanks, *Autobiography*, ch. 1.
11 *ibid.*
12 The Rev. Mayor's unpublished commonplace-book has many slightly startled entries about Anna:

May 23, 1875: Anna left Rome for Venice. Anna has the good word of all the English who come across her, but Robert [the eldest brother] is still murmuring at her for idleness and pleasure-seeking, so she has had to write and assert her own independence. [She was fifty-four.] She goes with a large party to the Dolomites.
1877: Anna has taken Rossetti's house in Rome.
1879: Anna in hot water; attacked by Miss Twining about London Artists' Home.
May 9, 1880: Stupid attack on Anna sent from Rome to Robert and John.
June 12, 1881: Anna satirized almost by name in novel about her in Rome. Anna wants to buy house in Rome for £12,000!

13 Professor Joseph Mayor's commonplace-book.
14 Robin Grote Mayor grew up to be a very distinguished man. His academic career continued to be brilliant; he became a Principal Civil Servant (in the Education Department), and was made a Commander of the Bath in 1919. His real aim in life, however, was to make a serious contribution to British philosophy. The friend of Lowes Dickinson, McTaggart, Bertrand Russell and G.E. Moore, Robin Mayor spent the last twenty years of his life writing *Reason and Common Sense*, Routledge & Kegan Paul, 1952, a work that radiates patience, integrity, lucidity and magnanimity towards those with whom he cannot agree. He finished it the day before he died.

Henry Mayor became Head of Classics and Housemaster of Watson's, Clifton College.
15 After *Mrs Hammond's Children*, c. 1904-1907, Flora Mayor wrote an attempted evocation of 'a child's impression of its ordinary life' based on her own childhood. Called *Reminiscences*, it was never published and the ms. has been lost or destroyed. The 'Quaker book' was *Reminiscences of My Life* by Elizabeth Sturge, printed privately, Bristol, 1928.

2.   TWO EDUCATIONS, 1883-1895

1 cf. Ellen Moers' discussion of Jane Eyre as 'rebellious slave' in *Literary Women*, New York, Doubleday, 1976.
2 cf. 'Women in fiction only rarely have the peculiar reality of the moral life that self-love bestows . . . But there is Emma, given over to self-love, wholly aware of it and quite cherishing it.' Lionel Trilling, *Beyond Culture*, Secker & Warburg, 1966.
3 For the history of the struggle to institute higher education for girls in nineteenth-century Britain, see Patricia Hollis, *Women in Public*,

1850-1900, Allen & Unwin, 1979, pp. 144-9; Bauer and Ritt, *Free and Ennobled*, Pergamon Press, 1979, pp. 38-44, 250-2; and Josephine Kamm, *Indicative Past*, Allen & Unwin, 1971, ch. 3.

The Sheepshanks parents did not approve of higher education for girls when they saw its effects on Mary — none of her four younger sisters were allowed to attend school or university thereafter. Flora Mayor's parents, however, did support the new movement — her father had even prophesied on her seventh birthday: 'For Flora, you know, will be Girton's pride/While Newnham spreads Alice's fame far and wide.'

4   Mary Agnes Hamilton, *Newnham: An Informal Biography*, Faber, 1936, ch. 8.

5   Alfred Marshall, Professor of Economic History, quoted in Rita McWilliams-Tullberg, *Women at Cambridge*, Gollancz, 1975.

6   Rackham Papers, Newnham, quoted in *Women at Cambridge*.

7   C. Crowther, quoted in Ann Phillips, *A Newnham Anthology*, Cambridge University Press, 1979, p. 39.

8   Fragment of an unfinished, unpublished short story by Flora Mayor.

9   Francesca Wilson, quoted in Ann Phillips, *A Newnham Anthology*, pp. 65-9.

10 Melian Stawell's fellow-Newnhamite, Clare Reynolds, for example, lived and worked and walked the Tuscan hills with her, nursing Melian devotedly through many illnesses and surviving her by only a few months. Clare Reynolds left her property to the citizens of Oxford as a woodland garden in memory of her friend, and her will ended: 'If possible I should like my body to be cremated and the ashes scattered on the grave of Melian Stawell.' 'Ugly as a witch, Clare,' Melian's nephew and niece told the author, 'but she was a first-class friend.'

11 Eglantyne Jebb, *Cambridge Poverty Survey*, Macmillan and Bowes, 1906: 'Children are being brought up here under circumstances which we would hardly tolerate were our own children concerned ... in our streets we meet occasionally with pitiful caricatures of men and women, poor puny wastrels, starvelings ... on whose faces the dull suffering of hopelessness has left its indelible stamp.' (Eglantyne Jebb later founded the Save the Children Fund, see ch. 10.)

12 Dorothy Muir, *Lift the Curtain*, Jonathan Cape, 1955, ch. 10.

13 cf. the youthful Boswell writing to himself 'Last night you was charming.'

14 In 1905 Mary Sheepshanks wrote to Bertrand Russell: 'Alys [Russell] returned *Villette*. I have often thought of late years that I was very like Lucy Snowe, but not so courageous.'

3.   OUT IN THE WORLD, OR BACK AT HOME? MARY AND
      FLORA, 1896–1901

1   See Charles Booth, *Life and Labour of the People in London*, 1st series,
     Poverty, 1902, vol. 1, Part IV, South London, pp. 275-290. 'South-
     wark Bridge Road, Gravel Lane, Union Street: — Many poor,
     rough waterside labourers in a network of old alleys near the river
     ... Blackfriars Road, Broad Walk, Great Charlotte Street: —
     labourers, hawkers, charwomen, sweeps, & ... with many bad
     characters among them ... Newington Causeway, Great Suffolk
     Street, Friar Street and Borough Road: — Many mechanics
     labourers, carmen, painters, hawkers, fish-curers, &. whose homes
     are often very dirty and bare, while others are very decent ... Two
     or three dirty little places, narrow enough to allow of clothes-lines
     being stretched across, inhabited by a very poor rough class ...
     Immediately round about St. George's Church and on all sides of it
     lie nests of courts and alleys ... still harbouring an appalling
     amount of destitution not unmixed with crime ... Among these
     courts, close behind the Church, was the Marshalsea prison, of
     which some part remains standing. To westwards as far as Black-
     friars Road there lives a population which is the despair of those
     who work amongst it. Not as being bad, but very low and difficult to
     raise.'
2   Somerset Maugham, Preface to *Liza of Lambeth*, T.F. Unwin, 1897.
     Preface added 1930, to the Heinemann edition.
3   Clarence Rook, *The Hooligan Nights*, Grant Richards, 1899, re-
     published by Oxford University Press, 1979.
4   See Charles Chaplin, *My Autobiography*, The Bodley Head, 1964,
     chs. 1-4.
5   Quoted by Peter Keating, *Into Unknown England 1886-1913*,
     Manchester University Press, 1976.
6   H.C. Escreet, Warden, WUS, Introduction to D.M. Brodie's
     pamphlet, *Women's University Settlement*, 1937.
7   *Cambridge Letter*, Newnham, 1887, p. 19.
8   Octavia Hill, 1838-1912, slum-housing reformer, campaigner for
     open spaces and founder of the National Trust.
9   Moberly Bell, *Octavia Hill*, Constable, 1942, ch. 17.
10   *ibid.*
11   D.M. Brodie, *Women's University Settlement*, 1937. It is significant
     that the Women's University Settlement, now re-named Black-
     friars Settlement, still exists as 44-46 Nelson Square. The work was
     grounded on such intelligent foundations that it has survived —
     but the need for such work has also survived. There are still Adult
     Literacy classes, 'sheltered' workshops for the handicapped,
     weekly social clubs for the isolated, elderly or blind; there are still

children being sent each year to a country holiday and some problems, like homelessness, fuel bills and school-leaver unemployment, are getting worse. (See Blackfriars Settlement Annual Report and Accounts, 1979 & 1980.)

12   Quoted in Brodie, *Women's University Settlement*.

13   E.M. Lawson, *Cambridge Letter* (Newnham), 1898.

14   cf. Flora Mayor's short story about a lady and a skivvy turned prostitute, *Miss Browne's Friend* (1914), see ch. 9.

15   Winnie Seebohm, *A Suppressed Cry: Life and Death of a Quaker Daughter*, Routledge & Kegan Paul, 1969.

16   Charles Booth, *Life and Labour of the People of London*, Vol. 1, Part IV, Macmillan, 1892-97.

17   'Colour, Space and Music for the People', 1884, quoted in Goodwin, *Nineteenth Century Opinion*, Penguin, 1951.

18   *ibid.*

19   See theatre reviews for the whole of Britain in the *Stage*, late 1890s.

20   J.C. Trewin, *The Edwardian Theatre*, Blackwell, 1976, ch. 1.

21   Quoted in Madeleine Bingham, *The Great Lover, Beerbohm Tree*, New York, Atheneum, 1979.

22   cf. Lena Ashwell, in *Myself a Player*, Michael Joseph, 1936, ch. 2. 'How can one ever express what Ellen Terry meant to us? There are just no words. The genius of charm, the lovely, gracious movements, the beauty of her face with its ever-changing moods, the ringing, brilliant laugh, her voice with its curious fascination . . . It is rarely that one hears a laugh which gives the sound of real, spontaneous, unself-conscious enjoyment, the sound that arouses happiness and joy in other people. Ellen Terry laughed like that.'

23   Roger Manvell, *Ellen Terry*, Heinemann, 1968, ch. 7.

24   E.g. John Stuart Mill's stepdaughter, Harriet Taylor, Eleanor Marx, Maud Holt, Janet Achurch, Elisabeth Robins and Florence Farr. See Christopher Kent, 'The Actress and Society' in Vicinus, ed., *A Widening Sphere*, Indiana, Indiana University Press, 1980, pp. 94-116.

25   'On the Living and the Dead' in George Bernard Shaw, *Our Theatres in the Nineties*, Constable, 1932.

26   Report in the *Daily News*, 1885, quoted in Denis Richards, *Offspring of the Vic*, Routledge & Kegan Paul, 1958, ch. 4.

27   Emma Cons, 1838-1912, friend of Octavia Hill, reclaimer of slum property, founder of clinics, crêches and libraries for her tenants, vice-president of the London Society for Women's Suffrage, co-opted as first woman Alderman on the London County Council in 1889, founder of Coffee Music Halls Company, provider of shelter for battered wives and children 'when farver came home boozed', etc. (Lilian Baylis, *op. cit.* below.) 'Emma Cons was a grand woman and we can do with many more like her' — Mary Sheepshanks,

Autobiography, ch. 4. See essay on Emma Cons by her niece Lilian Baylis in *The Old Vic*, by Cicely Hamilton and Lilian Baylis, Jonathan Cape, 1926.

28 Harold Nicolson, Foreword to Denis Richards, *Offspring of the Vic*.

29 Caroline Martineau, c. 1840-1901, Unitarian, friend of Emma Cons, scientist and benefactor to the college, she was Morley College's first Principal, and bequeathed it a physics laboratory.

30 Richards, *Offspring of the Vic*.

31 Richards, *Offspring of the Vic*, chs. 4, 5 and 6. Within a few weeks of Mary Sheepshanks' appointment, the College Principal, Caroline Martineau, fell ill with cancer, and Mary immediately had to take over the whole responsibility for the College and its thousand students. See Richards, *Offspring of the Vic*, ch. 8.

32 Richards, *Offspring of the Vic*.

33 Besier, author of *The Virgin Goddess*, Dent, 1906, *Don*, Fisher & Unwin, 1909, and *Lady Patricia*, Fisher & Unwin, 1911, was to have his greatest success with his *The Barretts of Wimpole Street*, Gollancz, 1930.

34 Three interesting studies of children had, in fact, recently been published — Frances Crompton's *The Gentle Heritage*, Innes, 1893 (about children still in the nursery), Kenneth Grahame's *The Golden Age*, L. Jane, 1895 and E. Nesbit's *The Treasure-Seekers*, Unwin, 1898. (See also the critics Roger Lancelyn Green, *Tellers of Tales*, Ward, 1965 and Marghanita Laski, *Mrs Ewing, Mrs Molesworth and Mrs Hodgson Burnett*, Arthur Barker 1950). Flora Mayor considered that all these late nineteenth-century writers idealised children and childhood, though in different ways.

35 'All hope of Aunt Georgie is given up now. Isn't it *fearful* for poor Aunt Fanny? ... [Father] says Aunt Fanny has been so specially dependent on Aunt Georgie ever since Aunt G. nursed her through illness...' (Alice to Flora, December 1897.) 'For us the loss is quite irreparable but what must it be for you? I cannot realise that I shall never see that dear dear face again. No one knows what she has been to me the last ten years ... God's ways are mysterious. I can only feel we have leaned too much on her. I have said constantly I could not get on without her monthly counsel and help and now I feel we are all at sea without our Pilot. Robert is terribly cut up — says he will soon follow her ... words are cold and stupid.' (Ina Mayor, wife of Canon Robert Mayor of Frating, to Fanny Mayor.)

4. 'MARY STRAFFORD', ACTRESS AND 'MISS SHEEPSHANKS, THE VICE-PRINCIPAL', 1901–1903

1 Contrast the Ibsen pioneers, Elisabeth Robins and Janet Achurch

discussed in Julie Holledge, *Innocent Flowers, Women in the Edwardian Theatre*, Virago, 1981, ch. 1.

2 Leonard Woolf, *Sowing*, Hogarth Press, 1960, pp. 163-4.
3 'Do you remember your Crofts scholarship at Newnham? Well, that was founded by my brother the M.P. He gets his 22% out of a factory with 600 girls in it, and not one of them getting wages enough to live on. How d'ye suppose they manage when they have no family to fall back on? Ask your mother.' (*Mrs Warren's Profession*, Act III.) In a later, undated letter, Flora praised Shaw's wit, his *clarté* and good stage construction in *Plays for Puritans*; she then added 'but his views are antipathetic for me'.
4 See Ernest Short, *Sixty Years of Theatre*, Eyre and Spottiswoode, 1951, ch. 1, for the fussy stage 'business' followed by actor-managers then.
5 Arthur Machen's own memories of joining the Benson Company were rosier than Flora's and are found in his autobiography, *Things Near and Far*, Secker and Warburg, 1923, ch. II.
6 J.C. Trewin, *The Edwardian Theatre*, Blackwell, 1976, ch. 4.
7 Gordon Craig was an innovative stage director and designer. He was the illegitimate son of Ellen Terry, and later the lover of Isadora Duncan.
8 For Edith Craig, illegitimate daughter of Ellen Terry, see Julie Holledge, *Innocent Flowers* Part III, *Edy and her Pioneers*.
9 cf. Noël Streatfeild and Antonia White twenty years on.
10 The Mayor family concealed the fact of Flora's attempt to go on the stage ever after. Thirty years later, when Flora's niece was considering a career in the theatre not one word was said to her by Robin, Alice or Henry of Flora's dire experiences a generation before.
11 See ch. 6.
12 Denis Richards, *Offspring of the Vic*, Routledge & Kegan Paul, 1958, ch. 8.
13 *ibid.*
14 *Morley College Magazine*, 1902.
15 *Morley College Magazine*, March 1903.

5. 'FLORA SHEPHERD', MARCH–OCTOBER 1903

1 *Morley College Magazine*, 1903, p. 116.
2 See ch. four, *passim.*
3 C.P. Sanger, the authority on *Wills* and his Dora, née Pease — fringe members of the Bloomsbury Group.
4 G.M. Trevelyan, historian, the biographer of Bright and Garibaldi.
5 Flora Mayor's unpublished *Grief Journal*, November 1903,

addressed to Ernest after his death.

6   Canon Howard, Ernest's uncle by marriage, writing to Flora.
7   Canon Howard writing to Auntie.
8   Sidney Irwin, Ernest's old teacher at Clifton, writing to Flora's father.
9   Auntie to Flora.
10   Fritz Shepherd, Ernest's brother, writing to Flora.
11   Isabella Howard, Auntie's sister, writing to Flora.
12   Mary Sheepshanks, writing to Alice.
13   Flora Mayor, *Grief Journal*, November-December 1903.
14   *ibid.*
15   *ibid.*
16   *ibid.*
17   Stephen Spender, *World Within World*, Hamish Hamilton, 1951, part III, p. 158.
18   Fanny Fawcett, letter to Flora, 28 October 1903.
19   Mary Bateson, History Don at Newnham, 27 October 1903.
20   Georgina Mayor, the pioneer nursing sister at Great Ormond Street Hospital, see ch. 3.
21   Flora's history tutor at Newnham.
22   Newnham Lecturer in History.

6.   PICKING UP THE PIECES — FLORA AND MARY, 1904-1907

1   Berkart, *On Bronchial Asthma, Its Pathology and Treatment*, J. and A. Churchill, 1878, ch. 2; and see H.H. Salter, *Asthma*, 1868.
2   Berkart, *On Bronchial Asthma*, ch. 7.
3   'Asthma is essentially, and with perhaps the exception of a single class of cases, exclusively a nervous disease . . . the nervous system is the seat of the essential pathological condition.' (H.H. Salter, *Asthma*, ch. 2.) Berkart, however, disagreed.
4   Julian of Norwich.
5   cf. Wordsworth after the death of his brother John: 'Why have we sympathies that make the best of us afraid of inflicting pain and sorrow, which yet we see dealt about so lavishly by the supreme governor? . . . Would it not be blasphemy to say that, upon the supposition of the thinking principle being destroyed in death, however inferior we may be to the great Cause and Ruler of all things, we have *more of love* in our Nature than He has? The thought is monstrous; and yet how to get rid of it except upon the supposition of another and *better world*, I do not see.' (Letters to Sir George Beaumont, February 1805, quoted in Mary Moorman, *Life of Wordsworth*, Oxford University Press, 1957.)
6   'Behind the Scenes' was performed at the Caxton Hall in Decem-

ber 1906 and February 1907, and was reviewed briefly, but kindly, by several papers especially the *Tribune*, the *Daily Chronicle* and the *Sunday Times*.

7   Flora's letters to Alice during the Clifton period 1904-1912 are full of such carping comments as: 'I went to D. She looked so coarse and old. All her charm gone. Of course it may come back.' Or 'I must say I do thank God I'm not a professional woman, I'm sure one would have got like them.'

8   Theodore was one of the six sons of the politically radical and theologically broad-minded Rev. J. Llewelyn Davies, Vicar of Kirkby Lonsdale — and lifelong friend of Flora's father, the Rev. Dr Joseph Mayor. Theodore's aunt was Emily Davies, founder of Girton, and his sister was Margaret Llewelyn Davies, pioneer worker for the Women's Co-operative Guild. For the Llewelyn Davies family background, see Andrew Birkin, *Barrie and the Lost Boys*, Constable, 1979, ch. 4. Leonard Woolf called Theodore Davies 'a man of extraordinary brilliance and great charm', *Sowing*, Hogarth Press, 1960. Bertrand Russell called Theodore 'the ablest and one of the best beloved of the family. Theodore and his brother Crompton were able, high-minded and passionate, and shared on the whole, the same ideals and opinions. Theodore had a somewhat more practical outlook on life than Crompton. He became Private Secretary to a series of Conservative Chancellors of the Exchequer, each of whom in turn he converted to Free Trade at a time when the rest of the Government wished them to think otherwise. He worked incredibly hard and yet always found time to give presents to the children of all his friends, and the presents were always exactly appropriate. He inspired the deepest affection in almost everybody who knew him.' *Autobiography*, Allen and Unwin, 1968, Vol. 1.

9   Mary Sheepshanks, unpublished *Autobiography*, ch. 7.

10   Russell, *Autobiography*.

11   *ibid.*

12   Personal communication to the author from a member of the Llewelyn Davies family. Meg Booth later married Billie Ritchie — grandson of Thackeray. (For the Booth family, see Belinda Norman Butler, *Victorian Aspirations*, Allen & Unwin, 1972.)

13   Russell, *Autobiography*.

14   Mother of Geoffrey and Hilton Young. Geoffrey Young (1879-1952) 4th Bart, and Professor of International Law. Hilton Young (1879-1960) married Scott's widow, created 1st Baron Kennet, Minister of Health 1931-5.

15   Virginia Woolf to Lytton Strachey, 4 January 1909, *Letters of Virginia Woolf*, 1975, Vol. 1.

16 Mary's friendship circle at this period included Lucy Silcox, the outstanding Headmistress of St Felix's, Southwold; Jane Harrison, the Greek Scholar; Amber Reeves, the lecturer in Philosophy and lover of H.G. Wells; Gilbert Murray, the renowned classicist; Beatrice Webb, the Fabian thinker; Erskine Childers, the Irish patriot; and the composers Ralph Vaughan Williams and Gustav Holst, as well as Bloomsbury's 'Friday Club' — for which, see Quentin Bell, *Virginia Woolf*, Hogarth Press, 1972, Vol. 1.

17 See Quentin Bell, *Virginia Woolf*, Vol. 1. especially Appendix for Virginia Woolf's *Report on Teaching at Morley College*, July 1905.

18 'Sheepshanks showed Wolf's fangs. ... Sheepshanks sat through the whole lesson last night, and almost stamped with impatience.' Virginia Woolf, *Letters*, ed. Nicolson, Hogarth Press, 1975, Vol. 1, June and November 1905.

7. MARY, FLORA AND 'THE SUFFRAGE', 1908–1913

1 Hannah Mitchell, *The Hard Way Up*, Virago, 1977, Part 4.

2 Mary Stocks, *My Commonplace Book*, Peter Davies, 1970, pp. 70-79.

3 Margot Asquith, ed., *Myself When Young*, Frederick Muller, 1938, chapter by Maude Royden (1876-1956), feminist, pacifist, socialist and pioneer advocate of the ordination of women in the Church of England, herself a Congregational Minister, later made Hon. D.D. and Companion of Honour. She was the outstanding public speaker on every humanitarian issue of the time. She could pack the Albert Hall and no one would leave until they had heard her. 'She was the most impressive woman speaker I've ever heard. When she spoke it wasn't rhetoric, it wasn't gesture, it was the sheer conviction of her personality that came across to the audience.' Lord Fenner Brockway, personal communication to the author.

4 Ray Strachey, *The Cause*, G. Bell & Sons, 1928, reprinted Virago, 1978, ch. 16.

5 *ibid.*

6 cf. Mary Stocks and Elizabeth Garrett Anderson in Mary Stocks, *My Commonplace Book*.

7 Elizabeth Robins, *The Convert*, Methuen, 1907; The Women's Press, 1980.

8 Ray Strachey, *The Cause*, ch. 16.

9 See Liddington and Norris, *One Hand Tied Behind Us*, Virago, 1978, especially chs. 4 and 9.

10 Virginia Woolf, *Letters*, ed. Nicolson, Hogarth Press, 1975.

11 *Morley College Report* for 1907.

12 *Morley College Magazine*, April 1907.

13 Bertrand Russell, *Autobiography*, Allen & Unwin, 1968, Vol. 1, pp. 153-4. Helena Swanwick has left similar accounts of encountering

mob violence during her and Dr Hilda Clark's suffrage campaign (*I Have Been Young*, Gollancz, 1935), and Hannah Mitchell suffered an acute nervous breakdown as a consequence of the intolerable strain of facing threatening rowdies over and over again: 'My nerves were so shaken that whenever I was in a meeting, however orderly, I found myself trembling for fear disorder would break out.' (*The Hard Way Up*, Part 4.) See also Linklater, *Charlotte Despard: An Unhusbanded Life*, Hutchinson, 1980, for an account of how her Votes for Women platform was stoned.

14   Mary Sheepshanks' unpublished *Autobiography*, ch. 8.
15   Anita Augspurg (1857-1943): teacher, actress, journalist, professional photographer, pacifist and Doctor of Law; outstanding (but also overbearing) leader, together with her friend and life-long companion Lida Gustava Heymann, of the 'radical feminists' of her time. Lida Gustava Heymann (1863-1943): heiress to a Hamburg 'Patrician' family; founded a soupkitchen, a crèche, a women's centre, and a technical school for girls. She unionised shop girls and actresses, campaigned against prostitution and for women's emancipation in general.
16   Mary Sheepshanks to Bertrand Russell, writing from Kalisz, Poland, May 1913 and see her *Autobiography*, ch. 8.
17   Mary Sheepshanks, *Autobiography*, ch. 8.
18   Mary Sheepshanks' letters to Russell, May 1913. These letters have only recently been unearthed in the Russell Archive of McMasters University, Hamilton, Ontario, and have never before been published.
19   *Morley College Magazine*, 1913.
20   Mary Sheepshanks, *Autobiography*, ch. 8.
21   *ibid.*

8.   *THE THIRD MISS SYMONS* (1913): FEMINIST TRACT OR HUMAN TRAGEDY?

1   Ruth Adam, *A Woman's Place*, Chatto & Windus, 1975, ch. 1, cf. Charlotte Brontë, writing c. 1850, over sixty years before F.M. Mayor: 'Look at the numerous families of girls in this neighbourhood: the Armitages, the Birtwhistles, the Sykes. The brothers of these girls are every one in business or in professions; they have something to do: their sisters have no earthly employment, but household work and sewing; no earthly pleasure, but an unprofitable visiting; and no hope, in all their life to come, of anything better. This stagnant state of things makes them decline in health: they are never well; and their minds and views shrink to wondrous narrowness. The great wish — the sole aim of every one of them is to

be married, but the majority will never marry: they will die as they now live.' (*Shirley*, ch. 22.)

2   The list could be much longer, viz. the anti-vivisectionist and champion of battered women, Frances Power Cobbe; the pioneer woman suffragist Lydia Becker; the pioneer doctor Sophia Jex-Blake; the agitator for girls' high schools, Emily Shirreff; the founder of Ragged Schools, Reformatory Schools and Industrial Training Schools, Mary Carpenter; the organisers of the Women's Co-operative Guild, Margaret Llewelyn Davies and Lillian Harris; the Textile Workers' Trade Union organiser Esther Roper; the founder of the Society for Promoting the Employment of Women Jessie Boucherett, etc. see Bauer and Ritt, *Free and Ennobled*, Pergamon Press, 1979, and Patricia Hollis, *Women in Public — The Women's Movement 1850-1900*, Allen & Unwin, 1979.

3   Anon: 'The Spinster' by 'One', The *Freewoman*, 23 November 1911.

4   The *Common Cause*, 30 November 1911.

5   The *Freewoman*, 11 July 1912.

6   Mary Doyle Springer, *Forms of the Modern Novella*, University of Chicago Press, 1975, ch. 5.

7   *ibid.*

8   D.A. Williams, *Psychological Determinism in Madame Bovary*, University of Hull, 1973.

9   E.M. Forster, *On Pessimism in Literature* (WEA lecture and pamphlet), 1907.

10 E.g. Virginia Llewellyn Smith, *TLS*, February 1981, wishing that the ending had been ironic.

11 Confirming the New Testament's 'Judge not, and ye be not judged' are Goethe and Jane Addams, among many others: 'Oh you people ... who, when you talk about anything must immediately declare: that is foolish, that is clever, that is good, that is bad! ... Are you sure you know how to get at the heart of the matter: why did it happen? Why did it have to happen? ... But we have the right to talk about a thing only when we can feel for it.' (Goethe, *Werther*, 1774.) I hate all pretensions of superiority. For anyone to despise any other human being is to me the unpardonable sin.

This was the only occasion on which I heard her speak vehemently. (Jane Addams, quoted by Mary Sheepshanks, *Autobiography*, ch. 16.)

12 Jane Austen, *Persuasion*, ch. 2.

13 *The Idler*, no. 36.

14 It is precisely the kind of tragedy that Euripides would have understood — he having been the first to demonstrate that suffering corrupts the sufferer, and that the emotionally damaged will do

terrible damage in their turn, committing just those atrocities they themselves once most abhorred (cf. *Electra, Medea, Orestes* and *Hecabe*).

15 The *Dublin Review* was also good in that it perceived Flora Mayor's grasp both of tragedy and of comedy: 'Only a true artist can depict a dull and futile life with such sympathy and humour as is shown by Miss Mayor in 'The Third Miss Symons'. Henrietta Symons was an everyday person without the gifts suited to everyday life. The tragic element in her character was her immense capacity for loving, joined to a strange incapacity for acquiring love. Her very longing for it made her tactless and overeager, and she was sensitive and prone to discouragement — enough material for misery. Her story might be tedious in the telling, but Miss Mayor has made it enthralling by reason of her sympathy and sense of humour and her artistic method.' (December 1914.)

16 *The Third Miss Symons* was nominated for the Polignac Prize. 'All the six judges wanted to place it first if a work of fiction were to gain the prize. Sturge Moore, Laurence Binyon, Professor Gilbert Murray and Professor Walter Raleigh wanted it to get it anyway, but Masefield could not press its claims, he having written the book's preface. Two judges did not want to award the prize to fiction again so Mr Hodgson's poem won.' (note in Flora's handwriting, December 1914)

17 *Tragedy is Not Enough*, Gollancz, 1952.

9. MARY SHEEPSHANKS AND THE FIRST WORLD WAR
    1914–1918

1 See the distinction made by Martin Caedel, *Pacifism in Britain, 1914-1945*, 1980. British women pacifists and/or pacificists in 1914 included Maude Royden, Crystal Macmillan, Helena Swanwick, Margaret Ashton, Dr Hilda Clark, Edith Pye, Alice Clark, Kathleen Courtney, Isabella Ford, Katherine Harley, Emily Leaf, Catherine Marshall, M.P. Stanbury, S.J. Tanner, Ethel Barton, Margaret Hills, C.C. Lyon, Lucy Deane Streatfeild, Dr Ethel Williams, Eva Gore-Booth, Esther Roper, and Mrs Charlotte Despard, as well as Mary Sheepshanks, Sylvia Pankhurst, Hannah Mitchell, Ada Nield Chew, Selina Cooper, Ethel Derbyshire, Margaret Llewelyn Davies, Lillian Harris, Mary Agnes Hamilton, Vernon Lee, Irene Cooper Willis and Ottoline Morrell. See: *Common Cause*, articles and correspondence, January-June 1915; Jo Vellacott, *Bertrand Russell*, Harvester, 1980; Mary Agnes Hamilton, *Remembering My Good Friends*, Jonathan Cape, 1944; Helena Swanwick, *I Have Been Young*, Gollancz, 1935, especially ch.4; Liddington

and Norris, *One Hand Tied Behind Us,* Virago, 1978, ch. 14; and Linklater, *Charlotte Despard: An Unhusbanded Life,* Hutchinson, 1980.

2   See Jon Stallworthy, *Wilfred Owen,* Oxford University Press and Chatto & Windus, 1974, and Ian Parsons, *Men Who March Away: Poems of the First World War,* Chatto & Windus, 1965.

3   Helena Swanwick (Mary Sheepshanks' second cousin and sister of Walter Sickert), *I Have Been Young.* Another friend of Mary's, the ardent internationalist, Sophy Sanger, pioneer co-founder of the ILO, was so appalled by the outbreak of the Great War that 'for a while she was literally stunned as with a blow on head and heart that stopped all action.' (Maude Allen, *Sophy Sanger,* privately printed, 1958.) 'People have no idea what a shock war was to us then.' (Dame Kathleen Courtney, aged 90, the *Guardian,* 11 March, 1968.)

4   *Ius Suffragii,* 1 September 1913. For Maude Royden, see ch. 7, note 3.

5   Frida Perlen, German Jewish feminist/pacifist from Stuttgart; Dr Gertrud Bäumer, pioneer sociologist, later M.P. and technical adviser to the German delegation to the League of Nations; Clara Zetkin, revolutionary Communist friend of Rosa Luxemburg and anti-militarist leader of the working-class women's movement in Germany; for Heymann and Augspurg, see ch. 7, note 15. Helene Stöcker, radical feminist champion of the unmarried mother and her child; Minna Cauer, leading suffragist in pre-war Berlin; Marie Stritt, President of the German Women's Suffrage Movement.

6   Mrs Fawcett, President of the British National Union of Women's Suffrage Societies and Vice-President of the International Alliance of Suffrage Societies; Mrs Despard, President of the Women's Freedom League; Mrs Pethick Lawrence, former militant Suffragette and editor of *Votes for Women,* expelled by Christabel Pankhurst and now a leading pacifist/feminist; Mrs Barton, President of the 32,000-strong working-class Women's Co-operative Guild; Mary Macarthur, trade union activist and founder of the National Federation of Women Workers, soon to become Hon. Sec. of the Central Committee on Women's Employment in Wartime; Madame Malmberg, the first Finnish woman M.P. who in her speech attacked Britain for supporting Tsarist Russia in 1914 — 'England is really being asked to fight to keep the Czar upon his throne' — and Rosziska Schwimmer, Hungarian pacifist orator who was to be a moving force behind the Women's Peace Congress at The Hague in 1915 — 'Women want a human world, not a man-made world; Peace Ministers, not War Ministers!'

7 *Votes for Women*, August 1914, reprinted in *Ius Suffragii*, 1 September 1914.
8 See Monica Krippner, *The Quality of Mercy: Women at War, Serbia 1915-18*, David & Charles 1980.
9 The American historian and former Ambassador to Moscow, George Kennan, has confirmed this analysis of the causation of the First World War: 'It was the momentum of the weapons race which carried the great powers helplessly along into the catastrophe of the first world war ... This not only can happen again. It *is* happening.' *UN Disarmament Times*, Dec. 1980.
10 *Common Cause*, 23 October 1914.
11 Dated 15 December 1914. Letter in the Fawcett Archives, Fawcett Library, City of London Polytechnic.
12 See Dorothy Muir, *Lift the Curtain*, Jonathan Cape, 1955, last chapter.
13 cf.

Private
Dearest Mrs Fawcett,
   It looks to me as if some of the dearest people in our Union — such as Miss Courtney, Miss Royden, Miss Marshall, and Miss Ashton — are bent upon a campaign of political education with regard to the attitude of the N.U. towards the war. They appear moreover to have strong leanings towards what the 'Union of Democratic Control' calls its 'policy'.
   This kind of propaganda — whether wise or not — is certain to have a most exasperating effect on a good many persons and it would be nothing short of disastrous to the N.U. if it becomes a centre or a medium of propaganda for any policy of any kind in connection with the war ...
   I have no doubt that we could string together miles of platitudes upon which there would be no possibility of disagreement in the Union but as soon as we come to the practical application of any of them I am certain we shall find ourselves in the arena of heated, party controversy, and this can only be disastrous to the one cause we exist to promote ...
      Ever Yours,
         Helena Auerbach.
(Treasurer of the National Union of Women's Suffrage Societies, 9 November 1914. Letter in the Fawcett Archive of the Fawcett Collection, City of London Polytechnic.)

14 See Ray Strachey, *The Cause*, G. Bell & Sons, 1928, reprinted Virago, 1978, ch. 18. The pacifists' extreme reluctance to break with Mrs Fawcett can be seen from this letter to her from her close

friend, the Quaker, Isabella Ford, also in the Fawcett Archive:

Dearest Millie,

... I would never really, never, be disloyal to any course of action you laid down ...

Please say all that you think — all you write to me, about Germany, I shan't look tiresome, and I shan't feel 'hostile', dear Millie — that's not the word ...I hate Prussianism as heartily as you do — and I long for it to go. But I do not think that war ever destroyed war — and real salvation can only come to people and nations from within ... I only wish I could feel as you do ...

Your loving I.O. Ford (Leeds textile worker organiser, see Liddington and Norris, *One Hand Tied Behind Us*.)

15   Personal communication from the late Dame Margery Corbett Ashby to the author.

16   Crystal Macmillan, M.S., B.Sc., was the Edinburgh barrister who had pleaded before the Bar of the House of Lords for the right of women graduates to vote, was a member of the Executive Committee of the National Union of Woman Suffrage Societies, Vice-Chairman of the International Women's Relief Committee, and a friend of Mary Sheepshanks.

17   Kathleen Courtney — full-time Hon. Sec. of the NUWSS. Emily Leaf — ex-Newnhamite friend of both Mary Sheepshanks and Flora Mayor, Hon. Press Secretary of the NUWSS. Catherine Marshall — friend of Mary Sheepshanks, Hon. Parl. Sec. of the NUWSS, later very active in the No Conscription Fellowship — see Jo Vellacott, *Bertrand Russell*.

18   At the meeting at Caxton Hall it was unanimously decided to support this Congress and also to make every effort to raise the necessary funds. The cost of the Conference will be about £1,000, and the German and Dutch women have agreed to contribute a third.

Miss Margaret Bondfield said that ... if the men will not make a start the women must. Each country had been afraid to speak of peace lest the reactionary press in the other countries should use that fact to its disadvantage. They were under a hypnotism which prevented them doing anything to stop this outpouring of ... blood ... It was the women who had to break the spell ... The peace they had in view was no flabby thing — not like a flabby angel in a damp cloud — their peace was going to be a robust reality ...

Miss Catherine Marshall said that all had the most passionate desire to serve their country in this appalling calamity ... They felt they had something definite, as women, to contribute to the problem of War and Peace. ... Women must have something constructive to put before the world, and in order to have something constructive they must come together. What they most wanted was to be able to stand outside their own national point of view, and try to understand the other person's point of view. This can only be done by coming together and finding out what our enemies feel about themselves and about us. It would be easier for the women to meet in this way while victory was still undecided than later on when one side was winning. The terms of peace would depend very much on the national feeling behind the few men who made it. The end of militarism, which was the end they all had in view, would not come by victory alone, but by force of an awakened and enlightened public opinion. It was time to begin [that] process of enlightenment ...

The sum of about £300 was raised on the spot towards the expenses of the Congress.

(The *Common Cause*, 23 April 1915.)

19   Helena Swanwick, *I Have Been Young*, ch. 10.
20   Daniel Levine, *Jane Addams and the Liberal Tradition*, State Historical Society, Wisconsin, 1971, ch. 14.
21   See Levine, *Jane Addams* and Allen Davis, *American Heroine*, Oxford University Press, 1973, chs. 12 and 13, as well as the internal evidence of the full report of the Women's International Congress *Towards Permanent Peace* (held in the Fawcett Collection).
22   See Alice Hamilton, *Women at The Hague*, New York, Macmillan, 1915, ch. 14.
23   Reported by Lady Courtney of Penwith, *War Diary*, printed privately, 23 June, 1915.
24   See Helena Swanwick on E.T. Morel in *Builders of Peace: Being Ten Years' History of the Union of Democratic Control*, Swathmore Press, 1924 (Morel had been the publicist who had earlier alerted the world to Belgian atrocities in the Congo).
25   Vernon Lee, 1856-1935 (pseudonym of Violet Paget), feminist, pacifist, writer and aesthetician, who wrote *The Ballet of the Nations*, Chatto & Windus, 1915; *The Handling of Words*, John Lane, 1923; *The Poet's Eye*, Hogarth Press, 1926, among others.
26   Margaret Bryant (c. 1880-1942) was an original member of the Royal Institute of International Affairs, founded in 1920;

Miss Margaret Bryant who died on February 14th, 1942, was in charge of the work of the Information Department at the time of her death. She had a passion for knowledge and a skill in using it which made her one of the best-informed experts in many fields. The readers of the *Bulletin of International News* came to recognise that the initials 'M.B.' were the hall-mark of competence. The Institute is indebted to her for the research which lay behind some of its best-known published studies, i.e., *World Agriculture; Unemployment;* and *The Colonial Problem*. She also assisted Sir John Hope Simpson in his *Refugee Survey*. (Extract from the annual report of the Royal Institute of International Affairs, 1941-42.)

27 *Ius Suffragii*, 1 April 1917.
28 Douglas Goldring *The Nineteen Twenties*, Nicholson and Watson, 1945. (The girl was Elsa Lanchester, cabaret artiste, singer, actress, later wife of Charles Laughton.)
29 *Ius Suffragii*, 1919.

10. FLORA MAYOR DURING THE FIRST WORLD WAR, 1914-1918

1 E.g., the former Clifton Headmaster, Canon Glazebrook, preaching to the boys about

the hordes of lust and cruelty which went forth ... from the North. It was as if God's voice were heard calling, 'Arise, shine, for your light cometh,' and lo! and in answer to the summons, the British Empire shone forth in its rainbow hues, offering hope and help to stricken humanity. (*The Cliftonian*, June 1916.)

2 Day by day our casualty lists grow longer with dreadful rapidity, telling the mournful and yet glorious tale of the deaths of Old Cliftonians on the field of battle. Already more than 100 Old Cliftonians have given up their lives for their country. ... There can be few Cliftonians who are not mourning sons or brothers or school friends. (*The Cliftonian*, June 1915, October 1915.)

3 Journal entry from a sixth former at Watson's House, February 1917.
4 *The Third Miss Symons*, Virago, 1979 ch. 6.
5 Her friend Melian Stawell wrote of Flora's dogged perseverance with her writing: 'She wrote continually when the grip of disease would allow it.' (Obituary on Flora Mayor in the *Newnham Roll*, 1932.)

11. MARY AND FLORA IN THE AFTERMATH OF WAR —
    1919–23

1   Dr Ethel Williams, report on conditions in Vienna, in *Towards Peace and Freedom*, WILPF, 1919.

2   See Francesca Wilson, *Eglantyne Jebb, Rebel Daughter of a Country House*, Allen & Unwin, 1967, ch. 9.

3   Philip Gibbs, Introduction to D.F. Buxton and E. Fuller, *The White Flame, The History of The Save the Children Fund*, Longman, 1931.

4   Kate Courtney, friend of Mary Sheepshanks and the Mayors, pacifist sister of Beatrice Webb and wife of the only peer to speak against the First World War in August 1914. See Mosa Anderson, *Noel Buxton, A Life*, Allen & Unwin 1952 and Kate Courtney's own *War Diary*, printed privately, 1927.

5   Francesca Wilson, *Eglantyne Jebb*.

6   See *The White Flame*.

7   Another eminently practical scheme with which Mary was also in close touch was that run by Mary's friend and fellow-suffragist, the Quaker, Dr Hilda Clark and her friend, the nurse Edith Pye. Throughout the First World War, Dr Clark and Edith Pye had helped women and child war-victims in France, setting up emergency maternity hospitals inside the French war-zone itself, for which work Edith Pye had been awarded the *Légion d'Honneur*. After the war, Dr Clark and Edith Pye went to the cold silent defeated city of Vienna with its population of over two million famished people. First Hilda Clark organised the dispatch of hard foreign currency to Holland and Switzerland with which to buy cows for the farmers outside Vienna. The cows were then kept alive on fodder that Dr Clark bought from Croatia and Czechoslovakia. The farmers paid for the cows by giving free milk to all the infant welfare centres of Vienna, and gradually the incidence of acute malnutrition, rickets and T.B. declined. (See Edith Pye, *War and its Aftermath*, printed privately and Francesca Wilson, *In the Margins of Chaos*, John Murray, 1944.)

8   For Maude Royden, see ch. 7, note 3.

9   Jane Addams replied, 'The Fight the Famine Council has been the brightest spot on the horizon for a long time ... I am ... quite clear that primitive human pity is not yet extinct among us.'

10 cf.

Could the League have considered Europe's multitude of starving children as its concrete problem, feeding them might have been the quickest way to restore the divided European nations to human and kindly relationship. If the coal, the iron, the oil and above all the grain had been distributed under international control from the first day of the armistice, Europe might have escaped the starvation from which she suffered for months, and the League could actually have laid the foundation for that type of government towards which the world is striving. (Jane Addams, *Peace and Bread in Time of War*, 1922, reprinted Boston, G.K. Hall & Co. 1960, ch. 10.)

11   Mary Sheepshanks, Report on her Fight the Famine Council Mission to Geneva, Nov. 1920, in the Leonard Woolf papers, Documents Section, University of Sussex Library.

12   Quoted in Bussey and Timms, *Pioneers for Peace*, Allen & Unwin, 1965, ch. 2. Mrs Pethick Lawrence had not been the only English-woman to denounce the continued Allied Blockade at that women's congress. Seventy-five-year-old Mrs Despard had also stood up and her 'passionate denunciation of the cold politicking which entailed such cruelty was received with exceptional acclaim by the starved defeated women of the Central European dele-gations. Her transparent sincerity and compassion pierced the barriers of language.' (Andro Linklater, *Charlotte Despard, An Unhusbanded Life*, Hutchinson, 1980.)

13   Quoted in *Towards Peace and Freedom*, August 1919, WILPF report of the Zürich Congress, in the Fawcett Archive, City of London Polytechnic.

14   Noel Buxton in the *Manchester Guardian*, 2 November 1920, 'It is nothing less than a disaster that we are weakening the German Revolution.'

15   Andro Linklater, *Mrs Despard: An Unhusbanded Life*, Hutchinson, 1980, re the equally ineffectual Women's Prisoners' Defence League in Ireland in the 1920's:

It is impossible to measure the importance of their work. Politically it was negligible, morally it was vital. Amid the barbarities of ... war ... the women gave a persistent voice to the standards of more humane times. They were as unwelcome, as unhelpful and as absolutely necessary as a bad conscience.

16   Psalm 15:

Lord, who shall abide in thy tabernacle? who shall dwell in thy holy hill?
He that walketh uprightly, and worketh righteousness, and speaketh the truth in his heart.
He that backbiteth not with his tongue, nor doeth evil to his neighbour, nor taketh up a reproach against his neighbour.
In whose eyes a vile person is condemned; but he honoureth them that fear the Lord. He that sweareth to his own hurt, and

changeth not.
He that putteth not out his money to usury, nor taketh reward
against the innocent. He that doeth these things shall never be
moved.

17. cf. that last cry of Kitty Howard's — 'Europe can smash up if she
likes, I shan't be in a position to care!' with Käthe Kollwitz' cry
about smashed-up Europe, also in 1920: '*Wien stirbt; rettet ihre
Kinder*!' (Vienna is dying; save her children!') When shall one ever
hear both those cries aright, or are the deepest needs of an individual always at odds with the basic needs of the mass?

18. In 1972, twenty-four years after Henry's death, Kitty was buried
beside him in Bicknoller Churchyard; on her grave was inscribed
some of the last words of St Paul: 'I have kept the faith.'

12. FLORA MAYOR'S *THE RECTOR'S DAUGHTER*, 1924

1   Flora Mayor had difficulty in finding a publisher for *The Rector's
Daughter*, until Leonard Woolf wrote to Flora, on 13 March 1924,
that he and Virginia would be glad to publish it on a commission
basis. Flora was to cover their total costs, estimated at £235, and pay
the Hogarth Press an additional 10% commission — 'because it
was a long book'. If Flora sold 900 copies, she would break even.
Her comment was: 'I know they're getting a good thing for
nothing, but I also benefit from their kudos.' The book sold better
than Leonard Woolf had anticipated and covered all its costs.

2   Wordsworth's Ode, *Intimations of Immortality* and *The Prelude*, Bk.
12. The whole of *The Rector's Daughter* attests to the truth of Wordsworth's affirmation in *Michael*: 'There is a comfort in the strength of
love 'Twill make a thing endurable which else Would overset the
brain, or break the heart.'

3   *Proverbs of Hell*, 1793.

4   *The Task*, 1780, Book I. Cowper was one of Flora Mayor's favourite
poets.

5   Canon Jocelyn and 'Dedmayne' itself owe much to Flora's
memories of her melancholy, reclusive uncle, Canon Robert
Mayor of Frating Rectory, Frating, near Colchester — 'Dedmayne
is in Essex', Flora later told her literary agent.

6   *Principia Ethica*, 1902, ch. VI, *On the Ideal.*

7   *Persuasion*, ch. 23. Flora Mayor once told Alice that *Persuasion* had
influenced her rendering of the emotional life more than any other
work.

8   'On the Passion of Love', *Miscellaneous Writings of Pascal*, quoted by
Walter De La Mare in *Love*, Faber & Faber, 1943, p. 96.

9   I use the term 'myth' to mean a necessary fiction expressing our sense of some inexplicable mystery of experience, in this case the oneness of lovers who are forced apart.

10   The portrait of 'Kathy Herbert' owes something to Flora's ambivalent response (compounded of jealousy, moral and intellectual superiority, pity and admiration) towards her young sister-in-law, Beatrice Mayor. Only when Beatrice was in the depths of trouble could Flora feel a rush of overwhelming, troubling sympathy for her. Flora deliberately gave Kathy the unBeatrician traits of Sporty Philistinism in order to throw readers, including Beatrice herself, off the scent. When Beatrice read the ms. of *The Rector's Daughter*:

> She wept at Kathy — the nursing home and her return. She likes Mary *so* much, thinks her like Kitty, can't believe she is really plain ... She thinks Kathy a wonderful creation. I said I should have been too shy of Kathy and she wouldn't have liked me. She said: 'You wouldn't have liked her. You would have thought her so hard in manner.' (Flora to Alice, 1923.)

11   It is instructive to contrast Mary Jocelyn and her father with another Mary in fiction, her near-contemporary, May Sinclair's *Mary Olivier* (1919) reprinted Virago, 1980. Both heroines are gifted and solitary and both are dominated by a draining relationship with an ageing parent — in Mary Oliver's case, her mother — of whose love they feel unsure. But in *Mary Olivier* the parent-child relationship is examined exclusively from the child's perspective, 'little Mama' being merely a clinical case-study of a neurotic, jealous, possessive life-sucker, hated by daughter, author and reader alike.

12   cf. the great Professor of Physiology working on the human bone-marrow in Chekhov's *A Boring Story*.

13   See Quentin Bell, *Virginia Woolf*. Hogarth Press, 1972, vol. I, p. 105.

14   Between 1917 and 1924, Flora Mayor had heard countless horror stories about the 'butchers of Russia', the raping of nuns, the campaigns against counter-revolutionary, upper-class women, both from her acquaintance with aristocratic Russian *émigrés* in France and from her reading of very conservative newspapers at home. Cf. 'Russophobia' in Northedge and Wells, *Britain and Soviet Communism: the Impact of a Revolution*, Macmillan, 1982.

15   George Eliot, *Middlemarch*, ch. 20. 'If we had a keen vision and feeling of all ordinary human life, it would be like hearing the grass grow and the squirrel's heart beat.'

16   *A Writer's Diary*, Hogarth Press, 1954, entry for 9 April, 1935.

17   cf. Jane Addams' concluding address to the Zürich Congress of the Women's International League, 1919: We may fail and fail again

but we must still go on learning to use that moral energy which we know is a vital thing — the only thing ... that will heal the world.

18 Quoted by Lionel Trilling in 'Emma and the legend of Jane Austen' in *Beyond Culture*, Secker & Warburg, 1965.
19 *Nation and the Athenaeum*, 21 June 1924.
20 *New Statesman*, 24 May 1924.
21 *The Bookman*, New York, May 1929 and September 1929.
22 *Guardian*, 18 July 1923, the *Church of England Newspaper*, 31 October 1924.
23 Late June 1924.
24 *Saturday Review*, 7 June 1924.
25 *Time and Tide*, 18 July 1924.

13. THE DARKENING WORLD OF MARY SHEEPSHANKS, 1926–1933

1   Rousseau, *Émile*, Bk. Two. First published 1768, reissued Dent, 1974.
2   *The Rector's Daughter*, ch. 1.
3   E.M. Forster, 'Post-Munich', 1939, reprinted in *Two Cheers for Democracy*, Edward Arnold, 1951.
4   Letter to Christopher Isherwood, 30 July 1936, published in Isherwood, *Christopher and His Kind*, Eyre Methuen, 1976.
5   The Women's International League had been founded after the Peace Congress of Women at The Hague in 1915, see ch. 9.
6   cf. Eleanor Rathbone's Presidential Addresses to the National Union of Societies for Equal Citizenship, 1920-7, on the need to reform British laws concerning divorce, widows, guardianship of children, women in sweated trades, etc.
7   Personal communication to the author from veteran American member of the WILPF, Muriel Olmsted.
8   *Pax International*, March 1926. (*Pax International* for the years 1920-1939 is held in the Library of the London School of Economics.)
9   Madeleine Doty pioneered Children's Courts in America c. 1915-1920.
10 & Mary Sheepshanks had first fallen foul of Heymann and
11 Augspurg, and they of her in 1913 — see ch. 7, and note 18 to ch. 6.
12 *Maternity* ed. Llewelyn Davies, first published 1913, reprinted by Virago, 1978.
13 See Mary Sheepshanks in *Pax International*, December 1927.
14 Dr Hilda Clark was Mary's friend, the famous Quaker relief-organiser in post-war Vienna, see ch. 11, note 7.
15 Former Professor of Politics at Wellesley College, awarded the Nobel Peace Prize, 1946.

16 *Pax et Libertas*, September/October 1928.
17 *ibid.*
18 *Pax et Libertas*, December 1928.
19 *ibid.*
20 *Einstein on Peace*, ed. Nathan and Norden, New York, Avenel, 1968, ch. 4, p. 93.
21 See *Frauen Gegen den Krieg*, ed. Gisela Brinker-Gabler, Fischer, 1980, p. 291.
22 *Einstein on Peace*, pp. 94-5.
23 For a full account of the allegations and the WIL's rebuttal, see *Pax et Libertas*, February 1929.
24 Personal communication to the author from Muriel Olmsted, veteran American member of WIL who had been a delegate to Prague in 1929.
25 See Bussey and Timms, *Pioneers for Peace*, Allen & Unwin, 1965, ch. 8.
26 On 11 February 1930, Mary Sheepshanks drafted the following memorandum to the Five Power Naval Conference in London on behalf of the WIL: 'Believing, as we do, that the late disastrous war demonstrated the error of trusting in armaments to give security, and being convinced that the peace and security, to which all the peoples in the world aspire, can only be attained by the development of institutions based on mutual confidence, we aim at the progressive attainment of universal disarmament by international agreement, and we urge that an immediate first step in that direction be taken by drastic naval reductions and in particular by the entire abandonment of the use of battleships and submarines ...'

   The Five Power Naval Conference did not reach any agreement on naval disarmament.
27 On July 1930, Mary Sheepshanks wrote to all National Sections of the WIL:

Dear Friends,
   We have today sent the following telegram to the British Prime Minister, to the Viceroy in India, to Gandhi and to Nehru ...
      'Women's International League for Peace and Freedom earnestly desiring peaceful solution to Indian problems urges truce to secure co-operation in Conference urges Government to withdraw repressive measures and grant amnesty and begs Indians suspend disobedience.'

28 Richard Rubenstein, *The Cunning of History: The Holocaust and the American Future*, New York, Harper Colophon, 1975, ch. I and ch. III. 'In the twenties and thirties, 'denaturalisation' and de-

nationalisation' were increasingly used by governments as ways of getting rid of citizens they deemed undesirable.' p. 14.

29   The first idea for this conference had come from the pacifist Roszika Schwimmer who had recently been refused American citizenship because she would not agree to take up arms for the US in wartime. For Roszika Schwimmer, see ch. 9. note 6.

30   *Pax et Libertas*, October 1930.

31   As late as January 1933 Lida Gustava Heymann, then 65, held a last small Peace Meeting in Munich, herself standing guard at the entrance to keep out the Brownshirts.

32   Jane Addams to Kathleen Courtney, when the British Section was thinking of leaving the WIL, 15 August 1932.

33   Alexander Herzen, *My Past and Thoughts*, ch. 25, English edition Chatto & Windus, 1924.

34   Jane Addams to the Quaker, Edith Pye, 17 August 1932.

35   For Lida Gustava Heymann's account of the WIL during this period see *Erlebtes, Erschautes*, Anton Hain, Meisenheim, 1978, ch. 8.

36   Mary Sheepshanks, unpublished *Autobiography*, and see ch. 7.

37   Mary Sheepshanks' official report to the WIL on her personal investigation in the Ukraine.

38   Mary Sheepshanks, *Autobiography*, ch. 20.

39   Mary Sheepshanks' Official Report.

40   Mary Sheepshanks' confidential letters to WIL Executive, 17 December 1930.

41   Mary Sheepshanks' confidential report to the WIL Executive, 17 December 1930.

42   *ibid.*

43   The text of Mary's letter to *The Times*, headed 'Ukrainian Minority in Poland', ran:

Sir,

I have just returned from East Galicia and found that:—

1. The recent police and military raids carried out in hundreds of villages were all done on a plan issued from Headquarters.
2. Wholesale and brutal flogging was inflicted on the male population without trial.
3. Contributions in kind were levied as well.
4. Cooperative stores and reading rooms were wrecked.
5. There was great destruction of tools, machinery and household furniture.
6. Priests and their families were beaten.
7. The authorities have taken strigent steps to prevent information being obtained as to the damage done. Doctors and lawyers have their houses searched for documents and

photographs, and anyone giving information to foreigners is liable to five years' imprisonment.

I spoke to many Poles as well as Ukrainians, who deplored the barbarity of communal punishment without trial and who were emphatic that it would make future peace and conciliation more difficult and play into the hands of revolutionaries.

The treatment of the Ukrainian minority is an international matter, as the minority treaty signed by Poland guaranteeing civil rights has been infringed.

It is also jeopardizing the peace of Eastern Europe, as Polish minorities have interested kinsmen across her frontiers.

On 28 February 1931, Mary published a second letter in *The Times*, answering allegations that she was anti-Polish — 'The Poles with whom I spoke felt that the present régime was not in the best interests of Poland and that it would be of benefit to the Polish people to have its actual nature realized in Western Europe.' In other words, she was anti-Pilsudski, not anti-Polish.

44   The text of the International Disarmament Petition, drafted and circulated by the WIL and presented to the World Disarmament Conference in Geneva in 1932 with 8 million signatures, including those of Einstein, Russell and Tagore, ran: 'The undersigned men and women ... are convinced that competition in armaments is leading all countries to ruin without giving security; that this policy renders future wars inevitable and that these will be wars of extermination ..., they therefore ask for total and universal disarmament and request their government formally to instruct its delegates to the next disarmament conference ... to take the necessary steps to achieve real disarmament.'

45   E.M. Forster, Letter to Christopher Isherwood, 30 July 1936. Published in Isherwood, *Christopher and His Kind*.

14. THE LAST YEARS OF FLORA MAYOR AND MARY SHEEPSHANKS

1   F.M. Mayor, Letter to the *Guardian*, 24 September, 1926.
2   *The Squire's Daughter*, Constable, 1929, ch. 3.
3   *The Squire's Daughter*, ch. 35.
4   R.L. Konigsberg, in the *Despatch*, Colombus, Ohio, 12 April 1931.
5   The *Saturday Review*, 10 February 1929.
6   The *Daily News*, 18 February 1929.
7   Published posthumously in *The Room Opposite and Other Stories*, Constable 1935.
8   *Christmas Night at the Almira*, published in *The Room Opposite* ...

9   Also published in *The Room Opposite and Other Stories*.

10   *ibid*.

11   Newnhamese for *Grande Passion*.

12   '... any discriminating reader of her books ... could see that though her inborn sympathies were with the dignities and decorums of the old order, the decencies of what used to be called 'gentle-folk', yet she had a large heart for those who broke bounds and for those who would once have been considered 'outside the pale'. That was one of the characteristic things about her: the union of a strong and convinced conservatism with a human sympathy that could take up, imaginatively, stand-points entirely opposed to her own ...

     This alertness of spirit was a prime factor in her equipment as a novelist.'

13   'Two of the six [novels], which did quite well when published are now forgotten, but are, I still think, remarkable, *The Rector's Daughter* by F.M. Mayor and *The Peacemakers* by Alice Ritchie.'

14   In November 1977 Susan Hill published her moving testimony to discovering 'A Lost Work of Literary Genius' in the *Daily Telegraph*, and in 1978 Jill Balcon read aloud *The Rector's Daughter*, most beautifully, on BBC 'Woman's Hour'. In March 1979 Susan Hill saluted *The Third Miss Symons* as another 'great work of fiction' in the *Daily Telegraph*.

15   cf. Leonard Woolf's conclusion to *Downhill All the Way*: 'The years 1930 to 1939 were horrible ... If one was middle aged or old and so had known at least a 'Sort of a kind' of civilization, it was appalling impotently to watch the destruction of civilization by a powerful nation completely subservient to a gang of squalid, murderous hooligans ... The last months of peace ... were the most terrible months of my life, for, helplessly and hopelessly, one watched the inevitable approach of war.'

16   At the memorial service held for Jane Addams at the Church of St-Martin-in-the-Fields, London, the pacifist orator Maude Royden, C.H., D.D., gave this address for 'the finest human being' whom Mary had ever known:

     Most of us when we believe we are in the right, even if all the world is against us, comfort ourselves with the reflection that we are right; that other people are insane or cruel or wicked ... We put armour on our hearts. And it was characteristic of Jane Addams that she could not put on armour. This is the very soul of peacemaking, when a person's very heart is not defended ...

     Her cause is not yet won, but she has shown us how to win it. No one will dare to associate failure with a life that justifies itself.

17   Hilda Clark's niece, Dr Priscilla Johnstone, remembers how in 1938, immediately after she had got married, she was summoned by Mary Sheepshanks to be told that a woman doctor was needed for three months on a project in India and that she, Priscilla, ought to go:

> We were both equally astonished — I that she should imagine that I could be willing, or indeed think it right to go off for three months and leave my husband and she that I was unwilling even to consider it. She was extraordinarily single-minded in her enthusiasms. (Dr Johnston to the author.)

But Dr Johnston did find herself giving English lessons to the Sudetenländers.

18   At the very time that Mary was writing that despairing letter, Anna Haag, a German member of the WIL was writing the first political pamphlet to be printed in defeated Germany. Headed: 'Thinking is Allowed Again!', it appealed to German women to give Germany a new human face by renouncing war and war-preparations for ever. The pamphlet ended by paying tribute to women workers for peace and demilitarisation outside Germany, citing as its two chosen Englishwomen, Helena Swanwick and — though she never knew it — Mary Sheepshanks.

19   Mary's political sharpness never left her. When the Korean war was nearing its end she noted that Persia would be the next danger spot, and when one of her nieces was uncritically enthusiastic about China, her eighty-year-old aunt, who had hoped so much from the Russian Revolution of 1917, thirty years before, counselled caution: 'I agree with you that the Communists in China have carried out great reforms, *but* so does every *new* regime — Chiang Kai Shek did — also in the U.S.S.R., it began by sweeping away abuses and developed into a brutal tyranny.' (Mary Sheepshanks, letter, 1951.)

20   'She set up a table in the middle of her sitting room, gathered all her material together and then wrote all day, day after day for three months . . . At the end of three months she said she had finished and would add nothing to what she had written.' (Dr Muriel Drew to the author.)

21   For Margaret Bryant see ch. 9, note 26.

EPILOGUE

1.   All these thinkers and writers based their ethics on the experiential *donnée* that humans do possess a redemptive capacity for fellow-feeling:

Sympathy, which convinces each human being that other human beings are sensitive as he himself is to pleasure and pain, which leads him sometimes and to some degree to feel pain at their pain and take pleasure at their pleasure, may ... lead him to a point at which he feels that he ought to take account of their pain or pleasure even when to do so is no longer pleasant or useful for himself. (Robin Mayor, *Reason and Commonsense*, Routledge and Kegan Paul, 1952, ch. 28.)

2   Rousseau, *Émile*, Bk. One. First published 1768, reissued Dent, 1974.

INDEX

325